One
In A
Million

AN IRS TRAVESTY

A Novel by
Pat Shannan

P<small>RESCOTT</small> P<small>RESS</small>

Prescott Press
P.O. Box 53788
Lafayette, Louisiana 70505

Library of Congress Card Catalog Number 98-68098
ISBN 0-933451-42-3

Dedication

To Eldon Warman,
who was the inspiration for this story,
and in memory of his "Sarah:"

CHAVALA PAULINE ATKINSON WARMAN
1942-1984

My special plaudits of gratitude go to
Marty, Linda, Colin, Carol, Dave, Henry, Vic, and Richard
in appreciation of their time taken and
their valuable editorial input.

Contents

Introduction

A new public opinion must be created privately and unobtrusively. The existing one is maintained by the press, by propaganda, by organization, and by financial influences which are at its disposal. This unnatural way of spreading ideas must be opposed by the natural one, which goes from man to man and relies solely on the truth of the thoughts and the hearer's receptiveness for new truth.

—Albert Schweitzer

In modern day warfare, the sword is always mightier than the pen, once the sword grows powerful enough to chop that pen to pieces. Meanwhile, to those in protest, the opposing silence is deafening.

Quite simply, the Bill of Rights was specifically designed to prevent the people of America from ever suffering the tyranny of a police state. The first ten Amendments actually amended nothing but clarified the exact entity which was most likely to become Public Enemy #1 and stressed the necessity of keeping the federal government out of the lives of the people of several states.

"Crime is contagious," Justice Lewis Brandeis warned in his 1928 Supreme Court opinion, *Olmstead vs. United States*. "When the government becomes a lawbreaker, it breeds contempt for law."

The following potpourri of facts and conjecture is a compilation of Justice Brandeis' prophesy coming to pass.

ONE

Prologue

In the library of the large mansion on Ward Parkway the two men sat warming their innards with a glass of vintage port in front of the roaring fire. It was the last week of the last year of the twentieth century. With the extravagant aid of antebellum chests, Hepplewhite chairs, French candelabra, carpets and wallpaper imported from Europe, Kirman rugs, Clarence House paisley prints, Chinese needlepoint, and a massive collection of Civil War books and memorabilia, the owners had turned the inside of their ninety-year-old, three-story home into a colorful antique palace. Outside, the early evening snowfall was filling the brown patches which had begun to appear on the lawn since the imprisoning blizzard a week before. The traffic was bustling on the boulevard as the city's work force rushed to the safety of their homesteads before passage became first difficult, then hazardous, then impossible.

The older man finished his glass first and stepped to the hand-carved French buffet for more. As he poured with his left hand, he loosened his tie with his right, and while striding back to their sitting area, began to unbutton his vest. He removed it and draped it on the brass hall tree over his suit coat before sinking into the leather desk chair, spinning to rest his left elbow on the edge of the credenza in back of him. His posture bestowed a defiant, imposing, almost intimidating atmosphere in the room before he began to speak.

"The last one was in Atlanta, and it was so easy it made it almost an anticlimax to a long-anticipated delight," he said. "Burr was his name, as in Aaron." The glowing nimbus that was blanketing the darkening sky outside was a fitting complement to his sullen mood. He was becoming visibly angry, just talking about it, and his powerful hands, with knuckles whitened, seemed about to crush the wine glass as he continued.

"It had just gotten dark. About this time of day. The sleazy pig opened the door and when I said, 'Hi, Leonard,' I guess he thought I was one of his neighbors and asked, 'What can I do for you?'

" 'Where is your wife?' I said as if I were the Tupperware salesman, and, in my suit and tie, I could have been.

"He said, 'In the kitchen washing dishes. Why?'

" 'Because I don't want her to see you die,' I whispered. I grabbed him by the collar with my right hand, and pulled him toward me. This animal must have thought I was going to kiss him until I jammed that ten-inch bayonet into his flabby belly with my left. He grunted like somebody had let the air out of him, and, before I let him drop to the ground, I pulled it out and pumped him again. His legs collapsed beneath him as he tossed forward, hit the concrete steps, and uttered a dying oath. I made sure he was dead by jamming the big blade into his face as hard as I could and left the handle protruding from his right eyeball. I knew it couldn't be traced. I had bought it months before in Denver, and, of course, I wore gloves the whole time. The front door was still open. As I jogged through the shadows toward my car, I heard his wife shriek. All I could think about was Maria screaming like that for hours after she found her mother that day. I had finally caught up with the last one who had sent her mother to heaven, and I knew he would never bother her there. I had just put his ass on a non-stop flight straight to hell—one way.

"Forty minutes later I had cruised around the west side of 285 to the airport, turned in the rental car, and was back on the eight o'clock flight to KCI. With the one-hour time change, I was home in bed before Becca finished up at her bridge club." The younger man was flabbergasted, not only by the story, but with the obvious incongruity of this peaceful, distinguished gentleman being able to, first of all, commit such a cold-blooded assassination and then speak of it with such unruffled composure—and there had been others.

The young writer really was no callow youth—almost thirty—and his subject, about to turn sixty wasn't that old yet either, and still not one to tangle with, the younger man noted. But, more than just by a generation of living, they were separated by two sets of American culture. The younger man had been educated in the public schools and could not quite comprehend the idea of someone bucking the ultimate authority of government. He stood and paced slowly around the library trying to digest what he had just heard, not sure what to say.

"Weren't you worried about getting caught somehow?" he finally asked.

"Not a bit. It had all gone without a hitch. I slept better than I had in years. Now, let's sign the contract, and you can turn on your tape recorder. I've got lots to tell you."

It was December 30, 1999. The agreement was that the older man would tell the whole story, with no holds barred, exactly as it had happened. The younger man could not publish it before the older man's death. It had been more than a year now since doctors had given him only four months to live, and the grim reaper could visit any day. At the time of his death all royalties would be split 50/25/25 between the writer and the two grown children of the deceased. The men read and signed the already prepared document. Then they settled in for the evening-long session, and the younger man turned on the recorder and asked about the twenty-two IRS agents who had mysteriously disappeared without a trace over a three-month period in 1987, in Orange County, California.

The old man sensed early in the conversation that it would not be a simple task of portraying to the young writer what life and its mental strife were really like in America in the 1980s for those who did not accept the government's edicts without question. He was straining the young man's credulity. This information just did not jibe with what the younger one had learned in school, watched on television, and read in the papers. What he would hear this night he had never heard before.

TWO

Even his closest associates said that Spike Thorsten would put his own mother in jail if it would help elevate him in the government bureaucracy. When he had made "All-City" as a high school linebacker in Youngstown, the other participants quietly voted him "the dirtiest player in the league." His classmates who had watched him cheat his way through law school at Kent State were not surprised five years later to learn that he had been kicked out of the FBI at age twenty-nine for "conduct unbecoming an agent."

The full story of that episode had never become available for public consumption, but the charges were that Thorsten—in whatever dementia he was currently wallowing—"had numerous times" over the course of two years on the streets of Washington posed as an undercover vice cop by flashing his badge, "arrested" the prostitute, and then agreed to release her in exchange for a sampling of her wares. When he was finally caught, he had agreed to a quiet resignation and a position in the Criminal Investigation Division in the Wichita Falls office of the Internal Revenue Service. He bragged later that the IRS commissioner at the time had remarked to J. Edgar Hoover: "Sure. Send him over. He sounds like just the kind of man we're looking for." If it took dirty tricks to move one's self ahead in the IRS, then it was dirty tricks that Spratlin Pike Thorsten would provide. He would quickly climb back up the Government Service pay scale ladder. But oh, how he hated the first name his parents had hung on him, and he long ago prevailed upon the Government Accounting Office to use only his first initial on his checks and all official correspondence. The nickname had long before evolved into *a sine qua non,* necessary for the feeding and caring of his ego.

Always ready to strike a Faustian bargain, one of Spike's earliest ploys was to intimidate banking officials into letting him look at the records of all their depositors—a clear-cut invasion of privacy. Sometimes he would browse through the business accounts, sometimes the personal. But whenever he came across something that looked as if it might smack of tax evasion—or better yet, hanky-panky—he would make extensive notes about the address, phone numbers, and reeking details for later use. One day spent in a bank could provide fodder for a month of harassment. There were, of course, similar ways of dealing with obstinate and uncooperative branch managers too, but as Thorsten's reputation spread, those types were rapidly curtailed in number. He later expanded this information base to include Visa, Mastercharge, and American Express.

With potentially damaging information in hand, Thorsten, never using his own name, would then call the target and say something like:

Mr. Jones, this is Harvey Gimlet of Internal Revenue. First of all we want you to know that you are not under criminal investigation. However, while we were inspecting the bank records of someone else whose name we cannot divulge, we came across some transactions of yours we would like for you to explain. Particularly, we are interested in this company check in the amount of twenty-nine hundred dollars payable to the Tropicana Hotel last October. Now we already checked with the hotel and they told us that this, uh, rather exorbitant expense was due to the fact that there was an inordinate amount of room service that weekend for food and beverage. But we still find it difficult to justify this large amount and are wondering what else might have been included. Also, your wife just told me that she was not with you on that trip because it was "company business," but your Visa card reflects that you purchased two round-trip tickets from Dallas/Fort Worth to Las Vegas with American Airlines. Would you like to explain all this?

By this time the "target" was sufficiently terrorized into putty-in-the-hands of the IRS. It was only a matter of stopping by to see Mr. Jones to pick up a check to "straighten out" this matter before it became a problem. IRS collections in Wichita Falls soared to record heights during the 1970s while S. Pike Thorsten was there, as did his personal bank balance and level of affluence. Five thousand dollars in cash was his standard fee to look the other way, and those unprepared for the Kafkaesque world of an IRS investigation, in which a presumption of guilt prevailed, were seldom reluctant to cough it up.

There were many fraudulent but workable methods at Spike's disposal with which to increase collections. After all, once the forms were filed, the signer was at the mercy of the IRS. A simple but effective initial attack was to pull the last tax form filed, change a "3" to an "8" or a "1" to a "4", and instead of calling in the filer for an audit, just send him a tax bill for the new amount.

A gross income of $80,000 with no additional deductions demanded a tax of five or ten times more than a $30,000 gross, and fixing the matter was no simple process for the taxpayer. The law said that in order to get the new amount corrected, one must first *pay the tab* before taking the case to District Court. Spike knew that most people could not afford to pay several thousand dollars more in one lump sum and would not take on the hassle and expense of Tax Court anyway. He lost the few cases that reached adjudication but won all the others because they went unchallenged.

Spike Thorsten was one of the first agents to discover how to enrich himself with his own inside information. He had first access to the list of all property confiscations prior to the quarterly auctions, supposedly public auctions. He would pick the one or two properties that had the most equity and least indebtedness and have a lackey do his bidding for him. Instructions to the others to "lay off" increased his odds of picking up the property for a "song" as most of his competition present at the auction were actually doing the bidding of another IRS agent anyway. His few years in Texas had made him—or rather his wife, since it all went into her name—a millionaire, and he soon moved on to the Dallas office.

During his grunt days in Texas, Thorsten had realized he had the only grip on a great idea and had expanded it to reach much greater heights—even to judges and jurors. His new duty was to zero-in on those sitting on tax evasion or willful failure to file trials. An evening phone call made to the home of one or two jurors who "might be found to have a problem" was most effective. They were told that a *guilty* verdict would go a long way toward stopping their own upcoming audits. A few federal employees or their family members always sat for an income tax case, and occasionally, with a little luck, an actual employee of the IRS could be conveniently placed on the jury panel, disclosing his occupation for the record only as "accountant" rather than bean-counter for the government.

Judges always got a personal visit from Spike. They already knew him and all his local contemporaries by name from being in the same federal office building and from their many appearances as witnesses in the courtroom. But sometimes when a "not guilty" verdict slipped through, the judge was gently reminded by Thorsten that it could increase the scrutiny of his personal 1040 form for the past several years, if such a thing happened again. Sometimes honorable men, such as U.S. District Judges Clay Bunn of Arizona and Dixon Walters of Mississippi, who

persisted in guaranteeing a fair trial for everyone in their court-
rooms, found themselves railroaded straight into the penitentiary. While it is almost impossible to coerce a scrupulous and
responsible person into committing a common law crime such as
murder or robbery, it is a simple matter to create a "crime" in
violation of some recently passed statute. Stashing drugs under
the seat in a target's car is one of the most frequently used. The
message on the wall of the courthouses to the other federal
judges nationwide was plain and obvious: "Play by our rules,
boys, because we have the power to replace you."

As the word spread, Thorsten's tactics had completely revo-
lutionized the *modus operandi* of the Service. During the Reagan
years, the Commissioner brought him to Washington, promoted
him to GS-16, and put him in charge of a special, but highly
secret, national program designed to forever stop the so-called
"tax protestors."

Spike was rewarded with a promotion to the headquarters in
Washington as a deputy director in charge of the Criminal Investigation Division (CID), with his own private office and a private
secretary, a few floors beneath the commissioner's. Bursting with
self confidence bordering on megalomania, he was a judicial
monkey at the controls of a legal spaceshot.

Thorsten constantly kept his eye on the high-profile leaders
of the money and tax movement, and his chief targets became
the authors and researchers—particularly those high on their
soapboxes spreading the truth to the masses. Their bank accounts were what he always hit first.

Thorsten continued his relentless attack until the people were
secretly meeting in small groups to discuss means of taking care
of the problem—means other than the traditional, peaceful
method of using the ballot box or the nation's court system. The
IRS had become a silent reign of terror, and someone had to
stop it.

*   *   *   *   *

In 1975, two men had sat beside a campfire in the Laotian
jungle sipping whiskey and complaining of the poor quality,
before tasting more. They knew and referred to each other only
by their code names—Tonto and Mountain Red. The two of
them had spent the last two days with an up and coming drug
czar of the Golden Triangle—a self-proclaimed monarch who
ruled a 60,000 square mile section of Burma, Laos, and Thailand
with feudal brutality. His name was General Khun Sa. Deserters
from his army were tracked down and shot, and informants were

buried alive. One tale had Khun Sa ordering wrongdoers hanged and drawn and quartered in the marketplace of Ban Hin Taek, his one-time Thai headquarters village. Another had him killing a barber for giving him a bad haircut. The two talked of the czar with disdain, each recounting the wild rumors, and questioning the wisdom of the U.S. Government's secret affiliation with this ghoulish ogre.

"Mountain Red" was a behemoth of a man nearly a foot taller and well over a hundred pounds heavier than his confederate. At age twenty-five, his hair was rusty orange, and his moon face carried the slight but customary map of freckles. His massive arms could snap a man's neck as easily as a twig and on occasion had done so. From the Smoky Mountains of eastern Tennessee, he spoke with the amusing twang and drawl of a mountaineer.

"Sumbitch seemed like a nice feller, Tonto. Makes you wonder if you can believe all that shit about him," he said before taking another sip.

His friend, who was twenty years older, brushed back the salt and pepper hair from his eyes and thought for a moment before replying. "Probably ain't true, not all of it. People of that caliber always have reputations that follow them. Just like General MacArthur. There's one thing we do know for sure now what no American outside of Washington D.C. knows, and that's that you and me and a handful of others are responsible for most of the heroin flow to the States."

"Tonto" had been the recipient of the Congressional Medal of Honor in 1951 in Korea. A PFC, his platoon had been overrun during a night long firefight, and he had awakened at dawn after an hour's sleep to realize that he was suddenly behind enemy lines. His C.O. in the platoon was a first lieutenant whose foot was nearly blown off. Of the thirty-three guys he had eaten chow and laughed with around a campfire twelve hours earlier, he and the lieutenant were the only ones left alive. Utilizing his innate Apache instincts, Tonto had carried his platoon leader on his back for ten starving days—eating roots, tubers, grubworms, and dried berries and suffering near-frostbite—before eventually slipping back through the enemy lines to freedom. En route, there had been two separate incidents where Tonto had quietly knifed to death two snipers and stolen their weapons.

When the lieutenant submitted the facts of the story to the war department, the American Indian was flown from the Tokyo hospital with the army brass to the White House in Washington for the presentation by President Truman. "You, sir, are the bravest man I have ever met," the President had told the Native American in the East Room of the White House.

The third quarter of the twentieth century had somehow passed since then, Tonto realized, as he snapped back into the present. The cheap booze that the general had given the two men was taking effect. They began to tell each other more war stories.

Tonto was now a sergeant-major, although for more than the last twenty of his twenty-five years of rising through the military ranks, he had never worn a uniform nor drawn a government check. Once a month, sometimes twice, he was paid from a Wachenhut Corporation envelope filled with cash and postmarked from a San Francisco suburb. Often it was U.S. currency, sometimes it was the funny-looking colored paper from the country in which he was currently based, but it always equalled to the last farthing the exchange rate of his pay in U.S. dollars. He always sent $500 or more to his family outside of Flagstaff, Arizona, before forwarding a large chunk to one of his coded bank accounts overseas. Twenty years experience in the CIA coupled with his heritage had honed his natural instincts of cunning and deception. In the crowded city streets he could spot a tail, and in a matter of minutes he could feel in his bones whether or not a new acquaintance was an enemy plant.

Even with the very few people on earth that he totally trusted, Tonto concealed his thoughts and feelings behind a plausible mask of easygoing coolness. In an era of galloping self-analysis and soul-searching, he was resolutely unself-knowing, coy, and aloof. Curiously, the mask he wore served two purposes. It prevented the world from penetrating his reserve, and it prevented him from penetrating certain levels of his own psyche. There was much about his past he preferred to just forget.

To the people who work for it, the CIA is known as "The Company." The big business mentality pervades everything. Agents, for instance, are called assets, and in 1975 there were 16,500 of them worldwide with an annual budget of 750 million, although they were not answerable to Congress. They were answerable only to the National Security Council, which was composed of the president and officials chosen by him. So it was really an instrument of the president to be used in any manner he pleased and with no legal restraints. Political assassinations were carried out with impunity. Having been involved in the Phoenix program, Tonto knew this better than anyone. The CIA, designed to provide international intelligence for national security, was now the president's secret army.

While he was somewhat advanced from the neophytic naivete of rookiedom, Mountain Red's three year's experience didn't begin to compare with that of Tonto, and he began to ask him some questions like *What does this army really do, and how did it get so much secret power?*

There were actually two reasons. The official reason was laid out in the National Security Act of 1947. It authorized the Central Intelligence Agency to collect and analyze foreign intelligence, ". . . which sounded innocent enough," said the leather-faced man whose eyeslits were beginning to narrow from the effects of the alcohol. "But there was an all-encompassing clause in the Act,". . . he went on to explain, which had allowed the CIA to perform other functions and duties related to intelligence and "affecting the national security . . . as the National Security Council (NSC) from time to time may direct."

"In other words, a private army in any goddamn private war the president wants to fight." He was confirming for Red what had been written in recent years by former operatives-turned-whistleblowers Victor Marchetti and Philip Agee. As the warm evening breeze mixed the rustling of the leaves with the normal jungle sounds of birds and bugs permeating the air, they poured another drink.

"What has been your most fun activity the last three years?" his Indian friend wanted to know.

Red took a drink, pondered for a moment, chuckled, and told him of the slick little Thai bastard who had been ripping them off by playing both ends against the middle—selling drug caches, stashing the money, and claiming he was robbed. At their last rendezvous in a Bangkok hotel, Red choked him into unconsciousness, tied a hallway firehose neatly around his neck, and threw him out a ninth floor window. The hundred-foot long firehose had left his victim dangling with a broken neck just inches from the sidewalk, a macabre testimony to others.

Tonto told Red about the time in South America when he and two compatriots had hooked metal pinchers to the earlobes, nipples, and testicles of their subject, plugging the other end into a wall socket for a few seconds periodically, until they had extracted all the information they needed. He said, "The old '110' treatment—one hundred and ten volts on demand—never failed."

On December 23, 1974, Seymour Hersh had reported in the *New York Times* that the CIA had been spying on congressmen and other government officials in violation of its charter, which forbade such activity inside the borders of the United States. When the agency heads admitted that it was true, few Americans understood with Mountain Red's insight just how close they were to becoming a police state.

"I'm getting out, Tonto," the big man said. "I'm quittin.' "

"You mean you're quitting the company?"

"Damn right. I've had enough. I've packed away fifty grand of their gott-damned dirty money, and I'm goin' to Tennessee, buy me an 18-wheeler, and marry my sweetie. Then I'm gonna be in business for myself and try to forget this filthy racket that gave me my nestegg."

The weathered Indian thought of the half million or so that he had secreted away himself in various banks in Switzerland and Australia. He had not told anyone, but he was about to come to the same decision.

"What about Ted? Have you told him yet?"

"I called him from Bangkok and told him this was my last mission. He told me to think about it some more and call him when we get back. I reminded him that I told him when I signed on that I wasn't going to do this shit forever. What I've seen the last few days didn't make me want to stay. It made up my mind for me to definitely get the hell out. What we're doing ain't right, Tonto. You know it ain't. If it hadn't been for the money, I would have been gone a year ago, but that means I'm no better than a whore. Matter of fact, come to think of it, it makes me a whore. I'm goin' home and get in a legitimate business where I can at least sleep at night and live with myself. Something's wrong with a government that would conduct this kind of secret, slimy business."

"It has been going on a long time, Red," Tonto replied. Johnson got rich with it, then Nixon, and now Ford and his boys will too. I figure Kennedy got killed over it. A lot of people forget that just a few weeks before they got him in Dallas he had announced that he was pulling out of Southeast Asia. That was plenty good enough reason for them to have went after him, you know. The bastards have been reaping millions from this harvest. You know you are going to have to convince Ted that you can keep your mouth shut."

"Ted knows that. I don't have any plans to go to the newspapers. Nobody would believe me anyway. Besides that, they know I don't know enough to write about it like Agee and Marchetti. I just want to go home and lead a normal life."

"That may not be a bad idea, Red. I should do the same thing. Maybe I'll save up a few more bucks like you and buy me a garage. You know what I mean? I don't know nothing 'cept hiding and killing . . . and fixing cars."

The two men drank themselves into a stupor and slept until daylight in their thin bedrolls. The campfire flickered and died.

In the morning light, they began to walk. Their only sustenance was the bland homemade bread given to them the day before and the raw fruit picked from the trees en route, as they walked the remaining eight miles through the jungle to their contact point at a boat on the river. That night they slept comfortably without benefit of booze at the Bangkok Hilton.

It had been a brief and peculiar association. Although neither knew the history of the other at the time, they would later learn from each other that one was a downline blood relative of a famous family of Indian fighters who had been named after Jim Bowie of Texas Alamo fame. The other was the great-grandson of the badass Apache Chief Geronimo. By a strange twist of fate, Tonto and Mountain Red would meet again more than a decade later—fighting together against the very government that had once employed them.

*   *   *   *   *

Two astounding research facts of ground-shaking significance uncovered in the mid-1980s which—in a land of free press—would have dramatically changed the course of history in America, went remarkably unnoticed by the national media. First, The Montana Historians, after years of exhaustive research, became convinced that the 16th Amendment—the one providing for an income tax in the first place—had not been properly ratified by the States in 1913. When they presented uncertified evidence to U.S. District Judge Paul Plunkett of Chicago, they were told to go out and get certified evidence that would prove the fraudulent ratification of the 16th Amendment. This scenario could be likened to a citizen reporting a kidnapping to the FBI and the FBI responding by telling the informant to go out and investigate the crime and return to them with evidence.

Federal authorities at all levels continued to ignore the reports. The Justice Department investigators said it was a matter for the courts to decide, and the Federal Court washed its hands of it by refusing to adjudicate the matter, saying that it was a "political matter" to be decided by Congress. The ball was kicked back and forth and never caught by either side.

Indeed it happened. The same people who reported the crime to the federal authorities were told to go back and investigate the case and to do it at their own expense. The Montana Historians had little choice but to do just that. They paid the expenses of former Illinois State Tax Auditor Bill Benson to travel to all of the forty-eight state capitols in existence in 1913 to dig from the archives the proof of the malpractice and fraud

by attorneys, judges, and politicians; and obtain the certified
copies. A year later he had done so and published the evidence
in a hard-cover book entitled *The Law That Never Was*. The federal judiciary not only ignored the evidence and continued to
send law-abiding citizens to long jail terms but also managed to
railroad Bill Benson into the federal penitentiary as well.

The lawful exercise of the First Amendment right "to peti-
tion government for a redress of grievances" had become the
political equivalent of throwing one's self in front of a rolling
cement truck.

THREE

Beneath the dam of ruthless federal rule, the stream of freedom was running shallow and muddy. The majority of the American people were never aware of what was happening, but some of those who knew had begun to realize that the time was at hand when men and women would have to make up their minds whether they were on the side of freedom and justice and the American republic; or if they would quietly submit to tyranny, oppression, and the New World Order. And the window of opportunity for making that decision was rapidly closing.

❦

Orange County, California, was a hotbed for the tax movement of the 1980s, and one Fourth of July early in that decade, the local historical group packed over two thousand people, at ten bucks a ticket, onto the floor of the Anaheim Coliseum for a "Freedom Rally." One of the interested people there was Brock Freeman, a forty-year-old multi-millionaire real estate developer from Kansas City who was visiting a business associate in the area and had come along only because his friend had an extra ticket which would otherwise go to waste. A lover of history and the law who already held attorneys and politicians in great contempt, Brock was quickly captivated by what he saw and heard.

Most of us have had the experience, either as parents or children, of trying to discover the "hidden picture" within another picture in a magazine. We are shown a landscape with trees, flowers, fences, and natural foliage. The caption tells us there is another, smaller but more important, picture hidden in the larger one and asks if we can find it. We cannot until we look at the answer on another page. Then it stands out so blatantly, we wonder how we could have missed it the first time.

Brock Freeman was one of those Americans who knew something was wrong in his nation, but he just couldn't put his finger on it. He had wondered in the past why we keep electing new presidents who faithfully promise to balance the budget, stop government waste, douse the fires of inflation, reverse the trend which is turning the country into a moral sewer, and generally become our savior the next four years. Yet each new administration, whether it is Republican or Democrat, continues the same basic programs of the previous administration, which it had so thoroughly denounced during the election campaign. Independent candidate George Wallace said in 1968 campaign speeches over and over, "there is not a dime's worth of difference in the two parties at a national level." But who could place any credence in anything a racist Alabama governor had to say, especially when truth is so cleverly obscured by the landscape painters in the mass media.

Brock was fascinated as he listened to Irwin Schiff's vitriolic attack on the IRS and chuckled with the rest of the crowd when he called them the "American Gestapo." Schiff said that history was repeating itself in the United States, as he compared us to thirteenth century Egypt. At that time slaves known as Mamelukes were brought to Egypt to serve as soldiers to the Sultan. In 1250 they revolted and overthrew the government they were supposed to serve, installed one of their own as Sultan, and ruled Egypt for the next two hundred and fifty years. He railed on about Americans being in the same yet worse predicament—worse because most people were not even aware of what the bureaucratic Mamelukes were doing to them.

In order to initiate this subterfuge, the modern Mamelukes had to destroy the very document designed to keep them in check and limit their power. They had nearly succeeded. Schiff said this was largely achieved by those assigned the role of "judges"—puppets whose strings were pulled by the invisible forces in charge. In addition, the key ingredient in the expansion and preservation of Mameluke control of America has been their success in illegally installing and enforcing the income tax. He called the whole IRS code book "utter subterfuge." The judiciary prosecutes people weekly for "willful failure to file," yet no place in the books can be found a law that requires one to file income tax forms. Compliance was voluntary, yet people were being turned into criminals for not volunteering. Schiff got everyone's attention when he made a standing offer of $100,000 to anyone who could show him a law in the code book or anywhere else that required individuals to file 1040 income tax returns. Previously he had printed flyers and sent them to senators, congressmen, and even the IRS commissioner making the same offer, but he never had a taker.

One of the many other speakers that day was F. Tupper Saussy of Sewanee, Tennessee. His self-published book, "The Miracle on Main Street," had sold over a hundred thousand copies without benefit of the corporate book stores, all of which had refused to handle it. Hundreds of copies would move out at every speaking engagement. The balance was being accomplished by word of mouth and mail-orders. Eventually, the book would sell out of its sixth printing—a remarkable feat in the underground market—before the author himself would be forced to flee, change his name, and disappear out of fear for his life.

Saussy was a soft-spoken, scholarly type whose delivery was the antithesis of the bombastic Schiff, but who spoke so matter-of-factly nobody doubted his say. When he asked the audience if anyone there had ever heard of Roger Sherman, only the ones who had read his book could reply to the affirmative.

"But you people who have been to college, maybe read a lot of history, and consider yourselves to be of above-average intelligence, should wonder why you have never heard of Roger Sherman. Why is his name not etched on your memory as keenly as that of Washington, Franklin, and Jefferson? Actually Judge Sherman was more instrumental at the founding of our nation than any of the others. He was the only American to sign all four historic documents: The Continental Association of 1774, The Declaration of Independence, The Articles of Confederation, and the United States Constitution. Renowned for his high intelligence and unswerving honesty, Roger Sherman was described by John Adams as being 'as honest as an angel and as firm in the cause of American independence as Mount Atlas.'

"Why then," continued Saussy, "does this great man remain completely unknown to all but a handful of early historians? I maintain it is because Roger Sherman, for all he did, would be best known for authoring the magic seventeen words in Article I, Section 10 of the Constitution: 'No State shall make anything except gold and silver coin a tender in payment of debts.' It is far better, from the viewpoint of the money creators, to allow this man to fade from history than to eulogize him as a hero in the history books and create a very big question in the minds of school children." Brock recognized that he was one of those with a college diploma—even a law degree and was an avid reader of history—who didn't know who in the world Roger Sherman was either.

"And why did our constitution mandate gold and silver as the only lawful money? Because it cannot be created out of thin air the way imaginary money can. Because it cannot fluctuate and be manipulated with the stroke of a pen or a computer controlled by a handful of plutocrats."

There were a half dozen other speakers that afternoon. Some ranted and raved, even cursed; others somewhat bored Brock but, nevertheless, made some good points. But none stirred his blood and gave him a thirst for more knowledge the way Schiff and Saussy had. How could such pertinent facts of history be shrouded from public view? Not one to impetuously dive into the pool, Brock decided he should check the water level first. He knew something about the law and history, and a broader spectrum of this subject had bugged him once in the past—enough to have changed the course of his life.

*   *   *   *   *

Brock Freeman was the modern Horatio Alger story. He had grown up in Independence, Missouri, Harry Truman's hometown, seven miles east of Kansas City. Ole "Give 'em Hell Harry" said that, for him, Independence was the "hub of the universe" and was always quick to remind folks in Washington and elsewhere that "Kansas City is a suburb of Independence. We were here first." It was true. The Santa Fe, California, and Oregon Trails—the southern, central, and northern routes west—began in Independence. Here in 1821, traders and then homesteaders left steamboats for overland travel to the West, spawning lusty trailhead towns. Kansas City blossomed later where the stockyards could more readily utilize the shipping up and down the Missouri River, and its great bend became the jumping-off place for more fortune seekers migrating from the East.

Brock's father had been a blue-collar laborer working as an electrician at the automotive plant before the war. He joined the marines in January of '42, survived the death march at Bataan followed by three and a half years in a Japanese prison camp, and returned home after the war a physically broken man but one whose dreams were still intact. The oil fields were where the big money of the future would be found, and Charley Freeman intended to be a part of it.

Brock's early childhood was a blur of nomad-like moves from one drab town to another in Oklahoma and Texas, of a series of rented apartments, and of long visits in the homes of various relatives. After working in the oil field for a short while, his dad became a wildcatter, moving from place to place in pursuit of the black gold. Brock seldom had playmates, and in his adult years could not remember the last name of a single friend he had had during his first decade of life. He had rarely been lonely, though, with so much to see and do and explore and consider. The turtles and frogs were his friends, and he had a name for each.

Johnny Mack Brown, Lash Larue, The Durango Kid, and Brock Freeman rode together through the mountains and plains of southeast Texas killing the imagined bad guys with a pointed finger, as the rabbits peeked from behind the rocks and the squirrels scrambled up the pine trees. His excited shrieks at catching his first trout brought his father running in time to grab him and unhook the fish before Brock tumbled into the stream. Was a man's son kind of an immortality? On rainy days his father stayed home, and they played cards, checkers, and chess; and every night his mom lead the family in Bible devotions whether his dad was home or not.

But the lure of riches in the oil business was never more than a dream never-come-true for Charley Freeman, and his pursuit never provided much more than the bare essentials of life for the family. When Charley died six years after the war from a recurrent attack of the malaria he had never shaken, Brock was still in elementary school. He and his mother soon returned to Independence.

However, the father had lived long enough to instill in the son the principles of treating one's fellow man fairly and the philosophy of "work hard, save part of everything you earn, and you'll get ahead." Brock cherished the large plaque his dad had made for him in the woodworking shop out in the garage in some Texas town long since forgotten. The oak letters were carved separately and crudely spaced and glued onto a smooth walnut backing—words Charley had first heard from his own father a generation earlier.

Dear Son,

Ordinary things occur every day. Extraordinary things do not. When you hear hoofbeats, first think of horses. But while you're busy meditating, be sure you don't get run over by the zebra, buffalo, antelope, and elephant.

Love,

Dad

Brock had already acquainted himself with a strong work ethic by cutting neighbor's grass in the summer and raking leaves or picking up pecans in the fall. Once they were settled again, he handled two paper routes—morning and evening—from age ten, in the fifth grade, through high school. His mother worked as a legal secretary and judge's clerk at the courthouse in Independence. And his secret love became Becky Burwell, but he could never muster the courage to tell her nor let on to anyone else, either.

When it became time for college, Brock had saved over two thousand dollars on his own—enough to take care of the first two years with frugal living, made easier by not joining a fraternity, and with some help from his mom. In the meantime he would figure a way to somehow finance the other two years. It would be at Kansas University, across the state line and forty miles to the west in Lawrence.

Then, as always, something happened that Brock had not taken into account. He was a young, healthy, attractive male and K.U. was a coeducational school. Girls, excluding the fantasies concerning his love from afar—Becky Burwell—had so far played no part in his life. Until now he'd considered his face too homely to attract a girl. Not only had he been otherwise occupied, but no one other than his mother had ever told him that he was a good-looking kid. God knows, that didn't count. Now he saw and was seen by Sarah Prince, the prettiest, brightest, and surely the most charming new girl on campus; who arrived a year behind him after attending a year of junior college in western Kansas. He fell in love—deeply, completely and forever in love—and Sarah was about to be smitten, too.

There was a rare and special quality about Brock's loving, and there was a special quality about Sarah herself. Hers was not the conventional prettiness of a nineteen-year-old, though she had her share of that—great gleaming eyes and a fine chin line softened by the gentle curve of her cheeks. Her face was made up of clean, distinct features that highlighted dimples when she smiled; a strong chin, and a nose the English would describe as patrician. But there was a glow about this girl, a promise. Every-thing—her young body, her manner, her eyes and smile—spoke of the woman she was about to be. She was that rare creation, slow to mature, that was to become more physically attractive at forty than she was at twenty. Beautiful, elegant, and discreet, her haunting mystique was already occupying Brock's mind for a larger portion of time each day than his studies.

Brock forgot he'd ever been shy. And he made a miraculous discovery: when someone thinks you are handsome, you are hand-some.

In Western Civ class every morning their eyes would meet, then with an effort withdraw. When classes were over, Sarah would tarry enough to just happen to be outside when Brock emerged from the building. In the evenings he called at the sorority house, and they would walk to the campus grill for a Coke. It was Sarah who led Brock into the real world and gave him a sense of importance and freedom. Now there appeared to be hundreds of paths he might follow, nothing he couldn't do. He began to pursue extracurricular endeavors, starring in the various intramural sports, including boxing, and became captain of the debate team, covering himself with honors. All this was suddenly done with a tremendous, contagious joy, for Sarah was a girl who was delighted with life and shared her delight with others.

No shrinking violet she, Sarah had always been curious and adventurous, and she was more than a bit of a daredevil. On a family outing when she was twelve, the family had camped out in a park at the foot of the Colorado Rockies. The next morning nobody could find Sarah. Her parents had searched everywhere, getting the whole campground management team in an uproar. About noon she came wandering back in, having decided to climb a mountain early that morning before anyone else had awakened. She would try anything once, as long as it didn't go against her moral code. Sarah should have been a boy, her dad used to say. She was a natural athlete. She could swing across the creek on a rope, hit and catch a softball like a boy, and run like the wind. Before she finished high school, she had even tried parachuting.

And yet all of her tomboy tendencies were far overshadowed by the feminine elegance of this enchantress.

All that spring and summer of their sophomore year there had been a new aliveness everywhere, a resplendent pink haze over the world, and—this may have been part of their blessing— they both knew it. He was her hero, she his inspiration.

Sarah Prince was a classic natural beauty. A tall, slender but buxom honey-blond, striking even without makeup, and looking more like a movie starlet with it. She had been the first girl in five years to take Brock's mind off of Becky. Having grown up in the conservative, Christian surroundings of her father's western Kansas farm, she had no aversion to hard work. In fact she thrived on it. Brock discovered when he visited the family that first summer he and Sarah had met that Mr. and Mrs. Prince had raised three other beautiful daughters—all named for heroines of the Bible: Miriam, Ruth, and Esther—but he had plucked the plum. Sarah's physical features were overcome only by her delightful personality and elegant charm. For him it had been love at first sight, and for the unpretentious Sarah, not much longer.

That first Friday night at the sorority house before Brock asked her to dance, he had already figured out the planned sequence of music—three fast ones and a slow one, three fast ones and a slow one. He had just danced with another girl to

Elvis's "Don't Be Cruel," Little Richard's "Rip it Up," and was happy when someone broke him in the middle of Jerry Lee Lewis's "Whole Lot of Shaking Going on." It had been his ploy for an hour to wait for the right moment to grab the pretty gal whose name, he had learned, was Sarah Prince. As they slowly spun around the living room dance floor, Tony Williams of the Platters sang in his strong falsetto:

> "Oh, yes, once in a lifetime you know, a love has been started below,
> though it may be rare, you and I, dear, share
> this love that has happened to few;
> for there's one in a million like you."

The two of them would forever remember it as "their song."

Another important element cementing their early relationship was Sarah's family. Her parents were unlike any Brock had ever known—both tough, second generation farming stock of Scandinavian descent who treated Brock as if he were a grown man whose ideas sincerely interested them. Such was the time when he brought up some of his own beliefs about the changes needed in the world. He found Mr. Prince agreeing and taking him a step further, hoping that Brock and Sarah would work and develop their minds, so that when the time came for them to strike out for change, it would be with force and meaning.

A time Brock would always remember was the evening after such talk that he and Sarah sat side by side in the porch swing for a while, neither of them speaking. Brock knew that she was mentally with him, going over in her head as he was in his what her papa had said—about how from the beginning, even the earliest and most primitive beings had wanted to be something more, to break through to new dimensions, to change, to improve. And he agreed with his future father-in-law's dinner table summation that throughout history there had always been evil men wanting to change the world to their own devious and selfish advantages, and there always would be. But the majority of times the world had been betrayed not by scoundrels so much as by decent men who had done nothing to correct the evils around them.

"I wonder what's waiting out there for us, Sarah," he said, as they held hands and gently swung back and forth. At the first feathery touch of the chilly night air, he had draped his cardigan sweater around her shoulders.

She paused and pondered deeply before replying, "Maybe what is waiting is what we are to do. 'Time and tide wait for no one,' Mama always says. If we aren't the most that we can be, then aren't we letting the world down by giving up too soon and falling into mediocrity?"

It was a declaration more than a question and one that Brock knew there was no need to answer, but he never forgot it. He also knew that this was the strength he wanted beside him as a life-long partner.

Much through the influence of his mother and the judge she worked for, Brock had decided to pursue a career in law. By attending year-round with a full load even in the summer sessions, he had hustled through all the pre-law requisites in just two years and a summer instead of the normal three years. And in the middle of the first semester of his second year of law school, he and Sarah had gotten married. She had waited tables at Bill's Cafe on Massachusetts Avenue and clerked at Sears before getting the receptionist's job at the campus library—all the while finishing up her degree in elementary education. Brock was ready to introduce the new Clarence Darrow to the legal establishment. After four years of study, increasing debt to his mother, and scraping and skimping at the Sisyphean task of simply making ends meet, he was ready for a job yielding tangible rewards, viz big bucks.

They were married in the little country church in Finney County on a rainy Thanksgiving morning in 1963. Mr. Prince had arranged for their short honeymoon stay at the world famous Broadmoor Hotel in Colorado Springs. Even with his new father-in-law paying for everything, Brock was horrified at the room cost of sixteen dollars a night and the prices on the dining room menu, but the weekend did serve him his first-ever taste of luxury in his life, and he liked it. "It's being billed to me, but spend it like was your own," Papa Prince had playfully admonished him, as Brock and his new bride had driven away that chilly afternoon.

They hiked, canoed, went horse-back riding, and learned how to make love together. During the 500-mile, all day trek back to Lawrence three days later, he came to the frightening realization that, for now and forever, he would be operating out of his own wallet again.

Brock got a job clerking in the Federal Court in Topeka and commuted the eighty round-trip miles each day while Sarah finished up her degree in Lawrence. While waiting to pass the bar, he had found time—and somehow the money—to pursue one of his life's dreams. He put in his required forty hours of flight time; soloed; did his "cross country" to Salina, Wichita, and back to Topeka; and got his cherished private pilot's license. It would prove to be an ace-in-the-hole later. In a short time he would become disenchanted with the whole legal industry.

During office coffee breaks in the morning and cocktail hour in the evenings at Poor Richard's on Kansas Avenue, the attorney's favorite Topeka watering hole, Brock got to know many of the young lawyers who had five to ten more years experience than he. He had found the tactics and business ethics of most of them to be disgusting. But more than that, he was appalled by the legal perversion of the law that had taken root during the last thirty years since the first administration of Franklin Roosevelt. The whole legal business seemed to be continually deteriorating from the once noble profession of Jefferson, Adams, and Madison to even less than what he had just been taught in law school. It just seemed so counterfeit.

From his Christian upbringing and study of the Bible in his early years and his recent law history courses, Brock well knew the difference between God's law and man's law. While few modern law professors mentioned it, Peter's admonition in Acts 5:29 had been well ingrained in him: "We ought to obey God rather than men," and he knew that the American Constitution had been born out of Old Testament law and the *Magna Carta*.

The first U.S. Chief Justice John Marshall had ruled in 1804 that any city, county, or state law passed contradictory to the Constitution was null and void. Brock could almost recite verbatim the "supremacy clause" of the Constitution:

> This Constitution . . . under the authority of the United States, shall be the supreme law of the land; and the judges in every State shall be bound thereby, anything in the Constitution or laws of any State to the contrary notwithstanding.

Why then, he wondered, were black people, who were "peaceably assembling and petitioning the government for a redress of grievances," not protected by the First Amendment, which is supposed to guard that right?

How was a local ordinance banning the possession of a firearm not an infringement on the people's right to keep and bear arms, supposedly protected by the Second Amendment?

How could federal authorities break down the door of a citizen's house and attack the people inside in the middle of the night without a warrant, without an affidavit by an accuser, but only on the *suspicion* of the possession of marijuana, which was a natural product grown on God's earth throughout history, and only recently ruled to be "illegal" by man? The common law held that there could be no crime without a victim. How could "possession" of anything create a crime unless men were playing god?

Judges in recent years had refused to allow a non-member of the bar to sit at the accused's defense table at trial. How had the legal profession usurped the sixth Amendment clause which protected one's right to "assistance of counsel" of his choice? The clause said nothing about having assistance of "only a licensed member of the bar who is beholden to the court and who practices there at the pleasure of the judge."

Brock had wondered: Are we a nation of laws or men? The countless list of double standards he saw displayed in the courtroom grated on his inherent sense of truth. He noticed that the federal judges, whenever a question arose concerning a statute that could jeopardize the control by government held over the people, did not behave fairly as the referees they were supposed to be but actually participated in the prosecution. He was repelled by the behind-the-scenes deals he saw made in the judge's chambers by lawyers time and time again as they sold out their clients in both civil and criminal litigations. In government "land-grab" or tax cases, Brock could see the trial rigged from the beginning while the poor, ignorant defendant believed all the while that his attorney was really acting in his best interests and doing the best job he could for his client. The "plea-bargains" especially nauseated Brock. "Just tell your client that, if he goes to trial and loses, he could go to jail for thirty years and be fined two hundred thousand dollars," the judge would privately instruct the defense attorney. "That should sufficiently terrify him into pleading to the lesser charge." And it almost always did.

After a year, when Sarah had graduated from K.U., Brock began to correspond with several of the commercial airlines to inquire about their commercial pilot-training programs. After considering several offers he settled on and was hired by TWA in Kansas City. The deciding factor was that Sarah would not have to give up the teaching job she had just taken in Overland Park, to which she had already begun commuting from Lawrence. They moved from their Lawrence apartment into a three-bedroom house with reasonable rent off of State Line Road near The Plaza. He had passed the bar but would never practice law.

The young lovers, both mature beyond their years, would lie in bed late at night and talk about the future. Rather than bemoan the fact that he might have wasted much time and money with law school and court work, Sarah instead preferred to back her husband in whatever endeavor he chose. Besides, having a law degree in his back pocket wasn't too shabby a beginning, and there were more lawyers in the country not practicing the profession than who were. So it was no big deal to change course.

Brock loved her a little more for that. Their happiness was the most important thing, she said, and airline pilots could make more money than most attorneys—and with a lot more freedom. Not to mention the travel benefits for both of them! With the family privileges, they could spend long weekends in Hawaii or the Caribbean as cheaply as at the Lake of the Ozarks. Of all the wonderful attributes his new wife possessed, Brock loved her ability to "roll-with-the-punch" the most. She maintained a positive mental attitude about everything. She was nearly impossible to fluster. "A cool head," said he.

One Saturday evening, shortly after they had moved into the house in Kansas City, Brock had grilled two costly bacon-wrapped filets on the outside charcoal pit while Sarah prepared the baked potatoes and vegetables in the kitchen. They had been planning to watch a special movie on television that night; one that they had missed in the theater a few years before. Sarah was already in the living room in front of her TV tray when Brock was pouring two glasses of the expensive burgundy he had bought for the occasion and placed them on the tray along side his plate of steak and vegetables. On the step-down to the sunken dining room he inadvertently dragged the legs of his TV tray and dumped the whole thing under the dining room table.

"Sheee-it!" he yelled. It was his favorite and almost singular curse word whenever he was perturbed about anything. The total frustration and helplessness of this situation, as he stared at the results of what he had done, left him no alternative but to scream it again—this time loud enough to be heard by everybody on the block.

"SHEEEEE-IT."

"What is it, Honey? asked Sarah, never rising from her living room easy chair. She was inured to these occasional outbursts and remained cool and calm.

"I just dumped my whole shittin' tray of food all over the floor," he yelled back to her as he gawked in a trance at the floor, the carpet now colorfully decorated with a huge splash of dark red.

"That's all right, Honey. Pick it up and eat it and don't worry about it. I just mopped and vacuumed this afternoon."

Suddenly Brock began to laugh hysterically, and when Sarah finally got up to investigate this maniacal howling emanating from the dining room, she found him writhing on the floor, bouncing from wall to chair in uncontrollable convulsions of laughter. Consumed by the moment, she dived on top of him and, screaming with laughter, began to wrestle his head and face into the wine and vegetables. He attempted to retaliate but in his temporarily weakened state could not readily get her off of him. After a moment, as she mockingly held his shoulders in a pinned position, he reached above his head and plucked a pinch from a soft, wet potato and began to gently smush it into her nose. She then planted a handful of mixed vegetables into his face and the silly war was on.

They didn't know exactly when it had happened, and it didn't really matter. But gradually, as they tired of their foolishness, the frivolous wrestling became, by slow and leisurely stages, a caress, then a wine-flavored lick, and a kiss. She felt his hand smoothing the back of her thick, blond hair and soon they were tearing their clothes off and making love under the table amongst the wine, steak and vegetables.

Age twenty-four might be "old" when you are eighteen, but it was still a long way from forty—the age when many men have to start all over with a career change. Brock and Sarah were as deeply in love as any couple had ever been and were totally devoted to each other. It was at this ridiculous moment that Brock realized that, with Sarah at his side, he could go anywhere and conquer anything. They would learn later that it was a memorable moment for one more reason. It was the night their son was conceived, and for months before giving birth, Sarah had teasingly threatened to name the baby "Shee-it."

Six years into the marriage, with two small children and Sarah at home as a full-time mother and homemaker, Brock had begun to invest in real estate as a part time avocation. Kansas City was sprawling into the suburbs and he had taken the plunge with a broker's advice that a certain piece of acreage near the new interstate highway interchange would be the logical spot for a shopping center. With a $100,000 investment, most of it coming from Shipmen's Bank, Brock bought it. Thirteen months later he sold it for a half million dollar profit. He was off and running and pursuing that seductive old whore, the American dream.

There was always something just a bit incongruous about the young man with his feet propped up on his desk, his boyish face appearing even more callow under the battered Royals baseball cap pushed to the back of his head, discussing multi-million dollar deals on the telephone while leaning back comfortably in his office chair. It was that touch of the midwest hayseed that never completely left him—in his speech, in his bright, friendly blue eyes. He was at ease, that was the thing. His love and respect for his fellow man was being reflected back to him. Men trusted him, talked freely with him, and began giving him tips and advice on the real estate market.

". . . And this is what I would do if I were a young man. . ." many old-timers were quick to offer, and Brock was eager to listen, sometimes taking the advice, sometimes rejecting it, but always listening, as he forged on to carve out a future.

Deals seemed to appear from nowhere, and Brock began cashing them like Midas. Positive thinking came as natural to him as sleep at the end of the day. When a shopping center sprang up, residential housing in the immediate proximity also came into demand. Condominiums were the new way for people to own a small apartment without throwing away money on rent. It also was a superb opportunity for real estate developers, and Brock cashed that ticket too. After another five years, the seventy thousand a year salary and all the benefits and prestige of being an airline captain were hardly worth his time anymore. Freeman Real Estate and Development, Inc. had assets in excess of twenty million dollars and was growing by leaps and bounds. At the time he had no way of knowing that in another two years his stock investments in a new Texas computer company would equal the value of his real estate business.

At the time of the California seminar, Brock had flown out West on the maiden voyage of his new jet plane, a Cessna Citation. He couldn't really justify the cost of the plane with enough usage in his own business, so he contracted with a charter company at the downtown Kansas City airport who guaranteed him enough hours to defray the overhead expenses and some of the bank note, which ran into five figures on the first of every month.

To meet the expanding needs of their family as well as to satisfy an inner desire, Brock and Sarah had also bought their dream home on Ward Parkway. It was a three-story mansion only a few blocks from the Mission Hills Country Club in the most exclusive area of Kansas City. Her 735 BMW, his 450 SL Mercedes, and their GMC Motorhome sitting in the driveway also attested to their arrival. Now son Brent would soon be entering high school and appealing for his own VW Rabbit convertible. Maria was only one grade behind. The family spent several weeks each summer and numerous weekends throughout the year at their *pied-a-terres* in Aspen and another overlooking the golf course at Lake of the Ozarks in south/central Missouri. "The only difference between men and boys is the price of their toys," Brock had mumbled with a sly grin when Sarah had wondered out loud about the wisdom exercised in the purchase of that private jet.

Brent and Maria were fine young teenagers. They didn't smoke or drink or foolishly experiment with hard drugs, and neither had ever cheated on a test. Brent had become an Eagle Scout before he was fourteen. Maria was as pretty as a young model and couldn't wait to get the braces off her teeth and find out what it was like to kiss a boy—really kiss one, in the dark when nobody else is looking. They both were straight "A" students and each was the most popular student in his/her class. Brock and Sarah were proud parents. They were finally living that slippery and elusive American dream.

Brock well understood the natural laws of giving and the meaning of "you reap what you sow." When his son was fourteen, Brock had been reading item after item about school kids getting into trouble, and he didn't like that sort of thing in the city where he was raising teenagers. Finally one evening when he read of one more story of a school boy chum of Brent's in a jam, he exploded.

"Doggone it," he roared, "why doesn't somebody do something about this? Why aren't these kids kept busy at decent things? Is this all Teddy has to do—steal his father's car and drive across the neighbor's lawns?"

Brent said, "There is a boys' club, Dad. But the old building is dying on its foundation. The ping-pong and pool tables are all but wrecked, and the toilets won't even flush. The kids would rather stay home and watch TV or hang out at the drive-in than go there anymore. Maybe someday somebody will . . ."

"You don't know the secret, Son. There is no someday. There is only now. You'll be an old man with a long beard waiting for 'someday'. Now just what would you do to change that place and make it fun again?"

Brent thought hard for a moment. "I would hire a plumber to get everything ship shape in the bathrooms and kitchen. Then I would hire a carpenter to replace the busted sheetrock and repair the old shelves. I would paint it inside and out and put in a new pool table and a couple of new ping pong tables with all new equipment. Then, most important, I would put in a juke box with all the latest records so the girls will come and we can dance.

"You mean like fifties music?" Brock jibed.

"No, awugh!" Brent overreacted, but he could tell his father was sincerely interested now.

"Can you find a half dozen of your buddies to do the painting next Saturday?"

"Sure."

"Good, because I know where the plumber and carpenter can be found, and some paint, too."

A month later the teenagers had a weekend meeting spot they could be proud of, and they were taking care of it because they themselves had done much of the work to put it in shape again. There was a new pride of ownership. An "anonymous" donor had silently paid for all the material and professional labor and lodged $10,000 in a savings account to provide for cokes, snacks, new records, etc., and perpetual care. The parents formed a small neighborhood association of volunteer chaperons on Friday and Saturday nights. Brent wrote some of the new rules of the club on a sign and posted it on the clubhouse wall. There would be a 5-cent fine for failing to replace the paddles and cuesticks in the rack after usage. Ten-cents for foul and abusive language and a quarter for failing to clean up after one's self in the kitchen or to flush the bathroom toilet. Any intentional destruction of equipment or graffiti on the walls meant permanent expulsion for the perpetrators—judged by a jury of their peers.

The neighborhood teen club became the weekend fun spot for the next several years, and fewer kids were out on the streets looking for mischief.

*   *   *   *   *

Brock's head was spinning with excitement as he fired up the engines on his Citation at Orange County Airport that Sunday morning following the seminar. From his California friend he had acquired reams of legal briefs and publications on the tax/money issue. At the Saturday meeting he had bought a dozen books, mostly from Saussy and Schiff, and stashed them all in a box in the luggage hold. The two had hardly talked about the $3 million oceanfront property they had purchased on Friday, the business deal which had lured Brock out west in the first place. "When the San Andreas gives one more good belch, we're going to be starting all over at fifty cents an acre anyway," he had remarked, only half-joking.

Brock had not wanted to talk about anything else except what he had gotten a taste of at the seminar. "Read," his friend had said. "You won't believe the deception that the American people have fallen for with all this. The whole money scheme was designed to steal the wealth and labor from the people and keep the power in the hands of the government and the money in the hands of the bankers." Brock was still skeptical, but his interest was definitely piqued.

He jabbered his aeronautical lingo to the tower, got the permission for take-off he was seeking, taxied to the end of the strip, waited for final clearance, hammered down, and before spending half the time and airstrip distance required for the big airliners, was airborne. *This baby jumps like a Corvette,* he thought, experiencing only his second take-off since acquiring it.

As happy as he was with his new toy, his mind was still occupied with deeper thoughts. As one of the speakers said yesterday, he remembered, *"Nobody in this modern day and age really believes in the conspiracy theory of history—except those of us who have taken the time to study the subject."*

Brock had first heard of the absurdity of the "conspiracy theory of history" over late afternoon beer at Poor Richard's during his year in Topeka and knew that whoever believes that major world events result from actual planning will be laughed at by the majority of his friends. But what evidence had those young lawyers used in forming their opinions, other than what some college professor had told them in a lecture one day?

When Brock thought about it, he concluded that there are really only two theories of history. Either things happen by accident, neither planned nor caused by anybody, or they happen because they were designed and somebody or a group of somebodies causes them to happen. Franklin Roosevelt said, "Nothing in politics happens by accident. If it happens, you can believe it was planned that way," and Franklin Roosevelt dang sure knew more about it than those bubbleheads back in Topeka. Matter of fact, this was a pretty good beginning reference point. Who could have known better than he?

In reality, it is the "accidental theory of history" preached to the fertile young minds in the Halls of Ivy which should be ridiculed, thought Brock. Otherwise, why does every new administration in recent years make the same mistakes as the previous ones? Why do they repeat the errors of the past which produce inflation, depressions, and war? Why has every politician at every level in every party bitched about "balancing the budget" and nobody has ever come close to doing it?

Surely there are individuals and groups of individuals who are working together in a cartel to deprive their fellow men out of their property, but that is nothing new. He remembered what Papa Prince had said about there always being men of criminal mind and there always will. But has the whole conspiracy theory been blown out of proportion all because someone suggested it years ago and it made wonderful typewriter fodder the last couple of generations?

Who cares? Brock whispered to himself as he flew over the Grand Canyon. A man could spend a lifetime in that swirling eddy of confusion and never be any farther down the road to

Truth than he was when he started. But something was going on. That was for sure. America had changed.

Could it be that the only reason for the politician's interminable movement toward gun confiscation is that they do have reason to fear the eventual use of force against them by the people? Brock figured this was too big for him, and the important thing is for one to take the steps to guarantee his own personal protection, whatever those steps might be. He wanted to find out.

He busied himself with the controls again, leveled out at his requested and assigned altitude of 29,000 feet, and began to consider the overall picture some more. What is the point of a captured nation fearing invasion by a foreign power? None, he thought, unless the people of that nation are unaware that they have already been captured. In that case, the fear factor can be very useful in the collection of taxes for their so-called protection.

But Brock thought about something else more specific that his friend had said before he bade him goodbye. It disturbed him all the way to Kansas City, and he promised himself he would find out the answer. It was a simple enough question. Why does no one ever ask his congressman? Or the president? Ha! Wouldn't that be great if a reporter at a press conference asked Reagan: "Mr. President, why are we taxed at all when government prints all the money it needs to do with whatever it wishes? I mean, uh, Sir, why do you need the income tax, anyway?"

But Brock already knew that you save a lot of unnecessary conversation if you remember that people aren't going to take your advice unless you are a lawyer or a doctor who charges them for it.

A seed had been dropped, and it had fallen on fertile and receptive soil. There is one ingredient in all great adventures that the adventurer will seldom acknowledge: The role played by chance. During his flight home, Brock became determined to satisfy himself through study. Had the escape from lawful money and the insertion of an elastic currency been a horrible mistake that even the smartest politicians found impossible to correct? Or had it been one gigantic scheme from its inception, designed to enrich a privileged few at the top?

There are moments in life which involve in themselves eternities. There are instants which germinate and continue to develop and bloom forever. Brock Freeman had been smitten again, and his new, intangible mistress was mysteriously elusive.

FOUR

"As I look back on it, I realize that there was no better place and time in history to grow up than in America in the 1950s," the old man wistfully reminisced. "With the circulating silver coin, we still had an honest system of just weights and measures, pastors unafraid to preach the truth, and the majority of the population was still a God-fearing people. Even if we had known that drugs and pornography existed— which we didn't—we couldn't have begun to know where to find them. And political assassinations were only something that you read about in books that happened in some other uncivilized time and place."

When Brock was fifteen, he was secretly in love with Becky Burwell. He hadn't matured very much yet and didn't have much self-confidence. He dreamed of being a football star, but, at five feet tall and barely a hundred pounds, he knew he didn't have a chance of even getting into a uniform and warming the bench. Besides that, the financial necessity of his afternoon paper route precluded most of the extracurricular activities his classmates enjoyed. At his little schoolhouse in the earlier grades he had been considered good at athletics, but here at Independence High School now, up against boys who had the time to really concentrate in sports, he felt clumsy and inadequate. But it was then that he developed an obsession. He'd show 'em. Someday he would be the best at baseball, or football, or something. No, he would be the best at everything.

Becky was a grade ahead of him in school, the head majorette in the marching band, daughter of a bank president, would be voted "Most Beautiful" two years in a row, and a straight "A" student. An absolute untouchable. There was no way she would ever go out with him. He didn't even have a car. What was he going to do? Ask her to take a ride with him on his bicycle? She was to remain on a pedestal, only to be admired from afar. The dark-haired, blue-eyed beauty never had a clue. Brock would forever remember these days of overwhelming loneliness that perhaps only boys of fourteen or fifteen ever know.

One chilly fall afternoon, Brock was on his bike and slinging his papers on Delaware Street. He had worn his old red, woolen sweater, which just happened to have large impressions of silvery elephants woven throughout the material. A block away President Truman strode out of his house at "219" embarking on one of his famous daily walks around the neighborhood. Several Secret Service Agents bounced into action behind him, struggling to keep up.

A moment later, Brock was face to face with the President of the United States, who had stepped off the curb to shake his hand.

"What's your name, son?" said the town's most famous citizen.

Somehow the boy was able to utter, "Brock Freeman."

"And where do you live?"

He told him.

Suddenly photographers were snapping pictures from three sides, and four reporters—two with "A. P." on a card extending from their hatbands—were taking down every word of the short conversation on steno pads. In a moment it was over and the President was hustling up the sidewalk again at 120 paces per minute. Brock continued on his route, hardly able to wait to tell his mother about it. He did, but it wasn't necessary. In twenty-four hours everybody in the country would know about him.

The next day's newspapers in most every city in the United States had a large photo on its front page of a beaming newsboy, still astride his bicycle with the basket stuffed with papers, shaking hands with Harry S. Truman. "Truman befriends Republican newsboy," announced the caption underneath, with an obvious reference to the elephants on Brock's sweater. They even printed his name.

Everyone in his class—students and teachers alike—were talking about it. His homeroom teacher asked him to autograph her copy of the newstory for her scrapbook. Brock was the school "hero" for a day. When he passed Becky in the hallway between classes, he hoped she had seen the papers and would comment, but all she had said was, "Hi," and kept walking.

A few afternoons later, on his route in Becky's neighborhood, Brock was accosted by the school bully, Butch Evans, who outweighed him by fifty pounds and was a budding young football player with the reputation of being "tough as nails."

"Gimme a paper, Shrimp," Butch said.

"Five cents."

"Five cents, my ass. If you don't give me one right now, I'll take your whole damned load."

"Look Butch," Brock tried to explain, "I have to pay for these papers, so if you want one. . ."

Before he could finish, Butch had him by the collar and was dragging him off his bicycle. The bike fell over, spilling some of the papers on the wet ground. With a sadistic smirk on his face, Butch slung Brock backwards, knocking him down into the watery mud in the small ditch between the road and the sidewalk. Then he picked up the bike and rode up the street a hundred feet before dismounting and slinging it into the ditch on the other side, *right in front of Becky's house!* He took one dry copy of the day's paper out of the basket and swaggered up the street, shouting back to Brock, "Hey, Mr. Hero. Go see your buddy, Harry Truman. Maybe he'll pay you for it."

Becky had been twirling her baton in the backyard when the commotion out front caught her ear. As Brock picked up himself and the few scattered papers from the mud, he was more concerned about whether Becky had seen the whipping he had just taken than about his wounded pride and soiled inventory. When he started walking toward her house to retrieve his bike, he was horrified to see her out there already picking it up for him.

"Hi, Brock. You okay?"

Feeling ridiculous in his torn shirt, wet and muddy pants, and a thoroughly diluted spirit, Brock scanned his brain for some pretentious cover-up that might enhance his position, but already he knew there were no words he could utter to improve this embarrassing situation. *Oh, God, why did Becky, of all people, have to see that?*

"Yeah," he meekly replied.

"Are you sure?"

If I say "no," maybe she'll take me in the house, put me in the guest room bed, give me a glass of ginger ale, fan me with palm fronds, and nurse me back to health for a year or two. No, forget that.

"Yeah, Becky. Thanks."

He rode off knowing that if his odds had been slim before, there was no way he could ever ascend that pedestal now. Becky would forever be the heroine of only his dreams. And first love never dies.

*　　*　　*　　*　　*

When Brock was a high school senior, he had finally started to grow taller. To improve his skinny physique he began to lift weights and drink homemade protein shakes, made with "super powder," ordered from the nationally renowned body-builder

Joe Weider. During his freshman year at K. U. he took up boxing and learned how to handle himself. He had grown to 6'1"
and 190 sinewy pounds. Only the few opponents who had fought
him in the ring knew of his devastating left hand and always
avoided bouts with him a second time. But by nature Brock
avoided physical confrontations outside of the ring and would
never intentionally provoke someone else into a fight. Except
once.

The favorite hangout for the college gang in Lawrence, Kansas, was called "The Stables." It was big enough for dancing and
eating, and was one of the few joints in town that could legally
serve beer. Even though it was only "three-point-two," it was still
beer. The original structure actually was a horse stable built in
the late nineteenth century and converted into a pub sometime
later. With the multiple pungency of the petrified horse manure,
college boy urine, vomit, and Mennen Skin Bracer; the stale beer
mixed with that greasy aroma of fresh hamburgers in the air,
most patrons agreed that the joint surely must smell worse now
than it ever had when it was full of live, flatulating horses. Nevertheless, The Stables holds more memories for the old alumni
than any place on campus, with the possible exception of the
small body of water beneath the Campanile—recalled by old
lovers as "the only pond in the world with a rubber bottom."

On football Saturdays, there was only one place to be. If the
Jayhawks were on the road, everyone who hadn't traveled to the
game was at The Stables, drinking beer and listening to each
gut-wrenching play on the radio. After home games, especially a
win, the joint would frequently jump until the wee hours, with
the celebration continuing in the parking lot after the doors were
closed. This was one of those Saturdays.

K. U. had just knocked off archrival Kansas State at the
homecoming game of Brock's junior year. Butch Evans had caught
the winning touchdown pass in the final minute and was wallowing in his glory at the bar when Brock walked in. Brock had
taken Sarah to the game and had just dropped her off at the
sorority house in order that she make herself beautiful for the
big homecoming dance at 8 o'clock. In just one more month—on
Thanksgiving weekend—they would be married. Brock had
stopped in at The Stables for a beer and to join in the early
evening celebration.

Something weird and unmanageable came over him. He never
did decide what. Maybe it was the excitement already in the air
or the fact that he had spotted but never acknowledged Becky,
who was still in her red and blue corduroy cheerleader uniform
at a table nearby. Maybe it was the courage augmented by the

first half-mug of beer he had sipped at the bar before realizing he was standing right next to Butch Evans, whose back was turned as he enthusiastically chatted with a few other swainish jocks and wannabes. It was probably a combination of all that plus what was etched on his subconscious from years before. Brock listened for another minute while Evans relived the winning play of two hours earlier and continued the report to his admirers of how wonderful he was. Spinning back to the bar on his swivel bar stool and reaching for his beer mug, Evans caught sight of Brock standing next to him.

"Well, if it ain't Freeman. Haven't seen you since high school."

"You owe me a dollar, Bozo," Brock retorted with scorn.

"How ya' figger?" said Evans, temporarily ignoring the disparaging sobriquet.

"Fifty cents for the ten stolen and damaged newspapers plus six years interest at my rates. One dollar, Clown," Brock said, with his right hand out, palm up. His left was cocked and ready.

Sensing the static in the air, Butch stood up. "You're serious, ain't 'cha? Then leaning right up in Brock's face, he said, "I hope you are serious, piss ant, because I want to see you take a buck offa' me." He was a full two inches taller and still thirty pounds heavier than Brock. Everyone within earshot got quiet and backed away.

"Your breath stinks, Bozo. Get out of my face!" retorted Brock, but before Butch could move or answer, Brock grabbed him by the throat with a right-hand choke-hold and fired three lightning-strike jabs with his left into Butch's right eye, the knuckles cutting through the eyebrow to the bone. He shoved back hard with his right before releasing, sending Butch off balance, and unleashed a combination of left-right-left-right-left; the last of which caught Butch on the chin and sent him skiing on his ass across the sawdusted floor into a table and chairs, which had been vacated just in time by four frightened and scattering patrons.

Down but not out, Butch Evans, football hero and BMOC, was livid. The blood trickling into his right eye only made him dizzier with rage than he already was with the thought of what his hero-worshipping entourage had just witnessed. Brock didn't charge but, gallantly complying with the Marquis of Queensbury rules, stalked from left to right and waited for him in the middle of the room. No one, not even the bartender, attempted to stop it. Instead, someone unplugged the jukebox and everyone rimmed the area for a close but safe look. All eyes were on the fallen hero, but no one uttered a word of encouragement. Somebody, they didn't know who, had just knocked big, bad Butch Evans around like a punching bag, and they did not want to miss round two.

Butch queasily pulled himself from the floor and brushed the peanut shells from his trousers. Reaching for a paper napkin at a nearby table, he wiped the blood from his brow. Brock stood poised with fists raised *au* John L. Sullivan, while Butch dabbed at his eye one last time, dropped the reddened tissue, lowered his head, and charged like a raging bull in an attempt to tackle his assailant. At the last split-second, Brock side-stepped, pivoted on the ball of his left foot while sticking out his right, and pushed and tripped the big tight end. Emitting a low animal-like moan, Evans clumsily stumbled to his knees and elbows through the furniture again, this time knocking over a large, sand-filled ash-tray. Brock had made the furious hero appear foolish once more in front of his now-worried worshippers.

"Do you want to fight or play football, Mr. Touchdown," Brock taunted from the middle of the room.

Butch got up and, in a rage of temporary insanity, charged with fists flailing. Brock ducked under and pounded the hard-ened midriff with devastating rights and lefts. Butch backed away as Brock again leapt in like a puma for his adversary's nose and eyes. One of those right jabs squashed Butch's nose against his face, flushing out a rush of blood. Butch, thoroughly beaten but still on his feet, never saw the final roundhouse left that put him back into the peanut shells.

Sitting on his butt in the middle of the room, Butch reached for his wallet, retrieved a dollar bill, wadded it, and flipped it across the sawdust to his antagonist. He had not landed a punch.

"Okay, Freeman, you win," he said. "There's your buck. We're even."

"Na na, Bozo, I only got a quarter's worth," Brock replied, leaving the dollar lay. "I am going to collect like this from you the next three times I see you, wherever you are, so be pre-pared."

With that Brock calmly walked to the bar, chugged down the remaining half-mug of beer, and—as the crowd parted for him out of respect, admiration, and fear—strode toward the front door. Somebody plugged in the jukebox, and Patsy Cline began to wail as if nothing had happened.

". . . *I faawwll to pieces,*
each time I see you agaahin. . ."

Standing near the door at the last table, slowly shaking her head and grinning from ear to ear, was Becky Burwell. Her face was perspired clean of makeup from an afternoon of cheerleading at the stadium, but looking ever so elegant and more intensely provocative than he could remember, with legs extraordinary and figure superb. Sarah was now his love, but Becky was still his fantasy, and he had long ago realized that she would always be that and nothing more. In a splendidly dramatic moment, he paused, started to speak, and then just gave her a wink before going out the door. Any utterance at this point would be empty and hollow. He knew that she alone was already aware of the whole story of this magnificent, avenging triumph. While touching her fingers to her rosy lips and flipping a gentle kiss in his direction, she discreetly returned the wink. He reflected a quick grin and was out the door. A quarter century would pass before he would see her again.

"*. . . you walk by, and I faawwll to pieces . . .*"

Fearing that there was only one way he could repay that remaining seventy-five cents, Butch Evans forever shuddered at the thought, skipped the homecoming dance that evening, and made certain that Brock Freeman never saw him again—ever.

FIVE

"The truth was that there was no money in the banks," the older man said, "and very little of that pretty green paper that they referred to as money was there, either. There were only electrons flitting around in the sub-conscious of the bank's computers, that of its board members, and that of the smiling people who worked the teller's windows; all of whom made believe that the uniformed guard with the pistol strapped to his hip was really guarding something."

The Kansas City summer of 1983 was its normal blistering hot. Three months has passed since the California seminar, and Brock was spending many spare hours in the air-conditioned comfort of various libraries confirming the theories of Saussy and Schiff. It bothered him that if it was true that money was created out of thin air by a small group at the top, then everyone else was a slave to those few. By studying the wisdom of Jefferson, he discovered a prophetic quote on the subject: "Whenever public servants begin to be paid by something other than what the people produce, the roles of master and servant become reversed." Had this already happened and nobody knew it? Brock's spare-time research was leading him to believe that it had; that the people had become servants of the government instead of the way it had been originally designed.

After dinner each evening in recent weeks, Sarah had seen him retire to his own reading room more often than usual, many times missing their favorite insipid diversion on TV, but she had not paid attention to what was so intently captivating him. She had tennis, bridge, the daily household grind, and the problems of two growing teenagers to occupy her time.

Brock had stopped by a Prairie Village coin dealer's shop one weekday afternoon on the way home from the office and purchased three old Federal Reserve Notes—each redeemable on its face for fifty dollars of lawful money, at least at one time in American history. One was a 1928 series, another 1934 series, and a 1950 series. In the upper left-hand corner where the small print outlined the redeemability clause, he noticed the print was regressively smaller with each series, making it harder to read and easier to ignore. He had paid from 25% to 50% over face value to acquire these notes, which the banks had been gradually removing from circulation since 1968.

On the way home, he pulled into Shipman's Bank and walked inside to the teller window, both to have a little fun and prove something to himself. He pushed the 1950 series bill across the marble counter top to the young woman in the cage.

"I would like to redeem my lawful money, please," he said.

"I beg your pardon?" she replied, and looked at him as if he had just presented her a bill from Mars.

"This note is one of the older ones guaranteed by the federal reserve to be redeemable in lawful money. See, it says right here in the small print that I can collect my lawful money at any federal reserve bank. You are affiliated with the federal reserve system, aren't you?"

After staring at it for a few moments she said, "I am sorry sir, but I have never even seen one of these and have no idea what you are talking about. Let me get the branch manager."

Brock said, "Fine. I'll wait."

The manager emerged from his office in a few moments with the fifty dollar note in hand and gave Brock a smile of recognition as he approached. "What seems to be the problem, Mr. Freeman?"

"That note of mine you have there says that it will be honored at any federal reserve bank or the United States Treasury, so I am here to collect my lawful money. What seems to be the bank's problem with that?"

"Mr. Freeman, you are joking aren't you?"

"Why no, I'm not joking." Brock said as he strolled to the writing station in the middle of the lobby, and the young man followed. Brock set down a file folder and removed a single sheet copy of 12 USC 152, which he had secured at the library. He read part of it aloud to him: "The terms 'Lawful Money' or 'Lawful Money of the United States' shall be construed to mean gold and silver coin of the United States."

Brock looked up to read the young man's reaction before explaining, "The same amount of silver coin will buy eight times what that paper will today, so you have to agree that it is hardly a joking matter. I would have to be crazy to take fifty bucks for that note when it is really worth four hundred. I'll take the silver coin, please."

"Mr. Freeman, we don't have any silver coin. All we can do is exchange that for a bank check, fifty dollars in cash, or deposit it to your account."

"But what about my lawful money that this contract guarantees? The bank or the treasury is supposed to be keeping it for me until it is demanded. Don't you agree that the contract here says that?"

"Yes sir, I agree it does."

"Then when did you stop honoring bank contracts?"

"I don't know. You are the first one to ask."

"Is your bank insolvent? Don't you have any lawful money, as defined by the United States Code, in your bank here?"

"No sir, I'm sorry, but we do not."

"Well then, where can I get my money?" Brock was firm but smiling.

"Mr. Freeman, I guess you will have to go the United States Treasury."

Brock grinned as he walked out the door, wondering if he had piqued the curiosity of the young bank manager the way his own had been piqued only a short time earlier.

Since the earliest of times there have been banks and bankers. The type of bank which was fair and honest operated simply to bring a person with money together with a person who needed it. Together they became partners in a joint-venture business enterprise. If the business failed, such as in a bad-crop year, the money-lender lost his investment, but, if the business prospered, the venture-capitalist profited along with the businessman/farmer. For this service the bank charged reasonable fees for their services. The system was natural and orderly and would never have fallen victim to the current deception that allowed government snoopers to have free access to banking records of its depositors.

The other kind of bank—which was usurious, unfair, and dishonest—operated on the Babylonian principle of lending ten and collecting eleven. When a borrower agreed to this, he had been sucked into agreeing to the impossible. Just as the earth cannot return more rain to the sky than the clouds deliver, a borrower cannot return to an only source more than was obtained. In this wicked system, the lender has no vested interest in the success of the farm or business. In fact it has a vested interest in the *failure* of it. The borrower must put up his land, livestock, and crop, and in the olden days even his wife and children, who were then sold into slavery following foreclosure. A system such

as this is bad enough on the surface in that sooner or later
everyone is going to have a bad year. But with failure manufactured by design, if but ten talents are in circulation, it would
always be impossible to repay eleven. The whole scheme was
deviously despicable. This was the system that had been foisted
upon the American people with the passing of the Federal Reserve Act in 1913 and the introduction of the central bank. It
would later acquiesce to any and all government scrutiny.

After dinner that night, when Brent and Maria had rushed
off to the pep rally at Southwest High, Brock spread the paper
notes out on the dining room table and began to examine them
with a hand-held magnifying glass. Sarah returned from the
kitchen to pick up the remaining dishes and condiments and
stopped in her tracks when she saw him.

"What are you doing with that money, Sherlock?" she asked.

Ignoring her sarcastic stab at humor, he said, "Honey, sit
down. I want to show you something."

"Okay, but let me get these things into the dishwasher and
get it started, and I'll be right back."

Sarah Prince Freeman was an idea woman, creative, enthusiastic, and sparkling. Had she not fallen in love with and married
Brock, her career choice would have been public relations and
communications instead of school teaching. By now she would
have been the local TV news anchorwoman or, maybe, even with
one of the national networks in New York or Washington. Looking ten years younger than her forty-two years, she was a beautiful woman—"a real head-turner," said any man watching her
enter a room full of people—who was a natural at innovative
advertising, and she handled people with tact and sensitivity.

More than that, she was a woman who *truly* liked people, and
such a natural trait of *giving* immediately magnetized others to
her. She never regretted surrendering her career in exchange for
sharing her life with this exciting man who was still her best
friend. Being the consensus "favorite mom" of her children's
friends was far more rewarding to her than fame and fortune.
Besides, her husband had already provided the fortune.

In a moment Brock heard the familiar clanging of the crockery being stuffed into the dishwasher, shortly followed by the
slamming of the door and the machine's susurrous hosing as it
went into its initial stages of the wash cycle. In another moment
Sarah came through the door, still drying her hands with a dish
towel.

"Look at this," said Brock. Have you ever seen any of these
before?"

Sarah peered over his shoulder for a quick look and said, "Sure. Yesterday I gave one to the cashier at Thriftway for that roast and vegetables you just ate. Why? Is it counterfeit?"

"No, not this one, but what you gave to Thriftway was," Brock replied matter-of-factly, "and what they gave you back in change was too."

"You're kidding. Am I going to jail?"

"No," he chuckled, "you aren't going to jail but only because the government has sanctioned its own counterfeiting scheme. It is not 'counterfeiting' that is against the law anymore but '*Illegal* counterfeiting.' Just like gambling is not illegal, but *untaxed* gambling is. It is only the *untaxed* marijuana and *unregistered* automatic weapons that are so terrible in this country. If Big Brother is getting his tax cut, suddenly they aren't so bad anymore. The government is playing 'god,' just like George Orwell warned. Can you tell any difference in these? Take a closer look."

Sarah scooped up the three fifties and gave them a desultory going-over. "Looks the same as any to me."

"Okay, Honey, sit down. Facts don't cease to exist just because they are ignored. I am about to give you the first-ever presentation of the 'Brock Freeman Ten-Minute Seminar on Money.' Remember the night at the sorority house and what became 'our song?' "

"Of course!"

"And on our wedding day at the reception dinner when I said you were still 'one in a million?' Now we're going to find out if you still are." He flashed her a sly smile. Sarah sensed a newly acquired neurosis in his obsession.

"Of course, I am. Who else would still be picking up your smelly socks and underwear after twenty years?"

Conceding the point, he ignored the question. "Please give me ten minutes of your undivided attention with no questions until I finish. Okay?"

"Okay."

Brock sputtered and stuttered at first, trying to get a grip on where to begin and where to go with his little roundtable symposium before giving a brief history on the evolution of money in this country.

"Remember the old saying, 'Not worth a continental?' " he asked. "That referred to the old paper continental notes that circulated in the 1780s. Tavern keepers would pay four thousand dollars for a barrel of whiskey and, by the time they had sold out, sell the empty barrel for eight thousand dollars. The paper had no intrinsic value, and, as the government printed more and more, its value became less and less. It took more of the money each month to buy the same commodities."

He told her about Roger Sherman and how the founders had declared in Article I, Section 10 that *"No State shall make any thing except gold and silver coin a tender in payment of debts,"* and, for that reason, how there was little or no inflation in the United States before the central bank was foisted upon the people in 1914. "It is precisely because we cannot foresee its disorders that we follow the direction of so-called economic experts and stumble blindly into these disasters," he said. "George Washington and the Continental Congress let it happen to them for the same reason."

Judge Sherman had brought the permanent antidote to inflation to the Constitutional Convention in Philadelphia, and it had met with little argument. The founders respected the wisdom of the man and his motion. Their personal experiences of the times had already taught them that he was right. The inherent problems surrounding an elastic currency had been solved for all time, or should have been.

"Now look at these *bona fide* Federal Reserve Notes. Any sophomore law student knows that a 'note' must contain four integral parts: a payer, a payee, a specified amount, and a due date. These notes have all that. They say, 'The United States of America,' that's the payer; 'will pay to the bearer,' that's the payee; 'on demand', that's the due date, whenever they want it; 'fifty dollars,' and that is the specified amount. Up here in the left hand corner, it specifies 'This note is legal tender for all debts, public and private, and is redeemable in lawful money at the United States Treasury, or at any Federal Reserve Bank.' 'Lawful money' is defined in 12 USC 152 as '. . . gold and silver coin of the United States.' So you see, Honey, these were *bona fide* receipts good for redemption in the real wealth at any time. These were the receipts for what was stored in the warehouse. But they are nothing like what you spent at the grocery store yesterday. Let's look at one of those."

Brock didn't have a "modern" fifty-dollar-bill on him, but he pulled a one, five, and ten from his wallet and spread them on the table and handed a twenty to Sarah. He explained that the U.S. government enjoyed such loyalty and trust of the American people, it was a simple matter to convince them into accepting notes that were not redeemable in anything. On all of the modern Federal Reserve Notes from the 1963 series to present, the "promise-to-pay" had been removed. "These are not notes," he said, "they're merely tokens, purporting to be something they are not. We have to work for what the money creators get for nothing. We are their slaves.

"The only way new money—which is not true money at all but 'credit' representing a debt—can get into circulation in America is by first being borrowed from bankers. When the state and people borrow large sums, we seem 'to prosper. However, the bankers 'create' only the amount of the principal of each, never the extra amount needed to pay the interest. Therefore, the new money never equals the new debt added. The amount needed to pay toward interest on loans is not 'created' and, therefore, does not exist." Sarah, still tracking, wondered: *If it doesn't exist, how can it be repaid?*

Brock said, "Under this kind of system, where new debt always exceeds the new money no matter how much or how little is borrowed, the total debt increasingly outstrips the amount of money available to pay the debt. Consequently, the people can never get out of debt. Neither can the government, paying interest to the bankers.

"The same is true with the coinage," he told her. "Since 1965, the coins have been minted not from silver, but cupronickel, a cheap mixture of copper and nickel. They're as counterfeit as the paper notes. No wonder the government can't balance the budget. They have us operating on an imaginary monetary system. Every credit dollar created also creates a dollar of debt. The rules of dual entry bookkeeping dictate it. The only real thing that the figures of the "national debt" tell us is how many phony dollars are in circulation.

"Under the old, honest system, a person did not have a hundred dollars *worth* of gold. He had a hundred dollars *in* gold. The gold was the money. When he put it in the warehouse bank and got a receipt, then he had a hundred dollars worth of paper which he could trade in the marketplace with other merchants. But paper currency must be 100% redeemable in wealth to prevent fraud and inflation."

Sarah could not resist asking a question. "So what difference does it make if I buy groceries with this or that," she said, pointing to the two different bills, "as long as the grocer is willing to take it?"

"Exactly. That's one of the basics that made the sham so easy to pull over on the people. Because, initially, there was no difference in purchasing power. But it gave a small cartel of plutocrats total control of an elastic currency. Now they can expand or shrink its value at will, thereby stealing the real property that has been mortgaged with it."

"And just what, pray tell, is a 'plutocrat'?" she asked.

"They are the super-rich who govern behind the scenes. The international bankers who buy and sell governments the way I do real estate. Their goal is global control with everyone else working for them, and they almost have it. They have controlled elections for generations and can create a war whenever they need one. Lincoln got on to them. So did Kennedy. Look what happened to them, but back to the sham.

"I have to trade my labor to accumulate and pay back what the bank created out of thin air, loaned to me at interest, and deposited in my bank account. If they decide to cut off the credit flow this year and create another recession, I may be unable to pay off the loan, and they will foreclose on the property. Then they will have ended up with something for nothing. Whenever they need or want more, they just print it.

"Such a system creates an enormous inflationary problem annually, some of which is then vacuumed back up with something called an 'income tax.' But this is a hoax, too. The income tax funds nothing, absolutely nothing, and it never has—except to breathe slight life into a dying system. Did you know that the whole income tax structure is unlawful, unconstitutional, ungodly, and that the money goes nowhere except to the federal reserve bank to be flushed down the sewer? They have been lying to us."

"Well, then let's hang the bastards!" Sarah said.

Brock laughed. "I wish it were that easy, Honey, but they own all the rope, and historically, tradition often overrides laws. Almost everybody in the United States has been brainwashed into believing that it is patriotic to pay income taxes. That's why some of the few who figure it out get railroaded right into the penitentiary. The judges don't let the juries hear the truth, and the jurors probably wouldn't understand the money issue anyway. The television, newspapers, and World War II movies have everybody convinced that the United States government is the most honorable in the world and would *never* cheat anyone. Therefore, anyone who cheats on his income taxes is not paying his so-called 'fair share'—at least in the eyes of the jurors—and is worthy of residence in the jailhouse. But the truth is, with no lawful money in circulation, the people don't finance the government any longer anyway, and the well-publicized cases of the few who do go to jail sufficiently terrify the masses into compliance. So the people voluntarily march right over the cliff like lemmings to the sea. An income tax has no function with lawful money, and in a system of legal tender, it is only used to clean up the government's inflationary mess, or some of it.

Since Roosevelt's creation of legal tender, the people have been like puppets on a string, at the mercy of the money creators."

This bonanza of truth, Brock already knew, was the exceedingly bitter pill for men to swallow. Most who had heard it still could not gulp it down. The government of the Land of the Free and the Home of the Brave for which hundreds of thousands had died to protect was actually in cahoots with the moneychangers? To steal the land and the wealth of the people? To increase the bureaucracy and dilute the assets of the common man? Outrageous! Who would believe it?

"This was the original fraud and the root of all our economic woes," continued Brock. "Let the banksters defend the practice as they will, the fact still remains that when they lend their credit at interest, they are creating private money which they can recall and destroy at will to the distress of the borrower, who periodically finds himself forced through artificial scarcity of credit money to pay back real property for the 'credit dollars' he borrowed."

Her face lit up as if someone had thrown a light switch. "Whoo-wee!" she gushed. "Brock! Now I see what you're saying. They don't have to work for their money, they just create it and lend it in exchange for collateral. This is how they get something for nothing."

It was almost eight o'clock. "Listen," she said, "there's a great movie that I wanted to watch coming on at eight, but I'll go set the VCR and watch it later. I want you to tell me more about this."

"Great," he said, "but you'd be better off to read some things first. Let me get your first primer. I've got something that you can almost finish before the movie is finished taping. Then we can watch it together later."

He reached into his stack of books and pulled out *The Miracle On Main Street* by F. Tupper Saussy. "Read this, and you will see the whole picture. Then we'll talk about it some more when you can ask intelligent questions."

"Okay, Mr. Rothschild," she said with a sardonic smile, "but I thought I was doing pretty well for a first-time student sitting under the tutorage of the sagacious guru."

"You certainly are. Most people never comprehend in a whole lifetime what you just have in one lesson, but Darlin', you have a long way to go yet, and you can't learn it all in a night or from any single person. You have to read."

"All right, I'll read, but I still want to talk some more with you about it first. I'll be right back. Hold that next thought,

Sage." They talked about it for another half hour before Sarah retired to read her first assignment.

Brock was silently thrilled that he had been able to get Sarah's attention with his mini-symposium, but what he had said the last few minutes had brought down around him a veil of inquietude, and he began to ponder his own revelations. He was his own best student. Every time he explained these facts to someone he rose to a higher level of understanding himself, even if they didn't. He thought that if everything he had just said was true, and he had already proven it to himself with his research and study the last few months, then the American people didn't have any more freedom than the slaves of communist countries; they only thought they did. He had hardly noticed the peck on his cheek from his wife as she passed his chair and headed up the stairway, book in hand.

Brock was wrestling with himself, finding it hard to believe the slick method by which his country had been captured from the inside. It was he who had said dozens of times in friendly debate—especially about the Vietnam situation—that "America is still the best country on earth, and if you don't like it, you can always leave." Only since reading in the Constitution about only Congress having the power to declare war had he realized both Vietnam and Korea had been initiated by the executive branch and not congress. He sheepishly admitted to himself that he had made a mistake with his hardcore stand of "America, right or wrong," as his car's bumper sticker had once reflected. The Fed, with the sanction of the United States Government, was perpetrating the greatest counterfeiting scheme in world history.

No, he didn't love his country any less, and he didn't hate the government. It was the *corruption* in the federal government that he was beginning to detest. The modern day Mamelukes. It was the subterfuge by those in authority who pretended not to know which disturbed him—chairmen and presidents of banks who stepped from their limousines and sailed into inner offices as though their right to wealth were ordained by the Almighty, as though nothing had changed.

He heard Maria come in around eleven and Brent shortly thereafter, but remained holed-up in his library, reading and writing notes until after midnight. When he reached the top of the stairs, he walked to the end of the hall to check their rooms just as he had done every night since the week they were born. When he stuck his head into the dark rooms, he could tell that they were already fast asleep. He smiled when he entered the master suite and there was his beautiful Sarah, sweetly sleeping, with the book across her stomach. The lamp was on and, with the VCR having automatically cut off, the television was blaring. He got undressed and changed into his pajamas, turned off the lights, and quietly slipped in beside her. Tossing restlessly, he began to think of ways to attempt to extricate himself from the usury trap in which he had allowed himself to be ensnared—now that he understood all the long term ramifications—and finally fell asleep.

Sarah arose first the next morning at seven and put on her housecoat to go downstairs to get the coffee pot started. On the dining room table, she noticed a book had remained open to the last thing Brock had marked with his hi-liter. It was *The Economic Consequences of The Peace* authored by John Maynard Keynes in 1920. She read the words and got mixed emotions, first feeling anger as one more piece fell into place in her economic puzzle, and then pride as she realized that her favorite person on earth had just become one of the men the author had described years before:

"By a continuing process of inflation, governments can confiscate, secretly and unobserved, an important part of the wealth of their citizens. There is no subtler, no surer means of overturning the existing basis of society than to debauch the currency. The process engages all the hidden forces of economic law on the side of destruction, and does it in a manner which not one man in a million is able to diagnose."

SIX

Kansas City sprawls into two states. The last Ice Age gave the Missouri River a mighty bend, and the wide Kansas River curls in from the west, availing the broad banks of both sides of each to become alive with man's industry. Straddling the state line, it is not truly one town, but a contiguous mosaic of fifty municipalities in six counties of hills and plains. Whenever people from Leawood, Lenexa, Bonner Springs, Prairie Village, or Olathe, Kansas—as well as those from Grandview, Lee's Summit, Sugar Creek, or Gladstone, Missouri—are vacationing in Florida or Las Vegas or wherever else and are asked, "Where are you from?" the answer is invariably "Kansas City." It is the home of K. C. steaks, baseball's Royals, football's Chiefs, golf's Tom Watson, The Plaza, Crown Center, and the once famous but now defunct Kansas City stockyards. It makes frocks, researches cancer, and assembles more automobiles than any city except Detroit. In all, the greater city's some eight-hundred square miles—home to more than two million people—encompasses a 40-mile sweep of landscape, an area so swelled in recent years that the weather service at times issues different forecasts for north and south.

Three quarters of the metropolitan area is in Missouri, but the new growth of the 1970s and the most modern construction had popped up in Overland Park on the Kansas side. The state line is the center line of a miles-long straight shot north and south appropriately named "State Line Road." People living on one side of the street face their neighbors in a different state. Kansans buy their gasoline, whenever it is convenient, on the Missouri side to take advantage of the lower tax, often saving a dime or more a gallon. Missourians like to go to the Kansas side for a night of—consensus opinion—better Mexican food, simple escape from the urban throngs, and more parking places.

If one is traveling from east to west in the city, he need not notice the street marker at State Line Road to become aware he has moved to another state. The green hills of Missouri almost immediately turn into the rusty plains of Kansas. The last hills available for hundreds of miles are right there at State Line Road and were long ago scarfed up by the ritzy Mission Hills Country Club and manicured into the finest golf course in the city, if not the whole Midwest. In the decade of the 80s "The Hills" was the entertainment center for Brock Freeman and his friends. Golf, tennis, billiards, lunch, poker, cocktails, and dinner. Some of each several days a week and always on Friday.

Vince Jaekel was sitting at the poker table with four others on Friday afternoon when Brock walked in, still wearing his golf spikes. He peeled off his shoes to his stocking feet and ambled to a vacant seat at the table, his bromidrosis trailing closely behind him. He reached for his wallet, plucked out a fifty, flipped it on the table in front of him, and took his seat. It was their regular Friday ritual. Brock was a little late today because he had had to take advantage of the mild weather for a quick nine holes of golf. Their poker games often went to the wee hours of the next morn and, on occasion, had been known to last until Sunday.

Vince was bitching, but that was nothing new. Vince was always bitching about something, if he wasn't cracking up the gang with his outrageous humor. Sometimes it was hard to tell which personality he was wearing at the moment. Vince talked at fifty miles per hour with gusts up to 110—often running his words together in unintelligible gibberish.

"Sunsabitches just emptied me, man. Came in and took my computers, typewriters, copy machines, FAX, anything that wasn't nailed down."

Brock, thinking Vince had been robbed in the ordinary fashion interjected. "Did they find out who did it?"

"Find-out-who-did-it? Chee-it. They announced themselves. 'We're from the IRS.' Showed their gott-damned badges and came on in like they owned the place. Said I owed thirty-three thousand bucks and that all my shit would go toward my debt after they sold it at auction. Whatever happened to 'innocent until proven guilty' in this country? I don't owe them thirty-three hundred, let alone thousand. It's one of them computer screw-ups. But do you think I can make them imbeciles listen. You can't tell nothin' to a robot. They said I could either pay it or tell it to the judge. Meanwhile, the leeches don't care if they just put you right out of business."

"Now slow down a second, Mozzarella," Brock said, the moment Vince finally took a breath. "When did all this happen?"

Vince was of mixed ethnic parentage—an Irish father and Italian mother. At a St. Patrick's Day party a few years ago when he had more than his share of alcoholic encouragement and the quintet had struck up "McNamara's Band," he jumped on the stage, grabbed the mike, and began to sing: "Oh, mee nyme is Mozzarella I'm the leader of the band . . ." That had been funny enough, but, when he got to the part about "Hennessy/Tennessy" and instead had said, "Old Mussolini tooted the flute, the music's something grand," it brought the house down. "Mozzarella" had been his moniker ever since.

"Yesterday, gott-dammit," he replied. "The bastids swept down on me like I was Al Capone or somebody."

One of the players was Dr. Joe Day, a successful southside dentist, friend of Brock Freeman and the others, and a regular player. He sat sober-faced, reacting neither positively nor negatively.

"You can't fight 'em, Vince," said Pottsie—Stanley Potts—another regular at the table and Brock's accountant. "They've got too many big guns, legal and otherwise. Just pay the damned thing."

"Bullshit. I-ain't-a-payin'-that. I-don't-have-it."

"So, what are you going to do?" Brock asked.

"Start all over, I guess. I'm still thinking about it, but the best idea I have come up with is starting a new company under an entirely different name, sell my furniture business to it, and keep operating like nothing happened. That won't get me anything back—I'll let my lawyers figure that one out. But at least, the next time they come a-lookin', I won't be the owner and they won't be able to legally snatch it. Deal the cards. I am tired of talking about it. I came down here to relax and forget about it until Monday. Go wash your rotten feet, Freeman. Nobody can relax smelling that funk." Vince picked up the phone and ordered another vodka and tonic from the bar. His cohorts all seconded his motion, and Brock was embarrassed into taking a shower before he could play cards with his friends, but he good-naturedly agreed with them and exited the card room.

He remembered the time the year before when Vince had been nursing a horrendous hangover and Brock said, "Mozzarella, why don't you cut down on the booze?"

"Well, Brockie," Vince had answered seriously, "sometimes I do get to feelin' mighty mean, and my stomach goes back on me, and I decide to swear it off. I go for two or three days without touchin' a drop, and then one morning I wake up, and the sky is blue, and the birds are singin', and the sun is all bright and warm—and then, by God, I rally!" For Vince, every weekend coming around the calendar was cause enough to celebrate the repeal of Prohibition.

Over the past six months Brock had begun to see through this money/tax sham and comprehend what few lawyers and fewer layman could understand. In the shower he began to think:

The Fourth Amendment protection of people to be secure in their "persons, homes, papers, and effects" is violated by any law that would require one to involuntarily declare all that information on a government form. It's like a forced confession. *Even if there is a law that requires people to file, and Irwin Schiff said over and over in several books and publications that there is not, the law is inapplicable to anyone who doesn't volunteer to fall under it.*

Now Vince faces an entirely different problem, Brock thought. He, like most everybody else, *did* volunteer into their jurisdiction. He is a documented slave in their camp. They've got him by the proverbials. Even though he did not earn any dollar of lawful money, he swore under penalty of perjury that he did, and anything accepted by the public *as* money *is* money by that acceptance, and even though it was through ignorance of the law, he contracted his way into their jurisdiction by filing the form.

The solution was so simple he could hardly believe his own conclusions: Ninety million Americans had been suckered into volunteering right into the federal jurisdiction under the shadow of belief that filing these forms was required, while even the IRS publications said it was voluntary. Various IRS commissioners through the years had been quoted as saying, "The system is voluntary." The answer for one who wanted out was to stop volunteering. But then that could present some problems, too, as then that person would likely be targeted by the government as an illegal tax protestor.

Brock toweled off, dressed, and rejoined his friends at the poker table. After a cold beer and a turkey sandwich, he decided to call it quits and go home. He just wasn't concentrating on the card game. Once, with no aces nor pairs showing on the board and holding only a king high, he had foolishly called Joe in a hand of five card stud. Dr. Day flipped the ace from the hole and took the pot. It was then that Brock thought he could more profitably spend this late afternoon at home reading. Besides, there was no point in attempting to explain all this to his friend. Vince hadn't read a book in years and was always more interested in pursuing his hedonistic lifestyle of wine, women, and song than in learning anything new. And even if his normal attitude had not been of a frivolous nature most of the time, he was too distraught on this day anyway. Brock excused himself with the knowledge that he wasn't going away a loser. Because the game never ended, there were never any winners or losers. The forthcoming session would be but the next chapter of a never-ending book.

*   *   *   *   *

The same afternoon that Brock was beginning to evaluate Vince's plight, the overall tax system, and himself; five hundred miles away in Indianapolis two grown men—one black, one white—were having some mischievous juvenile delinquency laughs in broad daylight by throwing half-brickbats onto the hood and into the windshield of a particular white Dodge parked in front of a certain residence. A few years ahead of Brock in the resolve department, the two took delight in this type of extracurricular entertainment.

The white man was hardly a hoodlum. Matter of fact he was a corporation president by the name of Samuel H. Prescott. A few days earlier he had strolled into a local printing office to get 500 quick-print copies of an envelope stuffer and overheard the owner expressing his consternation to another customer about current harassment from the IRS. The auditor had insisted upon coming to his house the following Friday, the print shop owner had said, "to peruse the books and records of the business." This meant that the owner would have to take a whole day away from his operation to tend to "this crap." Mr. Prescott listened without comment, waited for his turn in line, and placed his order to be picked up in two hours. During the extra hour he had spent having lunch, he had looked up the home address of the printer in the Indianapolis phone directory. Upon his return, Sam Prescott had confirmed the location of the residence in a brief conversation with a simple, innocent question.

"Aren't you the Blakeley who lives on Starlight Drive in Sunset Hills?"

"Yes, I am," the printer Blakeley replied innocently. "Been there for fifteen years."

"Yes, I remember you," bluffed Prescott. "My wife and I rented a house over there a couple of years ago while we were building our new home. I believe we met at one of those neighborhood parties. Well, thanks for the fast service, Mr. Blakeley. I'll certainly use you the next time I need some more." He had left without any further conversation. *Next Friday, huh,* Prescott thought as he walked to his car. *I wonder if Bill will be in town that day. Bet he'll want to have some fun.* With a few million in personal assets through shrewd investing over the years, Bill Banneker was no bum either. They were the last people in Indianapolis that anyone would have suspected of such hooliganism.

Bill and Sam had pulled a few stunts in the past for jollies. Nothing they could talk about except to each other, but what they enjoyed referring to as "reverse intimidation." One particular obnoxious auditor, who had harassed another friend of Sam's found out two months later, much to his dismay, that he had filed for bankruptcy at the local courthouse. It was news to the auditor, and it took him a year to get all his credit cards reinstated. Another one, who had made it a little too easy for a stranger to learn of his home address, was ostracized by his neighbors when over fifty letters had gone out informing them of the distasteful tactics the agent was using to confiscate property. "Did you know that a criminal is living in your neighborhood?" said the opening paragraph of the letter. Then it went on to explain in detail how the IRS agent had first confiscated homes for auction, then returned on the designated day and bought the property in his wife's name. The cross reference feature of the city directory made the contacting of his neighbors easy. Sam and his black friend had discovered a few other devious techniques for reverse intimidation.

"Sam," Bill said, as they cruised around the city on the I-465. "If you ever want to graduate to bigger things, I've got this friend down in Tennessee who, for about a dime or maybe even a nickel if we catch him in a good mood, will strangle some of these guys for us."

"I presume you are speaking in gambler's lingo of a thousand or maybe five hundred? replied Sam.

"No. Actually I was speaking in everyday terms of the slug coins. He hates the bastards so much he might even pay us for leads! Big, mean, red-headed sumbitch whose personal slogan is 'Have gun, will travel.' I'd rather dive in a sack of water moccasins than fool with him."

"No, thanks. I'll just stay in the minor leagues."

A little later on this Friday, the two upstanding businessmen were howling like high schoolers as the brickbats bounced off of the shiny finish of the new white Dodge with blue and white G-12 license plates.

"One point for the metal, two for the glass," Sam had decided, and they screamed with delight each time they made a pass with a over-the-top hook shot. No one came out to investigate, so they continued for nearly an hour. When they finally left the area, there was a small pile and a scattered array of shattered bricks next to a wrinkled automobile that looked like something out of the six o'clock news films from a bombing in Beirut.

*   *   *   *   *

During the short drive south on State Line Road, Brock thought about the money sham some more. *The scoundrels are defrauding us . . . out of our money, property and rights, and nobody even realizes it.* He remembered making that call a few days earlier to check on a billing mistake with his Visa card. Even though his social security card plainly stated, NOT TO BE USED FOR IDENTIFICATION, in order to pull up his account, they had to know his date of birth and social security number. *Surely this must be that Mark of the Beast from the Book of Revelation. It says something about no one being able to buy or sell unless he has the number.* He vowed at that moment to cancel all the credit cards in his name.

The first thing he did upon entering the big Ward Parkway home was go into the paneled library and pluck his Bible off the shelf. He sat down and thumbed Revelations but couldn't immediately find what he wanted. Upon checking the concordance, he went to chapter 13, verses 16 and 17, and there it was:

> And he causeth all, both small and great, rich and poor, free and bond, to receive a mark in their right hand, or in their foreheads. And that no man might buy or sell, save he that had the mark, or the name of the beast, or the number of his name.

". . . or *in* their foreheads," Brock muttered aloud, replacing the Bible on the shelf. Not *on* their foreheads. What American cannot recite his nine-digit social security number from memory? It's in his *fore*head, right on top of his memory bank. From the moment they mailed or handed him the card the first time, it was "*in* his hand" even if he carried it in his wallet or kept it in a dresser drawer. He sighed and leaned back in his chair staring into space. His computer-like brain was racing through every piece of data on the subject that had ever been pumped into it by preachers, teachers, his father, and the reams of books and papers in the recent months.

Brock was not a religious zealot. Far from it. But he was a mentally awake and morally straight individual who did believe that there were natural laws from which neither a person nor a nation should stray. To do so was to court disaster. He felt that most preachers were pious wimps who were more interested in numbers of tithing people sitting in the pews each week than practical application of Biblical law. There was, however, one minister in the city whom he respected, and he called him at home to put forward the questions. Brock did not fawn over this mortal or consider him some kind of religious guru. He did respect his Biblical knowledge.

"The civil government's origin is God," replied his preacher friend, "and, therefore, the government is accountable to God for all of its actions, for all of its policies, for all of its programs; it is accountable to its origin, whether it pleases a rebellious populace or not. So to say that civil government originates with God is to say that, number one, we as citizens have a duty to submit to that civil government's authority. We are to obey its laws. But whenever a civil government requires us to do something which in doing that would cause us to break the law of God, we must in that point disobey the civil government. Because the government originates with God, it too must be submissive to almighty God to rule in a way he has commanded."

Brock thanked him, hung up the phone, and began to piece the puzzle together in his mind. *The civil government must stay within the boundaries that God has placed around it or else it becomes a threat to the good and a comforter to the evil. The civil government is going to be a terror to somebody because it has the power of the sword. It is either going to be a terror to the lawless criminal or it is going to be a terror to the law-abiding citizen. Insofar as the states or the federal government do not enforce God's law, it has already become a terror to the law-abiding. What turns government into a beast? It neglects God's moral order and seeks to impose another. Whenever that takes place in a nation, there is revolution. The man who wears the seal of God in his forehead is a man who will not compromise and who will not bow down before any idol or any other claim to lordship and sovereignty and ownership other than God Almighty. To think or do otherwise would be idolatrous.*

Brock's memory bank was kicking up information at the speed of light. Just as George Orwell had warned was coming, this destructive principle of ungodly state taxation could now be seen in every area of life. Sales taxes were decapitalizing the lower members of society because they had to spend a larger proportion of their incomes than the upper income group. The state was taxing electricity, food, clothing, drugs, tires, and gasoline with no limit to the list other than that of the imaginations of the robots in the bureaucracy. The income tax was forcibly taking the labor and wealth of the producers and—in effect, at least—redistributing it to the bureaucrats. Taxes were eating up the entire salaries of Americans from January to June, making every person an involuntary slave to the state for the first half of every year. The income tax was punishing the successful, hard-working businessman by lessening production, raising prices, and decreasing earnings. "It's devastating," Brock mumbled to himself. "The power to tax is the power to destroy. 'Power corrupts, and absolute power corrupts absolutely.' " Vince's property had been taken away from him by the god he had voluntarily bestowed the power upon to do so.

And all this, Brock further realized, was without regard to the most destructive, the most vicious, the most hidden of all the humanistic taxes of all—inflation. *It decapitalizes and destroys all of society because it destroys the currency with which society makes its economic decisions and its fiduciary judgment. As a currency goes, so goes the nation. There was no inflation when the people had circulating gold and silver coin. No nation in the history of this planet has survived a paper money scheme. But how can we reform it? When the engines quit on your aircraft, you can't just jump out. You've got to finish the trip and try to find a place to put it down as gently as possible.*

Brock snapped out of his trance and rose to stroll around the library. "I've been talking to myself like I was the preacher," he mumbled to himself. But no, he thought, this isn't religion. It's law, pure and simple. And it's the *damned-by-God* laws that even the Christians have been willingly obeying that were destroying liberty in America. It was this moment that Brock Freeman began his personal rebellion against an unjust authority. He had sold his own soul to the devil by ignorantly filing those 1040 forms all those years. It was time to repent and retract the devil's jurisdiction over his life. He vowed to never file again.

On the wall hung a parchment document under glass in a large, expensive frame. In inch-high letters, the title announced it as THE GIFT OF ACABAR. It was from an inspirational book written by Og Mandino—Brock's favorite philosophical author—which Sarah had had an artist rewrite in old English script some time before and then had taken it to be framed before slipping it under the tree on Christmas eve. When Brock paused to read it once more, the three sentences on lines 5, 6, and 7 seemed to glow like neon lights.

Credenda

Turn away from the crowd & its fruitless pursuit of fame and gold. Never look back as you close your door to the sorry tumult of greed & ambition. Wipe away your tears of failure & misfortune. Lay aside your heavy load & rest until your heart is still. Be at peace. Already it is later than you think, for your earthly life, at best, is only the blink of an eye between two eternities. Be unafraid. Nothing here can harm you except yourself. . . .

Brock wasn't naive enough to believe that he could save the world. He did wonder how he might save himself and his family. *We are being ruled by God-damned tyrants,* he whispered to himself. *Damned by God as evidenced in His laws.* What could be more God-damned than that? And he knew there was nothing vain about his declaration. Framed under glass and hanging nearby on the library wall next to the time-worn wooden plaque constructed so long ago in the garage shop by his father was the cross-stitched embroidery given to him by his mother, shortly after they had re-settled back in Independence.

GOD HAS PROMISED FORGIVENESS TO YOUR RE-PENTANCE; BUT HE HAS NOT PROMISED TOMOR-ROW TO YOUR PROCRASTINATIONS. GET ON WITH IT, BOY!

SEVEN

Santa Ana, Calif.—(April 12) More than two dozen people were overcome Friday by toxic fumes from a liquid solvent that was fanned through the air-conditioning system of a new Internal Revenue Service building. Officials said twenty-five victims, including two who passed out, were taken to five hospitals for treatment of symptoms including severe nausea and headaches. Several other people were treated at the scene. About 150 people had to be evacuated from the IRS offices near the Orange County Airport. The incident occurred as the IRS was hosting an open house for the news media to show off its new mirrored-glass facility. (The Atlanta Journal and A.P. & U.P.I.)

Chattanooga is a big country town nestled at the foot of the Smoky Mountains and sitting barely above the imaginary corners where Alabama and Georgia meet Tennessee. For generations it has been famous for the spot nearby where one can "See Seven States." The old, wooden barns and houses—with the faded red, black, and white paint on the nearly indestructible roofs, advertising that fact—still decorate or desecrate, as the opinion may be, the backroads of most of the states east of the Mississippi and many west of it. That and "See Rock City." Johnny Mercer immortalized the area in song in the 1930s with "Chattanooga Choo Choo," and somebody else did it again in the 1950s with "The Chattanooga Shoe Shine Boy."

The city contrasts itself with ultra-modern shopping malls and rustic flea markets; supermarkets and roadside stands; or as likely as not in lanes next to each other at the stoplight, a proud yuppie in a BMW and a prouder redneck in a pickup truck with a couple of hunting rifles hung on a rack in the back window. On weekends the yuppies go to Gatlinburg, Nashville, or Atlanta for the sporting activities and nightlife, while the rednecks go to south Alabama for another load of fruit and vegetables or a day of squirrel hunting.

In early May of 1985, interested and dedicated people from all over the country came to a weekend symposium at the old, downtown Read House Hotel. Tupper Saussy had just been released from a fifty-day stay in the county jail. Because he had challenged the jurisdiction of the federal court to try him without a grand jury indictment, the judge had put him in jail for contempt of court. Along with many others, he was to be one of the featured speakers including Congressman George Hansen of Idaho, millionaire businessman Bill Kilpatrick of Denver, and Dee Kirk, the widow of Arthur who had been shot and killed in his front yard the previous year by state and county law enforcement officers in Nebraska, after he had refused service on a bank foreclosure suit. Mrs. Kirk would have a lot to say that day about the judicial power wielded by the banking community. Irwin Schiff was not one of the speakers at this function but had showed up to hawk his new book, *The Great Income Tax Hoax*. Brock spotted him the first day having lunch alone in the downstairs coffee shop and recognized him from the picture on the book jacket, TV interviews he had seen on video, and the seminar in Orange County two years before.

"How do you do, Mr. Schiff. I'm Brock Freeman from Kansas City. I've been an avid reader of your books for some time. May I join you?"

"Certainly," replied the gregarious Schiff, extending his hand. "Glad to meet you. Please, call me Irwin."

They talked discursively about the new movement in the country, money, and taxes. Schiff was delighted, of course, to learn that Brock had already read his latest book as well as all of the earlier ones. During the exchange, Brock noticed a nondescript, middle-aged man with a mustache sitting alone at the table to their right who appeared to have more than a casual interest in their conversation.

Before they had begun eating, they were joined by someone else—a giant of a man, maybe six feet eight inches tall and a muscular three hundred pounds. When he said, "Hi, my name is . . ." Brock expected to hear *Paul Bunyan*.

". . . Bowie Crockett," he said with a molasses-slow mountain drawl straight out of east Tennessee. Boooo-eee. "I've always enjoyed your work, Mr. Schiff, and I just wanteda' meecha'. "

"Holy Moses," responded Schiff with a good-natured smile, "could the Jets use you as a linebacker!"

"Yeah, people tell me that a lot," Bowie chuckled, "but would you believe I have never played football in my life? We had no team at my little school. My home town was so small, everybody who had a painted turtle was considered an art lover."

While the others were still laughing, he said, "How ya doin'," extending his big hand toward Brock, who told him his name and "from Kansas City." When Bowie Crockett one-handedly spun the chair backwards and straddled it, he was so big the chair seemed to shrink to half its size. He swept up one of the menus lodged between the salt and pepper shakers and the napkin dispenser. Brock told himself that this guy will probably order a dozen hamburgers and chomp each down as if it were a cheese cracker.

Bowie then asked Schiff, whose mind was like an attic stuffed with Americana, a technical question about the sixteenth Amendment, and the latter launched into a litany about Benson and Beckman's forthcoming book which explained how the confounded thing was never lawfully ratified by the states in the first place.

Bowie Crockett was the great-great-great-great grandnephew of the legendary Tennessee plainsman, Davy Crockett, who died with Jim Bowie defending Texas' freedom at San Antonio's Alamo. Although he carried the same name, he was not directly descended through the Crockett side, he said, but through a few grandmothers, one of whom later married another cousin named Crockett a few generations later. Without saying, Brock wondered if that might have been the incestuous touch which would genetically explain the latter creation of this gargantuan freak of nature sitting next to him. Freaks do not always spin forth as pathetically crippled carnival geeks or stammering mental midgets. A freak of nature can also be one of the positive meaning whose genes have homogenized his mind and body into an abnormal genius with both a photographic memory and superhuman physical strength and speed afoot. It was obvious to Brock where Crockett's parents had gotten his first name, remembering from history that Great-Uncle Davie had died at the Alamo in Texas with his best friend Jim Bowie in 1836.

The twentieth-century Crockett was red-haired and freckled faced, with farmboy-rugged good looks, now in his mid-thirties. His daddy had been a Tennessee rum-runner who every year moved his whiskey still to avoid the "revenuers." He had served three separate jail stretches—his mother always told Bowie and the siblings that their father was away furthering his education at "Pen State"—before they killed him in a shootout when Bowie was still in grade school. "He got two of them, though, and put another in a wheel-chair for life," Bowie said with disdain, "before they finally trapped him on the mountainside. Mama said twenty of them egg-suckin' dogs shot my daddy to pieces. We

had to have a closed casket at his funeral. I didn't even get to tell
him goodbye." Brock could see the hate flaming from Bowie's
brown eyes as he recalled his youthful tragedy.

Although he had taken a quick liking for Bowie Crockett,
Brock was driven back by the talk of violence and, while the
others finished their coffee, he chose this time to wander around
the coffee shop and take in the historic pictures on the walls.
Downtown Kansas City was full of this type of early twentieth
century tavern, and this hotel was about the same age as many
where he would often eat lunch back home.

They paid their checks and went into the meeting hall for
the seminar. During the mid-afternoon coffee break, Brock noticed Bowie talking rather surreptitiously with a conspicuous individual—a clean-cut, middle-aged black man whom Brock didn't
know—conspicuous because not very many black people were yet
involved in the Freedom Movement.

At five they broke for dinner, and Bowie and Brock got to
know each other a little better over another meal. He learned
that Bowie was a truck driver who owned his own eighteen-wheel
rig, who privately contracted for trans-continental runs, and had
not filed a 1040 form in seven years.

"Haven't they bugged you about that?" Brock asked.

"They did the first couple of years. You know, sending those
computer letters in the mail saying 'We haven't received your tax
form for last year' and that sort of crap. When I didn't respond,
they just made up some figure, probably from 1099s, and assessed me. They never collected. Four years ago I moved, and I
haven't heard from them since."

"Do you think you never will?"

"Oh no. I will. But I know how they operate, and I'm one
jump ahead of them. When they get around to me next time,
they won't bother with wasting any more paper and postage.
They'll go straight to the banks to try to lien any bank accounts I
might have. They won't find none. Next, they'll go to the courthouse and try to attach anything I own. They won't find nothin'
there neither. So then they'll file a lien with the courthouse to
attach anything in the future I might be stupid enough to file a
deed of ownership for. Look, here's how they operate. It's the
overall M. O. they practice on everybody: First they go after you
civilly. This takes care of about ninety percent of the people.
Sheeple, we call 'em. The sheeple will wilt and cough up whatever is demanded of them, after various degrees of bellowing of
course. Those who won't cooperate with them, like me, who tell
'em to go piss-up-a-rope and don't fall for their threats, and

arrange their business so the bastards can't steal anything; they, we, become potential targets for Level Two. That's a criminal investigation, and, believe me, if they choose to, they can make a criminal out of Mother Theresa. A jail-stretch of a year or two for a minuscule few causes most of those remaining to fall into line with the rest of the sheep."

"And the few that don't?" Brock asked.

"Then there is always the seldom necessary, but always effective, Level Three."

"What happens there?"

"They kill you."

Brock did not really think it very necessary at the time to be concerned about Levels Two and Three, but he did have great interest in what others were doing to protect their assets.

"What about your rig? Do you have it in your wife's name?" he asked Bowie.

"Nope. That dog don't hunt. They'll just grab it anyway and prove in court that it was really mine because I'm the one who uses it all the time. When I said that I owned that rig, I misspoke. I don't legally own it, but I control it—in that I make all the business decisions concerning it—but it is owned by an overseas company that conveniently hired me as their general manager. Wasn't that nice of them?" He gave Brock an overstated stage-wink.

Bowie began to explain a little about how the off-shore trust is operated.

"They wrote it into the tax code from the very beginning—at the same time they fixed it so the Fed would never be audited and the banks would never have to pay taxes. Old John D. and J. P. and the other super-rich took care of themselves and then made sure that nobody else would find out how to do it. CPAs don't know about it, and it's not taught in law schools either. Ask your attorney about it and he'll look at you like you're crazy, but there it is right there in the book. Section 892, I think, or something like that."

So in the specific situation where a guy has a potential IRS lien after a levy, when the government is making some spurious claim of a million bucks or so, what does he do now? Brock wanted to know. Bowie explained a little more without going into details. "The details vary with each particular situation," he said.

"Fred Forest, who designed these trusts in New York for decades, used to laugh at the situation Nelson Rockefeller found himself in when trying to be confirmed by the Senate as Gerald

Ford's Vice-President in 1974. Rocky claimed he had assets of some $34 million. Some news columnist wisecracked that 'Rocky must have thought they meant, 'How much do you have on you?' but the figure was accurate. The columnist did not know that the billions controlled by the Rockefeller family were actually owned by hundreds of separate entities called trusts, thereby avoiding any probate and estate taxes at the death of the principals as well. The trust never dies. And if you are using your friend's car, you cannot list it as your own on an asset sheet. So, of course, the honest answer to the question, 'Do you own that?,' is No."

Brock was very interested. Bowie did not yet know the extent of Brock's wealth. And while Brock had a good CPA who kept his taxable income at a minimum every year, he liked the idea of passing on the wealth to his children without the government taking an enormous estate tax bite when he died.

"So all this is legal?" he asked.

"Sure it is. The Carnegies and Fords and all them, like I said, have been using it since the beginning in 1913. But don't ask your accountant or lawyer to research it for you. They'll come up empty every time. Besides, don't forget, they take a huge cut in trumped-up fees along with the lawyers when estates are settled. It's in their own best interests to keep you ignorant. But Forest is a wizard who has been doing this for thirty years. The best way to set it up is to have him draw up the whole plan for you, and then present it to your accountant and lawyers and ask them to show you the fallacies. They can't."

Bowie thumbed his address book and gave Brock Fred Forest's New York phone number as well as his own.

Around ten o'clock that night, after the last speaker had finished, Brock couldn't find his new friend and began talking with a few other stragglers who were hanging around when he spotted Congressman Hansen. George Hansen had written a book in 1979 entitled *To Harass Our People* which described hundreds of cases of persecution of private citizens by the IRS all over the country. Hansen was now undergoing similar repercussions for exposing these atrocities and would wind up in jail the next year himself as a political prisoner. He would learn too late, as had Congressman Larry McDonald of Georgia, that the handful of honest people who slip through the election cracks and get to Washington are taken care of by other means.

Many people had begun in their own small and separate ways to handle some of the problems on their own. A man in upstate New York accepted the appointment for the IRS auditor to come to his house to go over his checkbooks and then blew him away with a blast from his shotgun as the auditor climbed the steps to ring the bell. A woman auditor in Atlanta had the back window shot out of her automobile as she pulled onto I-75 headed home during the evening rush hour. She was not hit but spent the next month in the mental ward before quitting her job for good. An agent in Cheyenne, Wyoming, who apparently was a child abuser as well, was shot and killed by his own teenage son as he drove into his garage at home. During the coffee break at the seminar, the people reported to one another with neither sadness nor glee the details of the latest attack of which they had heard in their home areas. All seemed to realize what was inevitable.

Brock chatted with a few other people in the lobby on the way to the elevator before heading up to the sixth floor. He got off alone and was rounding the corner in the hallway when he saw Bowie Crockett and another lean, wiry, and agile man of below average height maybe forty years old emerging from room number 609. Brock immediately recognized the stranger as the black man Bowie had been talking with during the afternoon break. They appeared to be in a hurry and slightly chagrined that they had been seen. Before Brock could say hello, Bowie displayed the "hush" sign by placing his finger over his lips.

"What room are you in?" Bowie whispered.

"Right here in 611, why?"

"Perfect. Let us use your phone a second."

"Okay. No problem."

Brock inserted the key, and the three of them entered. Brock had still not been introduced to the other man. Bowie went straight to the phone, sat on the bed, and dialed the front desk. The other two stood and listened.

"Call the police!" Bowie barked into the phone. There's one helluva fight goin' on in 609. I think two guys are about to kill each other. I know they're breaking up your furniture. I can hear 'em knockin' each other around. Yeah, 609. You're welcome."

"What was all that about?" Brock asked Bowie.

"Come on up to my room and I'll tell ya. We don't need to stick around here right now." Intrigued and anxious to know, Brock followed the other two up the back stairway to the seventh floor. When they entered his room, Bowie finally introduced Brock to Bill Banneker, who was from Indianapolis.

Banneker and Crockett had attended a trial in Memphis the year before where a husband and wife were being tried for "willful failure to file." Two of the witnesses for the prosecution were undercover agents for the Criminal Investigation Division of the

IRS who specialized in harassing helpless citizens. In recent weeks these same two had been instrumental in the IRS' kicking an eighty-year-old lady out of her home in Murfreesboro. Banneker had recognized them at the afternoon session and called Crockett's attention to them during the break. They both knew that these federal boys were up to no good again, and they needed to learn that it was not nice to spy. It had not taken Crockett and the shrewd Banneker long to plan a little mischief.

Banneker, much smaller than Crockett but no creampuff, had draped a towel over his arm and held an empty covered dish they had swiped off a metal cart found in the hallway. He then had rapped on the door with Bowie standing out of sight next to him.

"I intended to say 'Room Service' when they asked who was there, but they just opened the door without saying anything, and there were the two of them standing there begging to get their asses kicked," Banneker laughed.

Banneker had begun to work over the closest one with some quick, disabling blows while Bowie came in behind him and immediately grabbed the other one. *When he saw Crockett he must have been terrified,* Brock thought to himself as he listened to the other two tell of beating the two agents into submission. After rendering the agents unconscious and stealing all their identification, Bowie smashed a chair on the floor and spread the broken pieces over one of the men to appear as if the other had broken it over his head. Then they opened a bottle of cheap whiskey and dumped the contents over both before turning the dresser and mirror over on the other one. They had just been making their escape when Brock wandered onto the scene.

"Don't worry. Your secret is safe with me," he said. "Not only do I feel that it couldn't have happened to a nicer couple, but I know better than to get on the wrong side of you guys. Never fear. But you need to get out of here. They'll have thirty feds over here tomorrow trying to identify you two."

"He's right, Bowie. We ought to pack up and get out of here," Bill remarked as he stood at the basin washing the dried blood from his knuckles.

"Naw. First thing in morning is soon enough. They'll never get organized tonight. I'm going to sleep. I already paid for this bed, and I'm gonna use it. Man, that was great, wasn't it? I ain't had so much fun since I bit the head off that lizard." He grinned a tongue-in-cheek *it makes you wonder, don't it?* and Brock *did* wonder if he was really serious.

During the next few minutes before going downstairs, he got

to know Bill Banneker a little bit. The master salesman, Brock knew how to make a good first impression by getting people to tell him about themselves. How had Bill become interested in the government takeover of America? he wondered and asked him.

"Cause he's one rich nigger and he don't wanna lose his money," Bowie butted in.

"Listen here, you big honkey redneck, I told you not to call me that," Bill retaliated, while histrionically reaching into his pants pocket as if he were going for a knife.

Bowie feigned a run for the door, and for a moment until they both laughed, Brock thought he might be about to witness a cutting. Then he could immediately tell that far deeper than the racist jokes these two privately enjoyed, ran a tremendous respect for one another. He was yet to learn just how strong the bond really was between the two.

"To answer your question, Mr. Freeman . . ."

"Call me 'Brock,' please."

"Fine, Brock. But to answer your question, Black or White, we are all still Americans. And I'm not an African American, either. I'm an American—sixth generation, matter of fact, and not many of you can claim and prove that, but we are all still getting a raw deal, blacks and whites. I just grew to realize it by doing some of the same reading you did. When Lincoln freed the slaves, he didn't tell us he was putting us onto the federal plantation to chop and pick with the white slaves. But that's what's happened, Man. There's something ironic about all this, but I haven't figured out yet who gets the last laugh. Did we get freed to slave with ya'll? Or did ya'll get dragged down to our level and nobody toldya? All I know for sure about that is that we've all been captured, and most people don't even know it!"

Brock went back to the sixth floor, taking the elevator this time. Bill Banneker was right. Sarah's father hadn't gone around calling himself a "Scandinavian American." There were no German Americans or Hebrew Americans who described themselves as such, so why should there be African Americans? We were all Americans—emerged from the great boiling pot of the world in that purported "Land of the Free." And while the jury was still out on whether or not that amalgamation would ultimately work, Brock believed in granting common respect to all people until they had personally surrendered the right to that respect.

As Brock rounded the corner to his room, three cops were escorting the two irate agents toward him. Screaming that they had been framed, had not had a drink all night, and were special agents for the United States Government, one agent protested

violently, threatening the local constabulary with all kinds of
lawsuits for false arrest. The other slowly marched with his hands
cuffed at the waist and mumbled and whined in a voice not
unlike a bird's chirp, reminding Brock of Truman Capote. Brock
immediately recognized him as the mustached man who had sat
at the next table in the coffee shop at noon that day and now
surmised that he must have been trying to watch and listen to
what Schiff might say. The last voice heard was that of one of the
cops barking as they waited for the elevator, "Shutup, you drunk
ol' crybaby, I'm tired of listening to ya. Ya'll will have plenty of
time to sleep it off and get your story straight before you tell it to
the judge at nine o'clock Tuesday morning."

As Brock peered in the doorway of 609 to observe the wreck-
age, he saw what Bowie had meant by having had so much fun
and was amused to realize that if the prisoners couldn't reach
any of their superiors over the weekend, they would be the guests
of the City of Chattanooga for three nights. There was an amusing touch of irony in the recollection of the fact that this was the
regular ploy of the IRS/CID. They seemed to take sadistic pleasure in making weekend arrests, knowing that their targeted
victims would have to cool their heels in jail until early the
following week when the judge would be available for the next
bond hearing. This one would make for a nice twist of events.

At the meetings the next day, he listened for any small talk
about the incident. It was never mentioned, and Bowie Crockett
and Bill Banneker were long gone.

Traveling separately, Bowie had headed out I-75 toward
Knoxville and his home beyond in east Tennessee. Bill was traveling north in his black Chevrolet van toward Indiana. When he
got to Nashville, he stopped for breakfast at Denny's on the
north side. He thumbed the telephone book for the name and
address of the State Insane Asylum and called the Chattanooga
Police Department to see if the two men were still being held.
When the dispatcher checked and answered in the affirmative,
Banneker identified himself as "John Williams, the weekend supervisor" at the state home for the bewildered and named the
two individuals as escapees. He said that the two had fantasized
in the past about being "federal agents," and that the police
should pay them no mind. He assured them that he would see
that they were picked up by Tuesday.

"Thank you, Mr. Williams. We'll take good care of them until
you get here," replied the dispatcher.

Bill Banneker laughed half-way to Bowling Green.

EIGHT

Near the end of the twentieth century, without a public declaration, the United States government had quietly initiated open warfare against all dissenting American people. Some of the protestors were executed, thousands were jailed, their children put in state homes, and their property confiscated. The controlled news media never reported those incidents nor the fact that there were more political prisoners in jail in the United States than in Red China and the Soviet Union combined. When most of those who had been put in federal prisons emerged three to five years later, they found that although they had not been guilty of any violent crimes, they were now "convicted felons" and all rights had been taken away—i.e. voting and keeping weapons for their own protection.

❦

"And this tape will self-destruct in ten seconds," Spike Thorsten sarcastically muttered to himself and laughed out loud. As he stretched back in his big office swivel chair and peered out his window at the Potomac River, he was ecstatic. In Spike's warped and perverted mind the Deputy Commissioner had just given his silent approval to implement Spike's brainchild—Operation Loss Leader. "I told you the day you arrived that you are on your own, Spike," he had just reminded him, and that had been good enough for Thorsten. "You and your people be careful, *and no damned paper*," he'd barked at him with emphasis. "Any communication with your field force on this subject should be in person or maybe through public telephones and only when absolutely necessary. You'll get no credit for its success and all the blame for its failure. You are on your own, now understand that."

Spike had understood that well. He had been calling his own shots all along. Now he was attempting to stretch a little further knowing he didn't really need the approval of anyone any higher because no one knew the details of what his group had done to this point anyway. The commissioners were all political appointees who came and went with little knowledge of the internal workings of the agency. Most of them thought that the IRS collected taxes with which to run the country.

"No, Spike, dammit," the deputy commissioner said this day. "Have you lost your mind? We've got everything in our favor now to keep the people in place. Something like this could blow up in our faces. The people dutifully file their forms every year because they now think the law requires them to do so. You go to killing people and get caught at it and we might have rebellion on our hands."

"But Boss, I am talking about only the most disobedient of them. There are a few out there who are advising too many others with what the law really says. They have got to be stopped.

"No! It just isn't necessary. We've got the juries convicting ninety-eight percent of those guys anyway. When we blow it all over the news that this guy is going to jail for a year or two because he "didn't pay his fair share," it brings another million of them back into line. The few that you are talking about cannot hurt us."

"Yes they can," Thorsten countered. More and more are dropping out all the time. We've got to insure that they pay their fair share."

"Spike, you're so caught up in your own rhetoric you've forgotten what we taught you the first week you were here. There is no damned 'fair share.' Remember? We control it all at the top. So if a few don't cough it up each year, it's okay. We don't really miss it—we just make them think we do. Otherwise, the people will figure out that the whole damned thing is just a big bluff. The system makes up for the ones we miss this year by creating a little extra money next year, while we find some other sucker to take it back from. I am telling you that this proposed operation of yours is not necessary. Period. We never heard of Operation Loss Leader, and that's the last time the words cross my lips. And, if your people screw up and get caught by some sheriff's deputy or local cop with whatever they do, they are on their own. The Service will disavow any knowledge of the activities. The buck stops with you on this deal and you'd better not forget this. If a sacrificial ass has to be thrown to the wolves for any reason concerning this operation, it's going to be yours. You know what happened with Operation Leprechaun. Am I coming through loud and clear?"

Occasionally, investigations by congress had exposed outrageous IRS wrongdoing. Operation Leprechaun was one such instance. In 1975, Senator Frank Church headed an investigation into government operations which had included probe of the IRS's intelligence activities. The Church Committee uncovered Operation Leprechaun. As part of the Operation, IRS informants committed illegal acts under the supervision of the IRS agents directing them. Among other things, they collected details about the personal and sexual lives of various political figures in Florida.

That operation had been run by IRS Special Agent John T. Harrison out of the Jacksonville, Florida, district office. Harrison started out with an "imprest fund" of $30,000 from the IRS national office for the purpose of buying information from informants and for covering basic operating expenses.

Harrison cultivated a total of forty-two confidential informants in connection with Operation Leprechaun, and it was later found that five of these informants were requested to gather sexual information about their subjects, two were to create background files on targeted individuals, five were to gather political information, one was to get information on the drinking habits of various citizens, and four were to conduct electronic surveillance.

Two of the informants burglarized the office of a congressional candidate. Although a special agent named Harrison claimed ignorance of the burglary while under oath before the Church Committee, the files that were stolen from the candidate were found in Harrison's office.

Another two of Harrison's operatives used illegal electronic surveillance to record conversations with a former judge, the legal requirement for such activity being written approval signed by the Attorney General of the United States, and, of course, no such approval was obtained. Harrison's operatives were so out of hand that he himself did not know what his minions were doing, or so he claimed. Informants unknown to him were set up and paid off by other informants. It finally blew up in their faces with the senate investigation, but not before many people in the higher echelons of the agency were sweating. They had allowed Harrison free rein even when they knew of his questionable activities. After the smoke had cleared, he was allowed, apparently as a reward for his poor memory, to continue his work. It was the modern-day American way.

Yes, Spike Thorsten had understood the deputy commissioner perfectly. Harrison had let things get out of hand, out of his control. Spike would rule it with an iron fist. Maybe he would never get any medals or public recognition for its success, but

Operation Loss Leader would forever be the *private* badge of honor that would get him a director's position at a future opening and maybe someday, even a seat in the chair the commissioner had his proud butt in right now. But at this moment, now that he had the stamp of cachet—cryptic as it may be—he needed to start thinking about implementation. He would move ahead with his plans and piss on what the boss had said. Spike could read between the lines and he knew that the deputy commissioner was only mouthing a disapproval that he really didn't mean. After all, just like he had said, Spike had been on his own from the start and nobody had any control over what plans he carried out anyway.

*   *   *   *   *

Four months earlier Spike had begun to hear some of his drinking buddies out of the Drug Enforcement Agency gloating about what a free hand they had in utilizing the new forfeiture law passed by congress in 1984. The law said, in summary, that, if the authorities had only the suspicion of illegal activity, they could seize any property that might be connected with that "crime." The "criminal" would then have to post bond, go to court, and prove that he was not involved in anything illegal. The politicians, caught up in the hysteria of stopping drugs, had not only thrown the basic Americanism of "innocent until proven guilty" right out the window but had provided the opportunity-stage for authorities to make it next to impossible for an accused to prove anything in his own defense.

At the Top Hat that evening, one of the tipsy DEA agents confided to Spike. "Hell, if we see a yacht in Fort Lauderdale that we like, it's a simple matter to take a quarter-kilo or so from our last confiscation, conceal it on board late one night, and then tip the local authorities. A few days later, they call us in to report what they have found. Presto! The quarter kilo *and* the yacht are ours! Now how is the poor sumbitch going to prove he is innocent? We've caught him red-handed.

"That's how we nailed the mob big-wig in that little burg near Chicago last month. He had everybody in his pocket—the sheriff, the local police chief, the mayor, hell, probably even the governor. The FBI had been stymied for years. Your guys at IRS couldn't trap him because he did all his banking off-shore. Cheeit," he crowed. "It took us a whole week before we had his million-dollar mansion, his luxury motorhome, twin red Jaguars, and his cottage on Lake Michigan which came with four jet skis. Don't tell anyone, but my kid's fraternity at Boston College was the happy beneficiary of one of those."

Spike grasped the moment to exploit the drunk for more information. He learned that confiscated inventory was very loosely handled by the DEA's warehouses around the country. Because of the recording of deeds, it would be foolishly careless to attempt to take over any cars or real estate before they were legally auctioned, but incidental merchandise such as jet skis, lawn mowers, personal computers, copy machines, furniture, and of course, cash were often conveniently left off of inventory sheets and were easy to commandeer. Cops in various towns in every state were suddenly driving late-model Cadillacs, Lincolns, and Mercedes while they were waiting for the local auctions that might be conveniently set months in advance, before being quietly postponed indefinitely. It was a fact of life.

"Hey, Charley," Spike had asked quietly, "Do you think I could get a kilo or so for, uh, you know, proper distribution when I need it?"

"Call me," Charley had said.

*　　*　　*　　*　　*

Spike rocked in his chair quietly for five minutes or more before deciding that there was no better place to start than by locking in some contraband through Charley at the DEA. He was given the runaround as to Charley's whereabouts before using the clout of his office to learn the room number at which he could be reached at the Miami Fountainbleau. When there was no answer, Spike left his home number with the front desk. Charley called back and woke him up around midnight. After exchanging pleasantries, Spike, trying to mask his fear of getting a *non possumus,* got down to business and began to talk fast, directly, and emphatically.

"Charley, you remember my request a few months ago at the Top Hat, when you told me to call you when I was ready?

"Yeah, Spike. No problem. You caught me at a good time. We just made a big hit with the Coast Guard between here and Bimini. We got a ton of it. How much do you need?"

Spike had been hoping for a kilo or two but decided to overplay his hand. "How about ten kilos? Can you spare that without it looking, you know . . . uh . . ."

"Yeah, no sweat. There's so much here; it will never be missed."

"Great. Hey, Charley, one more request."

"Yeah?"

"I don't know anything about the shit. Can you cut it into forty quarter kilo bags, so we can, you know, utilize it the way you do sometimes?"

"Not without raising eyebrows, buddy. There are too many guys around down here. But I'll tell you what I can do. I can swipe fifty empty bags from our warehouse inventory when we get back to D.C., and you can put it up in any amounts you want to. Fair enough?"

"Great. When will I see you, or how do I get it?"

"We're finishing up here tomorrow, but some of the guys want to go spear-fishing in Grand Cayman over the weekend. We'll be back no later than Monday night. Give me Tuesday to do my pilfering, and I'll meet you at the Top Hat at cocktail hour on Wednesday."

"Super, Charley. I'm going to buy you the biggest steak on the menu."

"You're going to buy me the biggest steak on the menu every Wednesday for as long as you live, Spiko!"

"You got it, Buddy," Spike said, chuckling into the phone. "I really appreciate it. You're right. I owe you a big one."

By the time Wednesday came and Spike picked up his stash, he had laid all his plans for forty different "plants" in a dozen different cities. The trusted personnel were lined up and all knew the rules of secrecy. Operation Loss Leader was ready to go into action. Code name: OLLIE.

NINE

... Those, having not the law, are a law unto themselves.

—Romans 2:14

It was an irregularly warm late October afternoon when Brock wheeled his topless 450 SL south on Ward Parkway. At seventy-fifth Street he turned right and headed west the few blocks to the corner of Mission and pulled into the parking lot on his left at the office complex. He walked to the door near the center that announced *Stanley T. Potts, C. P. A.* and was again reminded, as he had always been whenever he saw the acronym, of the time a lawyer friend had told him that this actually stood for *Constant Pain in the Ass.*

Indeed, the whole tax system, bookkeeping, and the need for an accountant in a business was a definite "C.P.A."—not to mention the attorneys as well—but he had always been told and believed that these people were a necessary evil, an additional operating expense that in the long-run paid for itself. Stan had been a good friend as well as a great help to Brock over the last decade, and of course he had been paid accordingly. Stan and his wife traveled in the same social circles as the other "newly rich" of Kansas City, but he still drove a VW Bug to the same office where he had first hung a shingle twenty-odd years earlier. It was part of the game of maintaining the image. After all, the clientele mustn't think you are doing better than they are. Stan had beckoned Brock over this day to discuss a problem after hours.

"Hello, Mr. Freeman," greeted the pretty secretary/receptionist fresh out of the Arkansas Ozarks the year before, "Mr. Potts is expecting you."

"Hi," Brock replied, not remembering her name. "I'm a little early. He wasn't looking for me until five."

"No problem. He finished up with his last client some time ago. Go on back and I'll tell him you're on the way." She pressed a button on the phone, never taking her eyes off him, and Brock heard her twang as he walked away, "Mr. Freeman is on his way back." Stan was standing in his doorway when Brock rounded the corner.

They said hello, shook hands, and Stan told him a quick joke heard that day from a client; while he poured himself a drink from the foldout bar which was neatly built into concealed bookshelves. Without asking if Brock wanted it, he pulled out a cold Heineken's beer from the small refrigerator below, popped it open, and handed it to him. Excepting a couple of glasses of wine at special dinner occasions, beer was the strongest beverage Brock ever consumed, and Heineken's was his label of choice. It was always amazing to Brock that anything which in the end could drag a man so low could in the beginning could lift him so high. Beer and wine in moderation and his weekend poker games were Brock's only vices.

His abstention from hard liquor had nothing to do with any inborn sanctimonious religious stand. It was just that he had quickly discovered in college that the popularity of booze was due primarily to the fact that it charms people with their own personalities. The boozehound glows with self-affection—and takes for granted that you share his adoration for himself. He has a few drinks, and all of a sudden this dud achieves intellect, profundity, wit, and sex appeal. He becomes a raconteur, acquires a new-found singing voice, discovers how to rumba, and attains new and immediate stature and standing in the community. In fact, the fellows who were dull when sober were even duller when drunk; and the loud became abnormally louder. Both would just spread it around more audaciously.

Since the time of making that observation, Brock and Sarah had attended all the social functions that their rising status had provided, and while they found it far more entertaining to watch the drunken antics of their friends with a sober eye than to be one of them, they had never found them to be nearly as amusing as they were "crocked" up to be. Brock had been there a couple of times himself in his college days, and as far as he was concerned, that was enough for a lifetime.

Dark-haired, tanned, handsome, and still muscularly trim, Brock always had plenty of opportunity for participation in man's other favorite vice, but he always rejected it. He was too complex for recreational sex. When he had said to Sarah, ". . . and until death do us part," he had meant it. Whenever he had been traveling as an airline Captain, the "stews" were always trying to get him to go out on the town with them, but Brock had never gone any farther than the dinner table in the hotel's dining room. Now in his real estate office nearly every day, the female sales agents would halt their conversations and admire him as he walked by. Some faked a histrionic swoon and privately commented about his "cute tush," and all vied for his attention, but he always managed to maintain his distance and respect as "boss." He was again reminded that he still "had it" when Stan's secretary/receptionist stuck her head in the door to say she was leaving for the day unless he had something else for her to do.

"No, thanks, Belinda," Stan said. "I'll see you in the morning. Good night."

"Good night," she said to her boss, and then with an undressing look toward Brock that left no doubt about her desires, she drawled a syrupy, "Good night, Mr. Freeman. It was certainly nice to see you again."

"Good night, Belinda," Brock politely replied, shunning the come-on.

She shut the door slowly and gently, eyeing Brock until the last possible moment.

"Horny little devil, ain't she?" Brock mocked in a strained, country twang, and Stan guffawed and replied in the manner and voice of a stuffed shirt attorney, "Yes, we acquired her from the law firm of Lecher, Fondler, Chauvinist, and Pigg. By the way, Brock, what's the common denominator linking together termites, tornadoes, and women?"

"I don't know, what?"

"Sooner or later, one of them is going to get your house!"

They had another laugh together before Stan sobered and said, "Buddy, we got some problems."

Brock knew that the *we* his friend and advisor spoke of was not really *us* but more accurately himself alone. Just as lawyers don't serve the time, accountants don't pay the fine. In both cases the client does.

"What's the problem?" he said.

"Somebody down at IRS is monkeying with your returns."

"Personal or corporate?" Brock interrupted.

"Personal."

"Okay, go ahead," Brock said.

"I don't know what is going on, I haven't seen it, but I suspect they have changed some figures on your 1983 return."

"Why?"

"Why what? Why do I suspect it, or why did they do it?"

"Both. But for now, why do you suspect it?"

"Because of these computer letters which you will be getting in the mail by tomorrow. I've got a friend down there who lets me know when one of my clients is about to be hit, so when he phoned me about it, I asked him to send it here first. When I called the auditor about it today, all I got was the buck-passing runaround. You know, the mushroom treatment."

"No, I don't know, Stan," Brock replied impatiently, "What's the mushroom treatment?"

"Well, that's normal operating procedure around that whole confused organization. First, they keep you in the dark; then they cover you with manure. Then they cultivate you. After you get plucked, they let you stew for awhile. Finally you get canned." Stan forced a foreboding grin, but Brock neither smiled nor spoke.

"So," Stan continued, "yesterday, when they finally located your return, I nailed it down by making the woman read to me over the phone the figures in question, and it stinks. I've got a copy of your return right here where we declared one hundred and fifty thousand dollars gross income. We filed an honestly, correctly, and timely prepared return and paid the tax of just over twenty-one thousand on a net of sixty-nine some odd. I've rechecked it. The computations are correct. The problem is that their copy shows *four* hundred and fifty thousand for your gross. Some son of a bitch has changed the one to a four without touching anything else. The computer naturally kicked it out, and here we are. They want another two hundred thousand, roundabouts, in taxes."

Brock stared at him for a moment, deep in thought. "I fail to see the big problem, Stan. My corporation pays me one hundred and fifty thousand a year. Our bank statements reflect that, our copy of the 1040 and the computed tax reflects it—not to mention the same figures on the previous returns the last five years or so—and the corporate minutes dictate it. If someone has fooled around with a pencil, it should be simple enough for us to prove."

"Of course it is. That's not the problem. They don't have the authority to do what they're doing, but they've got the power. The bastards are out of control. The form is signed by you and Sarah. You have sworn under penalty of perjury that you grossed $450,000 and paid only twenty-one thousand in taxes. You are technically and legally delinquent. Now the law says you've got to pay it before you can go to district court to argue it. That's where they've got you by the short hairs. We can win, but you've got to come up with two hundred thousand bucks to fight it—plus legal fees, which could be considerable."

"Stan, you know I don't have a quarter million in cash laying around under a potted plant. Sure, I can raise it by selling or mortgaging something. But why should I have to? There has got to be some way to show the IRS that this is an error on their part, not ours."

"I'm telling you there is not. We can take our copy in and talk until we are blue in the face, but all they will do is say something profound like, 'That's not my department, you'll have to talk to so and so,' until finally ole 'so and so' tells us that we can only prove it in a court of law. The mushroom treatment all over again."

Brock already knew about Stan's opinion of most government workers, especially those at the IRS. According to him, the average bureaucrat was a time-serving incompetent, a drone interested not in serving the public but in protecting his own job long enough to retire on his pension. Shielded by rigidly protective civil-service rules, these workers had turned the bureaucracy into an army of professional deadwood. If a taxpayer falsely reports his income, he can be sent to prison for several years for tax evasion. But if an IRS employee misrepresents tax law in order to commandeer more of a citizen's bank account, he can get a bonus and maybe even a promotion.

"What if we ignore it and do nothing?"

"I can put them off, Pal, but it won't go away. That's for sure. They'll eventually get a judgment, lien some of your property, confiscate it, and have the sheriff sell it for taxes on the courthouse steps in Olathe or Independence."

"Stan, I want to think about this for a day or two. I'll call you next week."

"No rush, Brock. We've got ninety days from last week, and I can put 'em off longer if we need any delay tactics. They are pretty lenient as long as we try to work with them. But if we 'ignore them and do nothing,' as you say, they'll get tough, and they've got the power on their side."

"I'll let you know."

When Brock reached his car in the parking lot, the sun was gone, leaving the world to the magic of cool thin silver and shadow. At that hour in late October, Midwest autumn always sent out her two emissaries, chill and snap. Even in his wool sweater, he was chilly in the early evening air as he raised the convertible top on the shiny black SL before starting home. His mind was racing. *First they go after you civilly,* he remembered the big guy telling him in Chattanooga. *But why were they coming after him?* Was the IRS so out of control that they can indiscriminately tamper with the figures on anybody's tax return and get away with it? *I wonder if I was an intentional target or was mine just another return reflecting larger than normal income, and some jackass arbitrarily decided to create a little trouble for me.*

As he drove he thought for a moment that it might just be a mistake—that someone may have punched the wrong digit while pumping the information into their computers. No, because he remembered that Stan had said that someone had tampered with the actual return, probably matched it up with the same color ink. It is a pretty simple matter to turn a one into a four. Just check one of Stan's fours in some of the other figure columns and make it the same way he fashions his. Stan had filled in the data, and Brock and Sarah had signed the completed forms. Stan wouldn't make that kind of mistake. A junior rookie semi-trainee wouldn't make that kind of mistake, and even if he had, Brock knew it could not have slipped by his eyes before he signed it. Three years is a long time back to try to remember an insignificant incident in one's life, and Brock had done so much with Stan professionally and socially during the time frame, he could not remember signing this particular tax return. He had signed several other documents since then, as well as many other tax forms. But he did know that it was always his habit to read things in detail before signing. This simply could not be a mistake. It could not have slid by him and Stan, too. Somebody inside that IRS office was not playing by the rules.

He wheeled into his driveway at home wondering if he should mention this to Sarah, and he only took a moment to decide not to give her something to worry about right now when she couldn't do anything about it anyway. Maybe later.

Then he thought about Bowie Crockett again and had an idea. He went inside and straight to his desk in his library. Maybe he could still catch Stan at the office. He had left him only ten minutes ago. The recorder answered with Belinda's message that the office was closed for the day, the weekly office hours, and instructions to leave a message "if you wish."

"Stan," Brock barked into the phone. "This is Brock. Are you still there?"

He was relieved to hear the receiver rattle and Stan's voice say, "Yeah, man, but barely. I was just locking the door. What's up?"

"Stan, I understand that this is a personal income tax problem here. Is there any difficulty or complication in any way with the corporation?"

"Absolutely not. You are Boy Scout clean there."

Brock knew that he was. They had never even been audited since the business was incorporated. He had just wanted his bean-counter to confirm it.

"Thanks, Stan. Go on home and sleep tight. I think I know how to handle this thing."

"What are you going to do?"

"I'll call you next week and let you know."

Brock hung up, looked up Bowie Crockett's number in Tennessee and dialed it. Bowie's schedule as a trucker was so erratic, he was as likely to be home on a Wednesday as he was to be out on a Sunday, but maybe he could be located. A woman answered.

Reluctant at first to tell Brock much, Bowie's wife warmed up a little after Brock assured her he was a friend who had met her husband at the Freedom Symposium in Chattanooga. When he mentioned Bill Banneker's name, she felt a little better about trusting him, told him that her name was Stella and that Bowie was on his way to Phoenix.

"He'll be in Amarillo tonight, and he always stays at the Motel 6 there. Let's see. He reloaded in Memphis and got out of there about seven this morning, if everything went right, so he oughta' be a-gittin' in there about right now. It's about twelve hours for him. Let me git that number for ya."

The phone went blank for a full minute except for a radio in the background blaring Dolly Parton's "Nine to Five." Brock pictured Mrs. Crockett as a street-smart house frau close to six feet tall standing in front of an ironing board while the butter beans were "a-cookin' " on the stove. Stella returned and read the number to him and then repeated it.

"Now let me tell you this," she said. "Whenever he's in Amarillo, he likes to go eat at that steakhouse what has them humongous steaks. You know the one I mean? It's advertised all up and down the interstate. The place that has one so big that if you can eat it in an hour without gittin' up, they'll give it to you free?"

"No, I don't know about it," Brock said.

"Well, I cain't think of the name of it either, but anyway, that's where he'll be if he's not in his room. So you just call back to the room in an hour or two if you miss him, 'cause he won't go nowhere else. He'll be too tired, and he's got to git on into Phoenix tomorrow."

Brock thanked her, rang off, looked at his Rolex President, and immediately dialed the number of the motel in Amarillo. It was seven-twenty. The desk clerk confirmed that Mr. Crockett had checked in "a few minutes ago" and rang the room. After seven rings there was no answer, and Brock hung up. He dialed Amarillo information with an idea.

"Directory listings," said the female voice. "What city, please?"

"Uh, Amarillo. Tell me ma'm, are you in Amarillo?"

"Yes I am."

"Good. I'll bet you know the answer to this question. There's a famous steakhouse out there that serves a giant steak so big that, if you can eat it all in an hour, they'll give it to you free. Do you happen to know the place I'm talking about?"

"Of course. It's The Big Texan. But I don't recommend you try it. That's a seventy-two ouncer you're talking about. My big, dumb husband tried it once and he was sick for two days. I thought I was going to have to take him to the hospital to get his stomach pumped."

Brock laughed. Texas telephone operators were so much friendlier than most. Make a request like that in New York or Chicago and see what kind of brush-off you get.

"The Big Texan," he repeated as he wrote it down.

"That's right," she said, and Brock smiled again at her cute Texas drawl which actually delivered *Thas raat.* "Do ya want the numba?"

"Please. And thank you very much for your help."

"You are very welcome. Here's the numba."

She pushed the computer button and the synthesized voice slowly said, "The number is . . . Three, seven, two, seven, oh, oh, oh. Repeat . . . Three, seven, two, seven . . . thousand."

Brock rang The Big Texan and asked the cashier to page Mr. Bowie Crockett. Sure enough, his wife knew his habits. In sixty seconds he was on the phone.

"Hyat damn! Sure I remember you, Brock. How could I forget a name like Free-Man. But how in the world did you find me here?"

"Oh, I just called the C.I.D. at IRS. They always know where you are; watching you all the time," Brock joked.

"Wouldn't doubt it. I guess I'd better go back to eatin' at the Waffle House or "Hung Chow's" Chinese restaurant to keep 'em confused."

"You're not tackling that seventy-two ouncer, are you?"

"Man, naw. That would give me *hung chow,* for sure. I tried it once a couple a years ago and took half of it on the rig with me to eat the next night. All that meat at one time is just an invitation to colon cancer, I reckon. I am in the middle of a beautiful little ribeye, though. It's so tender I can cut it with a fork."

"Good. I won't keep you then. I just wanted you to know that I need to talk to you about those off-shore trusts we discussed in Chattanooga, and I'll call you in your room later, if you tell me what time you'll be back there."

"Oh, let's see. Give me thirty minutes. You've got the number?"

"Don't rush. I'll call you in forty-five. Yeah, Motel 6. I've got it right here."

When Brock reached Bowie later, they laughed again about the mischievous plot at the Read House Hotel the year before, and Bowie told him all about Bill Banneker's phone call to the Chattanooga police when he had posed as the weekend director of the state's looney bin. They had no way of knowing what kind of additional problems it might have caused for the two "IRS drunks," but they had some good amusement speculating.

Brock then got to the reason for his call. He related to Bowie all of the shenanigans by the mysterious someone in the local IRS office that he had learned from Stan a few hours earlier.

"That's a new one on me, Man. I knew they would stoop to anything, but some scumbag has come up with a whole new ploy."

"I know. Think of the ramifications of this. They can do this to anybody, and if the poor guy can't pay it or for any number of reasons, can't fight it, they'll just take his property without due process or just compensation."

"That's right, Pal," Bowie replied fatuously. Welcome to the real world. Now what do you want to do about it?"

Bowie Crockett was an enigma who wore many hats and never ceased to amaze others with his knowledge—especially those who thought they were talking to *only* a truck driver. But he could remove that hat and don the cap and gown of a scholar in a second's time. Those same massive hands that had strangled the life from Central American and Asian drug-runners could also massage "Orange Blossom Special" out of a fiddle at lightning speed. He had begun to study law and history on his own and had become a walking, talking paralegal. On a Nashville radio talk show a few years earlier, he had destroyed an IRS spokesman in debate to the point that the spokesman refused to come back the following week. Bowie and the host had agreed that there was no doubt that orders from higher-ups had been the real reason preventing the continuance of the discussion.

Bowie was out of his truck and had just put on his Intellectual Hat once more.

Brock said, "Let's talk about my particulars. Is it too late for me take advantage of that off-shore trust system we talked about last year?"

Bowie didn't hesitate. "Is it too late for you to sell any of your property to anyone else? I mean are there any liens on anything now or do they have any judgments against you?"

"Oh, no. It was just last week that they came up with their claim."

"Then now is the time to act. First, you've got to be empty-handed. If you can legally sell it to your next door neighbor, then you can legally sell it to the trust. The trick is in getting it out of your name but still maintaining control."

"And how do we do that?"

"Carefully. You'll need an expert to assist you in making sure that those transactions are organized properly and documented accordingly, so that you don't have to worry about ever being challenged for a fraudulent conveyance."

Just as he had explained in Chattanooga, Bowie reminded Brock that having the trust appoint him as the General Manager was a way to control his assets without actually owning them. "The Trust never dies," he said; "therefore, there is never any estate tax. If you have an income tax problem, that can all be resolved too, by distributing the excess profits to the foreign companies. So you can use the trust for the preservation of assets, tax avoidance, and estate planning."

Freeman Real Estate Development, Inc. could be sold to ABC Holdings Trust just as readily as to anyone else who wanted to buy it. No law against that. There might be a problem with capital gains though. Freeman Real Estate Development, Inc. was worth around forty million bucks.

"Forty million?" growled Bowie. "Are you kidding?"

"No," Brock replied modestly. "The Lord has been good to us."

"You can say that again. Wow, Man, all this time I thought you were just another peon like the rest of us, trying to preserve a few meager assets."

Brock smiled. "I am. Maybe a little more has stuck to me along the way, that's all. But forty bucks or forty million, the principle is the same. I don't want the government stealing it from me."

Bowie explained how the business trades its assets for shares of equal value in the domestic portion of the trust conduit. That way there is no capital gain and no incident of taxation.

Brock was ecstatic. His fingernails were making interesting little grooves in the left palm of his hand as he excitedly cradled the phone under his chin. "This is fantastic, Bowie. I didn't know anything like this existed. I understand it now. It's a complicated but legal way of side-stepping their even more complicated and illegal tax structure and holding on to what we earn."

"Of course," Bowie went on. "The money cartel had their legal eagles write it in for their own benefit from the very beginning when they designed the tax laws. They just didn't tell anybody else about it. But, as far as I know, it's the only way left to keep what is rightfully ours. And it is not expensive to set up—less than $10,000 bucks. A guy like you would save more than that the first year."

"Uh-huh. Hey, Bowie. When we were in Chattanooga you gave me the name of Fred Forest in New York. Is this 212 number still the correct one for him?"

"No. I'm afraid not."

"Well, how can I reach him. I want to set this up."

"You can set it up, but it won't be through Forest."

"Why not?"

"He's dead. They killed him."

"They killed him?" Brock almost dropped the phone. "Who killed him?"

"The IRS. They had been after him for a long time but could never find any law he was breaking. Finally, they just arrested him on some trumped-up charge when he was doing a seminar in Seattle, and the scumbags poisoned his food after they had him in jail. About six months ago now."

"So, what do we do?"

"Don't worry. We've got it all covered. Forest wasn't the only game in town. We've been working with a guy out in L.A. recently, and I like his ideas even better. He's spent the last fourteen years doing this full time, and I think he's got even a better product than Fred had. I'm an agent for him, so if you go through me, I can teach you all the basics, and he will handle all the intricacies, such as setting up all the foreign creators and trustees and everything else. He has done his research well and he earns his money. Now don't expect some magic package of "Overnight Cure-All." He is very diligent and meticulous in what he does, and he is very, very insistent in compliance with the rules so his clients don't have difficulty with the authorities later. His emphasis is that the individual is independent rather than *dependent* upon some licensed attorney or accountant, because he believes any individual is capable of managing his or her own affairs."

"I'm in. What do I do next?"

"Nothing yet. I'll put you two together. His name is Robert Summers, and I'll have him send you the forms, then you two can get together on the payment. He prefers to have it all up front, but he'll work with you."

"Not necessary. I'll give it to him whenever he wants it."

"He'll appreciate it, and, Brock, don't worry about trusting this guy. He's as good as his word. He's from the old school. If

Bob says it, he'll do it, and he expects the same from everyone else. He knows his business and will show you how to make the transfer without creating any capital gains tax. You'll be impressed.

"So what do I do next?"

"Nuthin'. I'll tend to it right away. You'll hear from him next week."

Brock did receive all the forms and instructions the following week from a company called Pacific Trust Consultants with a request that he call after he had received them. They came the same day the newspapers were carrying the story that Irwin Schiff had been found guilty of tax evasion, and Brock wondered if Schiff would be subjected to the same degrading death by torture as Bowie had said Fred Forest had been. A week later he was landing his Citation at John Wayne Airport to meet with Robert Summers at Pacific Trusts Consultants in Irvine to handle the set-up of his trust conduit.

TEN

Life-changing acquaintances and incidents appear at the most unlikely times in the most unusual places. While fleeting conversations with barbers, cab drivers, and bartenders normally cannot be recalled the following day, people such as these who always have an ear to the ground must not be discounted every time. Bill Banneker learned this as a young adult, and it had made him a wealthy man.

His insight to this source of information had first taken root in early December of 1971 when he was sipping a late afternoon brew at his favorite watering hole, The Sports Club on the south side fringes of the downtown area of Indianapolis. Marcel Gautier, a transplanted Creole from New Orleans and the night-time bartender, had just come on duty. Not only was Marcel dependable and conscientious, but he was also an articulate conversationalist, especially concerning all sports, and he was hard-nosed enough to double as a bouncer whenever the situation required it. This was seldom. His reputation had quickly become common knowledge with the younger and rowdier clientele. Marcel was the All-American bartender, the kind any club owner would give his toupee to have working for him. He also was one helluva horse-tipper in those days, and, in appreciation of a favor Bill had once done him—Bill had given Marcel a mobile home rent-free for several months after a tornado had blown away everything Marcel owned—he had passed on several "cinches" from the Arlington and Pimlico race tracks. Unlike most hot tips, Marcel's "cinches" were really cinches. It was only after Bill all but guessed it, maybe after two months of some miraculous wins, that Marcel had confessed that he had daily inside info from one of his old Louisiana buddies who was now a big time jockey. This particular December night, as Walter Cronkite was reporting from Peking about the upcoming visit by the president, Marcel was chatting with Bill Banneker, in between pulling fresh beer for the evening's new surge of customers.

"Why do you reckon he's goin' over there?"

"Who?"

"Tricky Dick! You don't believe that sumbitch is going to China to play ping-pong again, do you?" he said to Bill, as he delivered another draft beer.

"Oh! No, I guess not. I really haven't thought about it," Bill replied. "Is he supposed to referee or something?"

"Forget whatever the *official* word is that he is *supposed* to be doing. You can bet the real reason ain't got nuthin' to do with gyat damm ping pong.

Bill stared at him for a moment while he pondered the depth of that remark. "Okay, what do you think it is?"

"C'mon, Banneker, wake up. He's there to open up some import/export markets—probably foodstuffs and clothing. Coca Cola is already there. If I had a few thousand to blow, I'd go buy me some cotton futures tomorrow morning . . . probably go through the roof this year. Meanwhile, I'll bet you ten bucks the Bengals win Sunday, straight-up, no points."

"No deal," replied Banneker, "I like Cincinnati, myself, but I'll take the Lions against your beloved New Orleans Saints and give you the three. Tom Dempsey won't pull any miracles with that half-foot of his two years in a row."

"You're on," said the Creole barkeep, "but for twenty bucks," he said as he wrote it down, and his black friend nodded and smiled in agreement.

Bill finished his beer and headed for the house, unable to forget about Nixon's China trip. *Of course, he's not there to play ping-pong,* he thought. *Marcel has got to be right with that much. But is it really to open up markets? Maybe. Makes sense. And, if so, is it food and clothing? Yes, of course it is. What else could it be. If so, then cotton futures are a good gamble.* He decided to call his broker first thing in the morning.

Bill Banneker had learned another lesson as a young man: Never follow the crowd if you want to get ahead. Do the opposite of the majority and you will usually make the right decision. That's what had been preached by all the great teachers of success he had ever read. "Follow the multitudes to poverty," said they. There would never be a finer opportunity to test it, he decided. Whatever his broker advised, he would go against.

He was quite a little man, long-trunked with broad, high shoulders topped with a bull neck. The chiseled features of his face gave the appearance of someone older, but this was belied by the young spring in his athletic step and his flat and muscular stomach. While of average height, his disproportionately short legs kept his belt too close to the ground, and he often would attempt to compensate for this by wearing high-heeled dress boots. And he had offset his lack of formal education by becoming a voracious reader. This may have been the common ground for his friendship with Bowie Crockett.

"Hey, Bob," he greeted his commodity broker the next morning. "What's popping?"

"Good morning, Bill. Sugar and silver. Everything else is dead in the water and has been for a week or more."

"What about cotton?"

"Not much action there either. Let's give it a check here on the morning printout. Let's see . . . uh, no, ninety-dayers are down a little, uh, no, I don't think you want to fool with that right now. What are you looking for, short-term or a long-term flyer?"

"No rush. I can wait a year for a good return. What will a cotton contract cost me right now?"

"You're the boss, Bill. It's your money. But I would take a shot at silver right now. Cotton has been going down slowly all year, and there is nothing to indicate a turnaround at this time. I don't see any action there on the immediate horizon."

"Are you telling me that nobody has bought a cotton future this week?" Bill said, smiling to himself.

"I'm telling you nobody has bought a cotton future from me in at least a month, upside or downside. Everybody is laying off."

"Good. Gimmee a quote."

"Forty-three cents, down from forty-nine last month, fifty three in October."

"Okay, what's today's deal?"

"One hundred bale contract, 500-pound average, fifty-thousand pounds will cost you just under nine hundred bucks, give or take a dime."

"Shazam! I'll take twenty-five contracts," Bill said as he punched his desktop calculator for a few seconds. "I'm sending you twenty-two thousand bucks in today's mail. Send me the confirmation. If I'm short a little, I'll remit the rest. If I'm over, just credit my account, and I'll collect it on the next exchange."

"You got it, Buddy," said the gleeful but skeptical broker. "You've got my best wishes. Good luck." The broker hung up the phone and silently wished he had more contrarians such as Bill on his clientele list.

In sixty days, much to his broker's surprise, Bill had sold five of his contracts for a healthy $23,000 profit, which had provided him a free ride on the balance as long as the market kept growing. The U.S. open-door policy with Red China had exploded the volume of clothing exports and along with it, of course, the cotton market. When the price broke eighty cents, he sold another fifteen and, at ninety-three cents, he moved out the remaining five contracts. In just eleven months Bill Banneker had walked away with over two hundred thousand dollars in cotton futures profits.

One sunny afternoon soon thereafter, Bill spotted his Creole buddy walking toward the Sports Bar and gave him a lift in his new Jaguar. Marcel, who took plenty of good-natured ribbing about being the only "coonass" in the area, told Bill that he had the title for his book whenever he was ready to write it.

"What is it?" asked Bill, taking the bait.

Peering around at the plush interior of the new Jag, Marcel replied, " 'From Broke Barfly to Nigger Rich in only a Year.' "

The casual conversations with his favorite bartender and the playing of his hunch had laid the cornerstone for his real estate equities which would grow to nearly three million by 1985. Besides that, the Lions had blasted the Saints that following Sunday.

It was Marcel, the uneducated but street-smart bartender, and not any of the nationally known economists who had first pointed out to Bill the precarious economic position America had placed herself in by going totally off of lawful money in 1968. "No nation in the history of the world has survived a paper-money scheme," the Creole sage reminded him one day in 1975. "And this one won't either. The politicians will get a free ride for awhile, but we are doomed. This economy is built on sand. Buy silver while it's cheap. You'll pay off a lot of property mortgages with it someday soon."

And, indeed, Bill did. He had bought twenty bags of $1,000 face amount of pre-'65 silver coins at $2,350 each, following their barside conversation. In January of 1980, his stash was worth just under $39,000 a bag when he sold out. By the time he had finished clearing out most of his real estate debts, he was left with over one million bucks worth of property free and clear and was well on his way to building a small empire. It was during these years that the IRS became interested, attempted to hassle Banneker, and found out they couldn't touch him. And it was during these years that Banneker studied and began to discern the truth about money and taxes and how the hoax was protected by the federal judiciary.

He also knew from his conversations with Bowie Crockett how the American people had been tricked by stories fed to the controlled news media into believing that the "good guys" in this so-called Drug War were in the American CIA and DEA. Again and again, due to its ignorance of corruption by government officials all the way to the White House, the American public was blissfully suffering the consequences of the criminality of its leaders and particularly those attorneys and officials in the Justice Department.

Later when Bill met up with Bowie Crockett at the Memphis trial, more was confirmed for him. Bowie had worked for two years in Central America as a contract man with the "Company," back when George Bush had been its boss. At the time of the fall of South Vietnam, he had been doing similar work in Cambodia and Laos. It was not until he realized that he was on the wrong side of freedom that he quit and went back to Tennessee to drive a truck and "re-group." Bowie had seen from the inside that it was the American CIA that was drugging America as well as controlling ninety percent of the drugs world-wide. Drugs meant money, lots of it, and money meant power and control over those smaller, weaker nations. It was that simple.

"We were king-makers," Crockett said. "We toppled governments and established our own. All in the name of Democracy."

The two had been pulling apart a couple of slabs of dry ribs at a Beall Street restaurant when Bowie began to explain it to him.

"Sham drug busts occasionally occur to give the public the impression that drug enforcement agencies are carrying out their responsibilities," he said. "They plant it in a suitcase and put it on a bus. Then they meet the bus in the chosen city and have their dogs 'discover' it. The media people are always tipped first of course in order to be sure that the cameras are there. I know for a fact—some of my old cohorts were there—that one sham drug bust occurred in Miami to justify hiring more federal personnel and to make the new drug czar, Vice President George Bush, look good. Later they set up this huge bust in Sylmar, California, where they actually seized back twenty tons they had already allowed in. Now the purpose of this type operation is two-fold. One reason is for public relations, indicating to the American people that the enormous amount of money justifies the violation of constitutional rights. But there's another reason that nobody thinks about and that is to reduce the amount of drugs in circulation. See, at the time, the drug prices were plunging because of an oversupply, which restricted the CIA's income from its drug trade. If you understand money and taxes, you know what I mean."

"I know exactly what you mean," his new black friend replied. "The IRS is the collection wing of the Fed. They strip out the excess currency and credit in order to somewhat maintain the value of the money that is left on the street. So to hear that they do that with drugs, too, only tells me that they have learned that it works, for a while at least."

They both knew, too, of the horde of books being written every year by an illiterate cadre of imposters who otherwise presumed to be envoys of justice from the heavens. None of them ever told the truth about the inevitable, eventual demise of any economy based on imaginary legal tender. Most "economist" authors were not even aware, and the few who were, didn't dare report it.

Crockett's stories came to mind from then on each time Bill Banneker picked up the Indianapolis paper and read about the drug confiscations at an airport or bus station. If he had had any doubts, they were wiped out a short time later when former DEA agent Michael Levine, a twenty-five year veteran of that and other drug agencies, wrote *The Big White Lie* confirming all those tricks and more. He described how the CIA, the DEA, and other agencies blocked investigations and prosecutions of high-level drug traffickers and how the CIA was *primarily* responsible for the drug epidemic in America. He described how federal judges and Justice Department prosecutors dramatically drop the amount of bail for high-level drug distributors who are CIA assets and who have been accidentally charged, allowing those "assets" to then flee the United States. And the only people going to jail in America for drug trafficking were those who were in competition with the government.

When Banneker finished the book, he began to wonder how much time on this earth the author might have left. Almost all whistleblowers fare poorly, but none reach nearly the level of risk as do those who blow the whistle on the powerful Justice Department and federal judiciary. But now that the book was out, maybe he was safe. Most were killed to *prevent* the exposure, rather than in retaliation for it. Two of the better known examples became those of Karen Silkwood and Danny Casolaro, both of whom had been murdered under very strange circumstances just before exposing a story of government-shaking proportions.

Bill Banneker knew better than most people the risks involved with learning too much inside information about government crimes. When Bowie Crockett called to say he was coming to Indianapolis and wanted to meet, Bill already knew from previous conversations what the subject matter was to be. They decided on The Sports Club downtown at 5:00 P.M.

Bowie parked around the corner and walked two blocks to the former turn-of-the-century rowdy house remodeled in recent years into The Sports Club. Many of the old artifacts—guns and stuffed snakes, quail and pheasant—still adorned the walls. The downstairs bar was the original, a century old made of a now-refinished oak, thick and heavy, about twenty-five feet long, and which seemed to fit Tombstone, Arizona more than Indianapolis. The floor was the old black and white tile seen in many of the restrooms of buildings of that era and, "If it's not original, the remodelers certainly have done a great job of making everybody believe it," Bill remarked as they hoisted their first beers.

He had often wondered if his grandfather had ever frequented this joint. There had been a colored section in the back room in the Roaring Twenties when this was a Speakeasy. Before, during, and after that era, his grandpa had held down the custodian's job for fifty years in the office building only a couple of blocks north. He also doubted if 'joint' was a very accurate description of this gem even then. Only the blaring pop music seemed out of place, as the yuppies began to drift in after work.

They grabbed a second mug of beer and withdrew to a back table in a deserted vestibule. Bill had already noticed that his friend was piqued. Bowie lit a long stogie and rocked back in his chair to blow the first puff upwards, before leading right into why they were there.

"It's time to go on the offensive," the big man said, rocking forward toward Bill.

Bill said nothing but turned his palms up and wiggled his fingers on the table with a "C'mon" signal to silently say *Tell me more*. Bowie proceeded.

"Somthin' strange has been going on in recent weeks, and not even my guys on the inside can learn anything about it. But three prominent men who were active in the Freedom Movement have died mysteriously. Two car wrecks and a shooting on the street sloppily made to look like a robbery. You know who is responsible."

"The agency, sure, but what do we do to find out exactly who?" asked Bill.

"Well, I've got some more feelers out, we'll find out who the individuals are, don't worry, but meanwhile, we're gonna retaliate, big time."

"Just how big time?"

"By leveling some bricks and mortar. Are you game?"

"I thought you'd never ask, big guy, I thought you'd never ask."

Bowie spent the next forty-five minutes outlining a secret plan that was already in its preliminary stages in central Florida. A small band of Vietnam vets, working in pairs, had set out to capture any IRS agents who were harassing the American people. Only those from the Criminal Investigation Division (CID) were targeted—those who were raiding homes and offices and taking property without due process.

When found alone going to work in the mornings, coming home in the evenings, or out to lunch, the agents were captured and placed under citizen's arrest. But instead of being taken to the local sheriff, who would only release them almost immediately anyway, the new suspects were taken bound and gagged in the back of a van to a remote rural property near the Gulf on the northwestern edges of Hernando County, Florida. A thousand acres were enclosed in a ten-foot high, electrically charged cyclone fence.

At trial, wherein evidence would be submitted before a judge and jury, the accused could speak in his own defense. Almost invariably, the only justification for the action would be, "I was just following orders." Ignorance of the law being no excuse, the jury would return a guilty verdict, and the judge would pass the same sentence each time. The convict would be stripped to the waist, given a hunting knife for survival and an hour's head start in the enclosed wilderness; and hunted for sport by the twelve jurors, who were all middle-aged former military men, seasoned in guerilla warfare.

The cost of participating in this new game was $1,000, but for obvious reasons, only a select few were invited. Bowie knew the landowner, whom he identified only by the code name of "Mr. Roark," and extended an invitation to his pal, Bill Banneker, who jumped at the chance.

Handing over the ten hundred-dollar bills, Bill remarked, "And I suppose when my plane lands, I'll be met by a three-foot dwarf named 'Tattoo!'" Bowie, who only recently had acquired the first television set he had ever owned, had no idea what his friend was joking about.

"No", replied Bowie, "his name is Raoul, a Cuban freedom fighter I worked with years ago in the Company."

"Okay," Bill said, "let's get back to the bricks and mortar detail. What, where, and how?"

Bowie lowered his voice. "The What is IRS offices, particularly those remote CID locations housed outside of the federal buildings. We want to send the message to the public that this is not a group of kooks bent on destroying their government, but rather fed-up citizens just like them who are rebelling against a confiscatory tax system. If we handle it properly, the P. R. result will be silent approval instead of public outrage. We hit in the middle of the night where only buildings and records are destroyed and nobody is killed. The Where will always be several hundred of miles away from Indianapolis. You will already be on your way out of town before anyone knows you were there."

"How soon do we start?"

"Immediately. Let's go out to your farm. I've got some supplies we need to unload."

Bowie trailed the Buick station wagon as the two drove the half hour north to Bill's farm near Noblesville. Heinrich, the attack-trained Doberman, yelped a friendly greeting from his pen as they emerged from the car. They tended to the unloading, ate a sandwich, and went to bed. Bowie departed for St. Louis before daylight.

* * * * *

The Florida hunting expedition ran into unexpected problems before it got a good start, operations were called to a halt after only a few trials, and Bill and Bowie's hunting excursion never came down, at least not in Florida. Their cash was returned a week later with the simple note of explanation signed by Raoul that there had been some problems and "they would be in touch."

Six weeks later they learned that the whole operation had nearly been torpedoed when it was almost infiltrated by a government snitch. One of the operatives, upon receiving the entrance fee, recognized the address stupidly used too often by one of Spike Thorsten's OLLIE operatives in Atlanta. This was the only fee not returned. Instead, "Jim Wood," the phony name used by the Atlanta agent, was lured to the Orlando airport by Raoul and taken by private plane to what he believed would be the secret location of the camp. While Raoul, who was piloting, had him absorbed in conversation in the co-pilot's seat, another compatriot garroted the agent from the rear seat of the Cessna 172 with a four-foot piece of rawhide. The body of "Jim Wood" became piscatorial nourishment in the Gulf of Mexico, two miles off the coast somewhere between Apalachicola and, appropriately, Deadman's Bay.

Consequently, the location of the camp had to be changed. Because it was still secret, it could be used later, but it was "too hot" to risk now. Only the operation had been compromised, not the names of the operatives. Because Raoul had used as a contact point a different motel with a different name each time, the FBI would be stymied, and their investigation would lead nowhere.

"Mr. Roark" would settle on a remote ranch outside of Virginia City, Nevada, as their future site. It enveloped over five thousand acres of both mountains and plains. The remaining twelve prisoners were soon transported in a Boeing 727 whose flight plan had been logged as a "gambling excursion to Reno." A school bus met the plane a furlong away from the terminal, and the prisoners were loaded for transport to Virginia City without observation. The hunting excursions would resume in a few months, but Bill Banneker would never get a chance to participate in the fun and games. At least not in the advertised manner. The lords of chance held a larger role for him as well as Brock and Bowie. He did, however, become better acquainted with "Mr. Roark." It was an association that would develop into a valued, trusted relationship between themselves as well as their affiliates. Banneker also convinced him that between the two of them they could well afford to finance the business of the camp. It would not be necessary to attempt to bring in money by including outsiders and along with it the potential to jeopardize the whole operation. As good fortune would have it, they later found some other like-minded people with the funds to lighten the financial load.

Pre-fab buildings were thrown together, new electrical fencing was put in place, and Banneker and Crockett soon had a branch office out west.

ELEVEN

Spike Thorsten was bursting with enthusiasm as he drove through the post-dawn mist toward Washington National Airport. Arrests and collections were up, and he was glowing with pride in the new tool he had discovered which was successfully instilling fear around the country. He had gotten a phone call from the commissioner on Friday personally congratulating him on his general success. Spike still wondered if he or anyone else beyond the deputy had any knowledge of the secret mission but could not ask. Regardless, as he pulled into the secured parking lot, he gloated to himself with righteous and aggressive superiority about how close he must be now to that promotion.

The stillatitious accumulation of rainwater on the tile floor was making yet another mockery of the ongoing struggle to fix the roof and, for that matter, the whole shabby structure of the aging airport terminal. Spike cursed it one more time, hurried through the terminal, and took his customary seat in the first class section on the early Monday morning Delta flight, this time to Kansas City. His normal, irritable mood was boosted with the tickling of his nose and lip by the new, phony stick-on mustache which he had applied in the men's room before boarding.

After an uneventful two hours above the rainstorm, he drove away from KCI Airport and Hertz in his newly rented Lincoln Towncar. Forty minutes later he pulled into the IRS/CID headquarters above the Cellular One offices overlooking Shawnee Mission Parkway in Overland Park.

He flashed his badge to the receptionist and was directed to the correct office. Spike handed the agent the requisite tesserae: his picture I.D. and a handwritten note on the back of his business card which bore the solitary word—"OLLIE."

"Well, Boss, so we finally meet. I'm Don Handy, handy-dandy Don at your service. Happy to meet you."

Spike was not impressed by the agent's capricious cockalorum. "Yeah, good to meet you too," he said with a look of vacuity as he shook Handy's hand. For a moment he thought he was gripping a dead fish. "Let's get down to business, Don. I've got to fly back to Washington tomorrow night, and I believe we have a lot of miles to cover."

"Yessir, we do. We've got a farmer near Hutchinson—the one we talked about—who needs our attention. That's about three hours each way plus whatever more we need while we're there. Maybe another hour or two. That will pretty much shoot the daylight hours, no pun intended. We've already gotten the rumor started that he is heavily indebted to the gamblers in Wichita. Then late tonight we are paying a visit to the real estate tycoon who snookered us out of our assessment."

"Tell me more about him."

"Brock Freeman. He's about forty-five, a former airline pilot who quit when he made a jillion in property development on the south side. We almost had him cold last year after we did a slight manipulation with his return, but the sly bastard moved his property into a trust before we could grab it. The courts held that he had done it in ample time to avoid our liens, so we've got no civil recourse. We've got over four hundred thousand on him that's growing with interest and penalties every month, but he doesn't give a damn. He knows we'll never collect. He'll never own anything in his name again as long as he lives. We need to teach him a lesson."

"What are his habits? Have you got a plant on him?"

"Yessir. A golf and poker-playing buddy of Freeman, a dentist named Dr. Joe Day, and we've got him eating out of our hands. He's a Napoleonic little prick who thinks we're going to pull off him because he's feeding us information. Hell, we never made any deals with him. We made a routine call to his office because he hadn't filed in years, and, all of a sudden, he began to chirp about all these illegal tax protestors he's associated with. Turned out that when we asked about the trust he had established, he mentioned that he was best friends with Freeman, and that's where he learned about how to establish the trust. Anyway, Dr. Day says that Freeman is a family man, home every night relatively early. The only thing that might keep him out is a business appointment or an association meeting with the protestors, which is only one night a month. Third Tuesday, we found out, at Shoney's over on Independence Avenue."

"So, are we proceeding with Plan "A" or Plan "B?"

"With Freeman, if we ever get around to him, definitely Plan 'B.' It'll be after dark, and his big place is isolated enough that we don't have to worry about neighbors eavesdropping. One five gallon can of gasoline after midnight will send him a message he'll never forget. If he doesn't take the advice therein, I figure we can move him up to Plan A later. With Walter Jenkins, the farmer, even though it will be broad daylight, probably "A" is better because he'll be alone. Besides, the hard-nosed son of a bitch will never knuckle under. We already have seen that. He will be in the field on his tractor this afternoon, finishing the last days of harvest. Johnston and I did a little surveillance late last week, and we know Jenkins is finishing up in a field where we can have perfect range from the road—three hundred yards, maybe less. If we get moving, we can have a little lunch in the local cafe, tend to business in the early afternoon, and be back here for a beer and some ribs before dark."

"Then let's get going. We can talk more in the car." *This guy Handy talks a good game,* Thorsten thought on the way to the car. *Let's see how he handles it under fire.*

Nickerson looks like any other tiny, dusty, midwestern town that might be found ten miles from Sterling or twenty from Inman. A few more miles north in Lindsborg, one is as likely to see a family traveling by horse and wagon as by automobile.

There are two gas stations in town now—both became self-serve in recent years—along with one Ma and Pa all-purpose store, one combination barber/beauty shop where all the new county gossip can be learned each week; and the pre-war, wood frame building housing the Sunshine Cafe, serving fresh vegetables along with the special entree of the day—either country fried steak, fried chicken, or meat loaf. This day the sign in the window said it was meat loaf, and in a glaring portrait of incongruity, a horse, complete with western saddle and silver-laden bridle, was tied to a parking meter out front.

The shiny white Lincoln looked conspicuously out of place as it pulled to a stop across the street from the Sunshine. But the two men emerging from it did not. Handy had worn overalls and cowboy boots. Thorsten had peeled of his coat, vest, and tie, and, in his white shirt and slacks, appeared as if he were no more than either a city-dwelling land owner who was taking his tenant to lunch or a traveling salesman, maybe out of Wichita or Topeka, eating with a farmer client. Either assumption would be fine with Thorsten and Handy. They both knew that country Kansans are respectfully curious but not nosey people, and that no one would be questioning them.

At 12:25 P.M. as the two attempted to enter the door of the cafe, it opened in front of them and out walked a grimy, grey-haired man who greeted the two with a "howdy" and walked toward his pickup truck. The two strangers returned the greeting and strode inside to a vacant table.

"Guess who that was," said Handy, after they'd pulled up their chairs and grabbed a menu.

"You mean going out the door?"

"Yeah."

"Jenkins?"

"Jenkins."

"I'll be damned. Do you think he recognized you?"

"No way. He's never seen me. We've been observing him from afar with telescopes and wiretaps. The old fart thinks we pulled off him since he won that tax case two years ago. He'll be blissfully tending to his crops when we get there."

An hour later, the white Lincoln crept down the gravel road, surrounded by the sun-bleached wheat fields of bucolic tranquility. As it coasted to a stop, the powered glass on the driver's side buzzed down, and the muzzle of a .308 rifle with a scope attached extended from its window. The cross-hairs centered on the head of its target for a second or two as Don Handy, on the passenger side, placed a finger in each ear. The carbine exploded with its report, and, a furlong away, the tractor began to weave off course for fifty yards before stalling in its tracks. The barrel of the gun receded into the car, was thrown into the back seat, the power window buzzed up, and the Lincoln disappeared over the horizon into its own spindrift. The first OLLIE immolation was completed, and no one had seen a thing.

The driver of the tractor had been listening to his transistor radio, which was blaring at its highest volume to overcome the noise of the machinery, and the local country station had taken a music break to announce the news headlines on the half hour. The last earthly words Walter Jenkins, age 58, heard were from the recorded voice of Vice President George Bush saying something about "a kinder and gentler nation."

*   *   *   *   *

Brock was continuing his education wherever he could outside of the traditional methods. Most of what he wanted to know could be found only in the used book stores anymore. The details had slowly been eradicated from the public school books and libraries since he and Sarah had attended—to the point now that his son Brent and the younger generation didn't have a clue to the truths about monetary realism. However, it was more difficult for the re-writers of history to remove some of the basics such as Article One, Section 10 of the Constitution. Roger

Sherman was still in the history books but his actions with the preservation of hard money at the founding of the nation had been glossed over.

During Brock's early quest for knowledge he had briefly met researcher and writer Dave Littleton at the conference in Chattanooga and had later subscribed to his newsletter—*American, Wake Up!* Brock had found it to be the most informative piece of monthly advice he had ever seen. When he had had the problem with the IRS changing his corporate tax return, he had written to Dave, reminded him of where they had met, and explained a little of his problem following with a plea for a little fatherly advice. Months later, a letter arrived with the apology for not responding sooner but Brock's letter had gotten buried in the papers on Littleton's desk and had only recently risen to the top. Brock skimmed over the first paragraph and got right into the meat of the letter. Nobody had ever told the obvious truth more boldly and succinctly than Littleton in his newsletters, and his personal letter was no different:

> Brock, the first step is to become a monetary realist, and it seems that you have taken that step. Once you understand what was corrupted and how, the current deception is as conspicuous as the wart on a stranger's nose. And whatever you do, don't get involved in a confrontation with the enemy. You will lose. Their legal guns are too powerful today. Just use your knowledge for your own family's benefit and protection. The trap is well laid

> Revolution operates above the threshold of the intelligence of the people. So few filter through the knowledge net that the number is insignificant. The truth is that the so-called income tax system in America and the world is a massive cover-up for the most devilish chicanery of the ages. The system and the IRS have nothing to do with collecting taxes, and whether or not we as private persons are "liable under the tax code" is *not* at issue. But the "tax system" and the IRS have a vital part in the government money monopoly. In fact, the tax system is absolutely essential to the money creators. The money monopoly cannot survive without it

> So, you must understand, the government gets no money from taxes. The government *needs* no money in the form of taxes. It is impossible to pay taxes with your computer symbol credit. The tax system destroys some of the banker created-credit so that the Fed can continue to create more credit and with this credit continue to get unlimited goods

and services for nothing. THIS IS THE GREAT SECRET. The point is that every "dollar" created represents infla- tion. Inflation is an euphemism for thievery. It's pouring water into the milk. Theft is theft is theft. Anybody who creates credit steals from the producer because the money creators get for nothing what the producer has to work for. Don't be foolish enough to think that you can reason with these gangsters. They enjoy a silent monopoly now and will stop at nothing to maintain it. This includes the termination of your life.

What is the other main function of the IRS? All illegiti- mate authority must have information on the citizens. What better information system could they have? And all under the pretense of collecting taxes. What liars the politicians are about is so-called Tax Reform. If you could create unlimited amounts of credit for yourself, would you really be worried about big deficits and how much taxes you could collect? And would you not be able to "buy" any number of politicians to help you keep your secret system concealed from the public? Sincerely dedi- cated, honest, and idealistic people are corrupted in a very short time, once they get elected to congress. It is all done with legal tender

And so, Brock, you now have the basic premise of every- thing I have ever written since the beginning of *American, Wake Up!* nearly twenty years ago. The message has reached thousands, maybe even millions by now, but only now and then does someone understand. Your correspondence sug- gests to me that you are becoming one of those people. I hope so. Once again, I apologize for taking so long to respond to your kind letter.

                                                In liberty and law,
                                                Dave Littleton

                    *   *   *   *   *

   Don Handy sat terrified in the booth in Lynn Dickey's Sport's Bar in Westport nursing a beer with shaking hands. During the ride back to Kansas City, his mind and body had been invaded by the full grasp of what they had done. Although he had been honored and intrigued with the appointment to the OLLIE team initially and had jumped at the chance to be a part of it without a second thought, he had never seen anyone murdered before and was already having second thoughts about the wisdom of his decision to participate. Older, tougher, more dedicated, and less empathetic Spike Thorsten sensed from Don's conversation and demeanor that his confederate was about to vomit. He could readily see Handy's weakness and lack of appetite for violence. While Thorsten thrived on his new license to kill with OLLIE, he also knew that he mustn't flaunt it but rather be a "father" to the team members. A well-trained deceiver, he knew how to motivate with half-truths.

"Calm down, Handy Dandy, there were no witnesses. No one will ever know." Spike knew exactly which retort would be forthcoming. He had heard it a dozen times in Texas.

"I'll know."

"Of course you will. But you must look at it like this, we removed one more obstacle to the success of the United States. That guy was no good. He wouldn't pay his taxes—his fair share. That's unAmerican. You know our nation can't survive without everyone paying taxes. In the long run, you have to admit that the country is better off without the likes of Walter Jenkins in it."

This deranged explanation was IRS personnel's *raison d'être*— their only justification for existence. U.S. Attorneys had been successfully snowing juries with that line in "willful failure to file" trials for years. Because this freeloader didn't pay anything, they would have to pay more, the jurors were led to believe. It was just another prevarication designed to perpetuate the Big Lie. The whole bureaucracy had bought it, too. It kept them employed.

"Yeah, I know it, but . . ."

"And you are the first to go forward with me on OLLIE, Man," Thorsten interrupted. "Five years from now this will be like Armstrong walking on the moon, at least in our private government circles. `Don Handy was along on the first one,' I'll be able to whisper to the commissioner, and don't think this isn't going to move you up in years to come. You're going to be in Washington with us before you know it. Maybe a district director's job is down the road for you, if you just hang tough."

Spike Thorsten had studied psychology and understood brainwashing techniques. He well knew that humanity is a predicament of ignorance and fear made tolerable by self-deception and diversion. Of all creatures, man alone is a threat to his environment, an intruder to the balance of nature. Man alone is a threat to his own species. He alone envies, hates, steals from, hoards from, lies to, tortures, and wantonly murders his own kind. Man alone is a threat to his own person—animals don't have nervous breakdowns. Man's most irresistible drives are often self-degrading and self-destructive, resulting in a myriad of physical, mental, and emotional disorders. He fears the future—what it will bring and, moreover, what it will take. He knows he must lose everything, sooner to catastrophe or later to time. The prospect of death to the humanist without a rulebook is depressing, and judgment is terrifying. And if he is at all honest with himself, all of his striving and pastimes, his remedies and answers, both for this life and beyond, are products of his vain imagination, neither convincing nor satisfying. "Vanity of vanities, saith the preacher, all is vanity," but Spike's worldly wisdom did not include anything from the Bible. Nor had he been inside a church house since being dragged there on his wedding day.

The life of the typical bureaucrat is about as purposeful as a careening pinball, and his control of it amounts to the operation of a lever. He absorbs his senses in the excitement of bells and lights and numbers; and strains to keep the ball in play as long as possible, but inevitably, the ball eludes his touch and drops in the hole. There follows a curse or a sigh, a quick glance at the scoreboard to declare him a winner or loser, and all is soon forgotten. Of all of nature's animals, man alone has the rational capacity to contemplate ultimate questions, yet with no ability to answer them. Man alone wonders about the beginning, the meaning, and the end of the universe, history, and himself.

Spike was reaching Don, but it was sluggish progress. After an hour, he decided to call off the second mission of the day and have a couple of more beers and something to eat. Don Handy objected mildly, saying that he understood and was okay and "ready to ride." Spike knew better. OLLIE was too important a mission to have Phase II of it destroyed on the first day by something as trivial as the potential emotional breakdown of a dispensable pawn. Brock Freeman and Plan B would have to wait. Spike had had a long day and was tired. They got drunk instead.

TWELVE

The young writer was flabbergasted. His head was spinning more from the overdose of legal knowledge than from the fruit of the vine, and he requested more of each.

"How long could these government agents expect to get away with breaking all these laws?" he asked.

The older man contemplated that for a moment as he filled their glasses. "A long time ago," he said, "Meyer Rothschild, an international banker and maybe the richest man in the world, said, 'Give me the control of a nation's money supply, and I will care not who makes its laws,' and he set out to prove it. He bought and controlled governments by lending money at exorbitant rates of interest which eventually bankrupted them all. Don't you see that when one controls the money, he controls everything—the public schools and what is taught, the news media and what is reported, and the politicians and what laws are passed. With unlimited resources he can buy any thing and anybody. But understand, while the OLLIE team could not function in any way except undercover, most of the big power grab by the government was done above board and legally right under the noses of the large majority of unwitting and ever-patriotic Americans who all the time were continuing to pledge allegiance to their flag and congress. You are in a sad state of affairs when your society has sunken to a depth where the average person cannot tell the difference between Biblical truths and political lies."

***

Bowie Crockett's big eighteen-wheel rig rolled off the interstate into the green hills of Pasadena at 7:15 P.M. *Good timing*, he thought, about his run from Phoenix. The loading dock boys would have shut it down at seven, and he would be first in line to unload cargo at 7:00 A.M. tomorrow. Ten minutes later he had backed the trailer into the loading slot, unhooked, and had lit out toward Long Beach, fifty miles to the south but more than an hour in the freeway traffic.

"Baby Needs Shoes" was painted in gold across the front of the black, chrome-clad, diesel truck. On the doors it advertised, "Alamo Trucking Company, Rt. 1, Bluff City, Tennessee." A fresh bumper sticker issued the suitable caveat: "You toucha my truck, I breaka you face." He was on schedule. Bill Banneker would meet him in Orange County at a popular beachside restaurant, Maxwell's, in Huntington Beach, between 8:30 and 9:00 P.M.—and give him his assignment.

Banneker was seated at the bar and flirting with the pretty black barmaid, when the colossal truck driver strode in at 8:45.

She whispered, "I hope he's a friend of yours, 'cuz I sure wouldn't want him as no enemy." Bill smiled and, as Bowie was seating himself, glanced at the menu.

"I'll have a quickie," he said to her.

Bowie snatched the menu from his hands. "Lemme see that!"

Bill pointed to what he meant, and Bowie barked, "That's *quiche*, man!"

Banneker grinned and uttered a fatuous, "Oh," alerting the other two that he had just victimized them with a put-on "gotcha'."

The barmaid retreated to her station, giggling, to repeat it to her bar patrons.

At the bar Bill paid for two more large beers, ordered a couple of cheeseburger plates, and adjourned to the booth in the rear where Bowie had sat down. There would not be time to relax with any full course stuffed flounder dinners and desert tonight. They would have to be ready to depart on short notice.

"Where's your truck?" queried Banneker.

"A block up the beach at the Jack in the Box hamburger joint. To legitimize it, I bought a burger and fries and told them I would leave it there just a coupla' hours. The manager told me it would be no problem, just to have it out before closing at midnight. The cops get snoopy during the late hours. What's your plan?"

"No rush yet, Big Un. Sit tight and enjoy your beer. They'll be here in about an hour."

Banneker and Crockett had become best friends since their Chattanooga prank, and their rendezvous at the Indianapolis sports bar had sealed the relationship even tighter. They kept in close contact by phone and FAX. Each had a private "branch office" line—a pay phone less than five minutes away from their homes—by which they could converse without fear of eavesdroppers. When one got a call from the other asking *How soon can you be in your branch office?* he knew it was important and confidential. From home the precarious subjects were discussed only by FAX with a *"P.S. BURN"* reminder added at the end of each message. They had decided months earlier to watch for the right situation on which to act again, this time more seriously. Bill had shared his knowledge of the Florida hunting expedition and what he had learned about it since. Bowie had been intrigued to learn that there was another private but well organized war going on against the IRS and had prevailed upon Bill to make a concerted effort to find and befriend this "Mr. Roark."

Bill never learned Mr. Roark's real name. From other sources, Bowie did but never divulged it to anyone else, always keeping everything on a "need to know" basis, and it just wasn't necessary for anyone else to know that particular piece of information. They did learn other interesting data on the distinguished-looking septuagenarian. Roark had made literally hundreds of millions of dollars in the 1950s as a movie producer who moved into television sitcoms in the sixties and seventies. If the right script were presented to him again, he still might consider doing another . . . "strictly for the money," but for all intents and purposes, he was retired. His current residual weekly income from the re-runs was astounding.

And he was bitter. In a short time the two men became trusted allies of the wealthy film producer, and both had now become loyal undercover operatives in the bigger game. Mr. Roark would remain forever behind the scenes.

In 1983, Mr. Roark's thirty-year-old son and only heir had culminated a two-year battle with IRS auditors with suicide after having everything he owned fall levy to a multi-million dollar assessment. The young man's pregnant wife had hanged herself in the front foyer of their home the next day. Following a brief investigation, Mr. Roark had discovered that the original assessment had been but an arbitrary figure drawn from the air which had then been multiplied with penalties and interest. When one of the auditors made the mistake of saying to him that his son had just "made their job easier," the older man had furiously decided it was time to retaliate. The idea for the Florida hunting excursions, which were later moved to Nevada, was born.

Instead of hiring help to eliminate the guilty parties, he had settled on the "sporting" idea and common law trials for everyone involved in the whole fraudulent system, from wherever they came. Money was no problem. Mr. Roark had no place else to leave it anymore and was delighted to learn that Bill Banneker was also a man of means who was dedicated enough to the cause of freedom to be willing to lighten his financial load of fighting for it. This current trip had worked out perfectly in that Bowie happened to have a run to the west coast booked at the time Bill needed him there. Mr. Roark would be paying their expenses for the next forty-eight hours, but Bill would be handling most of the future endeavors of himself and Bowie Crockett.

Along with the Indianapolis commercial properties, Banneker's crafty speculation with midwestern farm land had made him a ton of money in that see-saw market of the early eighties, and his holdings—protected now by the intricate off-shore trust conduit introduced to him by Bowie—still exceeded two million when measured in what he referred to as "those imaginary dollars." But millionaires in this inflated society are just "the upper middle class," he would often say, only half-joking. He had no social security number, no bank accounts in his name, and had never in his life filed a 1040 form with the IRS.

Several years earlier he had refused to renew the Indiana driver's license he had held since his teen years, when he learned about the national computer which stores massive data on individuals and is triggered through a driver's license check. In its place he carried an international license acquired in Europe and good for ten years. This prevented hassles when he was traveling in the trust's automobile or when he needed to rent one.

How had he escaped detection from the IRS? Bowie had wanted to know when they first talked about it. "I've heard of millions dropping out, but you're the first one I've ever met who never dropped in."

"I just never got around to it in the early days, and, when I started making good money, I just didn't see any point in sharing it with those war-mongers. They never came calling because they never had a starting place. I had never volunteered into their system in the first place. When they finally did pester me, they didn't have a legal leg to stand on because I had never contracted with them. Of course, they tried to coerce me with threats for a year or two, but it didn't work. I just kept writing them back asking for the law that required me to file, and they never replied to that. They apparently had figured out by then that I knew that their law applied only to U.S. citizens and not state inhabitants."

By having no bank account, dealing in barter and often making change in gold and silver coin, and cashing rather than depositing any checks, Bill Banneker had left no paper trail for the enemy to follow if they ever attempted to build a case against him. As far as he knew, they never had.

"*Who* will be here in an hour?" Bowie was now itching to know.

"Our quarry," said Bill, with an ever-so-sly grin.

The best-organized underground unit in the whole freedom movement was in Orange County, California. One of the reasons was their "plant" within the IRS's own CID unit in Irvine. He was a Whistleblower who had seen what had happened to other loud and visible reporters of the government's atrocities and had decided that he could be more effective by remaining on the inside and gathering information to be used later in a court of law, or for other reasons. It was only in recent months, after the numerous frustrations of seeing the culprits whom he knew to be guilty to be free to continue their rapacious assault on unsuspecting and innocent people. When he had anonymously fed the information to the U.S. Attorney without action, he had become disgusted enough to resort to more drastic measures. Now he had seen the folly of attempting to prosecute Caesar in Caesar's court. Bill knew him only by the name of "Jason," and both were happy to keep it that way.

"What's he look like?"

"Don't know. Never seen him," Bill said, "but he'll be wearing a blue blazer with a red tie and will come in with one other man. That will be our target. The message from Jason was that he would seat himself on the outside of a table on the wall near the center of the room, and, to prevent any mix-up with anyone else who might be wearing a blue blazer and red tie, he would fiddle with his right sock and roll it down to his shoe top. He'll order a Moosehead in the bottle. Remember, he doesn't know what we look like either. Probably would never guess it's me over here in this black disguise."

Bowie grinned. Bill Banneker did not speak with the Ebonic accent and on the telephone sounded just like anyone else from the Midwest. As a matter of fact, with his southern, mountain twang, Bowie Crockett's voice would sometimes sound to be more likely of that of a black man than Bill's. Bill's accent was common. Bowie's definite.

"He'll only be sending the signal for identification," Banneker went on to explain. "They will then stay for only one drink and leave in separate cars. We follow the target. Jason's never seen me, either. We have only talked on the phone after being brought together by a certain someone else you will meet later tonight."

"Okay, then what?"

"Jason says he'll go south and our man will go north up Pacific Coast Highway. A couple of miles up, near the library, there's a desolate area where I'll have a minor accident with him. When he gets out, you put him in a hammerlock, and I'll take his gun. I've got chloroform, cuffs and gags for him, and gloves for us, in the trunk of my rental car. Then we swing back south to Newport Beach where I've got a little surprise for you."

"Listen, Banneker. So far it sounds easy enough, but I don't want no damn surprises in a deal like this. Spill it."

Bill exaggerated an impish chuckle under his sleeve. "Now don't get bent out of shape, Big Un. You're not going to mind this surprise. In fact it will make your whole, otherwise dull, day tomorrow. You're rolling empty to Reno, right?"

Right."

"Jason and I have a small load for you to drop in route, that's all."

"Contraband?"

"Of the vilest kind."

Bowie grinned with satisfaction and nodded with beaming eyes like a child in anticipation of his birthday cake.

After the waitress had delivered the cheeseburgers and fries, two strangers walked into the lounge. One was wearing a blue blazer and red tie. They sat next to the plate glass window overlooking the ocean and ordered two mixed drinks. *False alarm* thought Banneker but watched them closely for any hand signals. None came forth.

Ten minutes later, Bowie had finished his burger first and was squirting ketchup over his remaining fries with all the energy of a firemen. Soon his head was cocked back washing down the final bite with the last swallow of beer when he spotted them.

"Don't look now, but I think this is our boy," he softly said to Banneker. With the Muzak mixed with the numerous, muffled, and indiscernible conversations, it was hardly necessary to whisper, but each was careful to gauge his volume at a level at which the other could hear but no one else from nearby tables could pick up.

"They're sitting in the right place this time," Banneker said, as the man in the blue blazer and red tie pulled up the chair on the outside. The other man appeared to be about thirty years old, of average size, and with a pussy cat face. *A piece of cake,* Big Bowie said to himself. They could not hear what the two men ordered, but, as the waitress walked away, the man on the outside began to tug at his sock. A minute later, he rolled his right sock down to his shoe top and began to scratch his leg as he continued light conversation with his partner.

"That's our boy," said Banneker. The waitress then confirmed it by placing a bottle of Moosehead in front of the man. Bill stepped to the bar and asked the friendly barmaid for their check, paid it, stuffed a fiver into her hand, and with all the histrionic aplomb he could muster, kissed her knuckles and turned on his charm.

"I wish I could stay longer only to spend more time with you," he said, still holding her hand firmly, "but I shall return. And your mission, should you choose to accept it, will be to run away to Fiji with me. I believe in grand gestures and don't bother with small details. When I come back, you surely will be over-whelmed by my charisma, my personal aura, my sense of the spontaneous—and I expect you to fall hopelessly in love with me."

The pretty, bronze-skinned barmaid responded with that frivo-lous repartee mothers have taught daughters from generation to generation. "Lawdy, lover boy, with a line like that, I already have! Now you hurry back and take me away from all this!" It was spoken with that two-edged, barroom insincerity which always says *Forget it, Jerk* in such a way that a wisp of hope still remains, and Bill found himself wishing he weren't so busy later.

Bowie was lingering at the front door and the two went outside to wait for their prey while sitting in the rental car. It had been strategically positioned in the parking lot for a close view of the front door. Banneker removed a plastic shopping bag from the trunk and sat down in the driver's seat.

Within twenty minutes the two strangers emerged. Banneker and Crockett watched Jason drive away first. He did not appear to want to see them and looked only straight ahead as he pulled out of the lot, paused for the stoplight, and headed south on the coastal highway. After watching the other man get into a late model green Toyota, Banneker pulled his rental Buick out first and turned left—north—on the beach road, traveling slightly less than the speed limit. He watched the Toyota pull out behind him thirty seconds later and unwittingly follow. A half mile later, the Toyota passed them and Bill increased his speed with a gentle acceleration.

A mile farther up the beach, the Toyota stopped for the light, and Banneker quickly surveyed the situation, saw no other cars in the darkened area, and made the decision to go into action. As it slowed to a near-stop, the big Buick popped the rear bumper of the green Toyota. The blow was hard enough to startle the driver but soft enough to not inflict any visible dam-age. Banneker engaged the hand brake, immediately jumped out, and began apologizing as he approached the infuriated young man emerging from the Toyota ahead.

"I'm terribly sorry, Mister. It was my fault. I was talking with my friend and not paying attention. Are you okay?" His courtesy temporarily disarmed the other driver. Bowie Crockett had al-ready emerged from the other door and was walking around to the front of the Toyota.

"Yeah, I'm okay. But let's have a look at my bumper." He led Bill to the space between the cars. Bowie, at the front of the Toyota now, followed them to the rear.

"I think it's okay," the young man said, straightening up after kneeling to have a look at the bumper, "but you need to be a little more careful when you're . . ."

"So do you, Shitbag," Bowie growled, as he wrapped his big right arm around the young man's neck from the rear, lifting him off the ground. Bill grabbed the snubnose .38 from the exposed shoulder holster with one hand and slammed the chloroform-soaked handkerchief into the startled face with the other. Their victim struggled for five seconds before drooping silently into Bowie's arms.

They handcuffed him behind his back, stuffed and taped a gag into his mouth, and Bowie dumped him into the trunk of the Buick with little more effort than would have been necessary to handle a suitcase. Bowie, wearing his gloves, jumped into the Toyota and drove it back to Maxwell's parking lot, leaving the keys in the ignition and hoping someone would steal it. The parking attendants had gone home at ten o'clock, and he saw no one else outside to observe him. Bill drove the Buick again and waited on the beach highway a block south of the Jack in the Box until Bowie could walk up from Maxwell's and get his rig rolling. Bowie then followed the Buick five more miles south to a warehouse behind a mechanic's garage on the outskirts of Newport Beach.

The fading sign over the door said, "Henson's Engine and Body Repair." Bowie was particularly amused at the message underneath, in smaller, fresher lettering: "We do not collect any sales tax on our goods and services. If you believe that the government has any right to tax your purchases, send an additional 7% of the amount of your bill to Sacramento yourself."

Bowie parked his diesel on the gravel in front and walked to the rear where he had seen Bill stop the Buick. In the dim light outside of the warehouse, he saw Bill talking quietly with another man.

"Bowie Crockett, meet Cochise Henson," Bill said when the big man strode forward. The two new confederates shook hands. At first glance Crockett thought he had never met a meaner-looking son of a bitch in his life. Then as he stared momentarily into the cold black eyes, he realized in a second he had shaken that oversized hand extended from this heavily muscled old arm sometime in the past. As their hands clasped, Bowie began to scan his memory to clarify this hint of recognition. The smaller man's hands were as big as his own. That didn't happen to Bowie very often, and in another second his mind had searched and found the right answer. It had been in the jungle in Laos more than a decade earlier.

"And his code name is Tonto," barked Crockett.

"Mountain Red!" shouted Cochise. "I thought you looked familiar. You haven't changed much. Just got a little bigger! I'm glad to see you. This calls for a drink, after we tend to business, of course," and began to lead them inside. "Mountain Red," he repeated, shaking his head in disbelief. "I'll be damned!"

Cochise wore a tee-shirt, grease-caked jeans, and had a bullwhip coiled into a snap-release on his belt. The American Indian's pyknic build brought to mind an image of a former middleweight boxer. Now 56, his snow-white hair and leathery face, which looked ten years older, topped a body that could have been the envy of men twenty years younger. He invited the other two inside.

The front half of the building appeared to be just what it was supposed to be—a junk storage area stuffed with automobile body and engine parts. Carburetors, fenders, bumpers, door panels, and engine blocks were stacked on the concrete floor to the eleven-foot-high ceiling. Bill and Bowie followed Cochise to the rear of the hazard-filled building, as he picked his way through the incidental parts strewn on the pathway. He put a key in a large padlock on a wooden door, snapped it loose, and pulled the heavy door open.

Four feet ahead of them was another door—this one of solid steel and seven feet high—and between it and the first wall was a four-foot-thick section of asbestos insulation which reached seven feet up and curled over the top, shrinking the size of the next room they were about to enter. When Cochise pulled open the big steel door, Bowie saw that it was an iron bar cage, not unlike the drunk tank he was once thrown into in Knoxville years earlier. A score of terrified men and one toilet were inside. They immediately fell to their knees and bowed their heads when they saw their captor enter.

"Here they are, Gentlemen. Nine of the worst pieces of shit on the face of the earth. Prisoners of war. Yours makes ten, and with the dozen already waiting for you up the road, a grand total of twenty-two. Bring him in."

In less than a month, twenty-two agents from the Criminal Investigation Division of the Orange County Internal Revenue Service offices had literally dropped out of sight, and not a word about it would ever get beyond the rumor mill to make the news. The three conspirators knew that this latest one wouldn't either. For years the IRS had kept a control on what news about them was reported and when. Convictions in those cases of tax evasion or willful failure to file were trumpeted in the headlines. The acquittals were never heard by the public. The men knew that the stories of the multiple disappearances would go unreported by the government indefinitely out of fear of giving others some ideas.

Bowie retrieved the last one from the trunk of the Buick and watched as Cochise and Bill stripped-searched him before throwing him naked into the cage on top of his clothes. Cochise uncoiled his bullwhip and administered three hard lashes across the man's back as he lay whimpering, and then instructed him to be prepared for another dose of the same if he didn't bow down as the others did whenever Cochise was in their presence. He relocked the cage and door, and the three men returned to the front office.

Seated behind his little office desk up front, Cochise pulled a bottle of Jim Beam from the bottom drawer and began to pour the bourbon into three styrofoam cups. "There's a water cooler over there if you want to thin it," he said as he slid two cups three-quarters full of whiskey across the desk. He took a mouthful of his own and swirled it around his gums a couple of times before downing it in one gulp.

"Emm-ehh," he grunted. "Firewater make Indian boy do crazy things," he grimaced, showing grimy teeth etched dark brown from a lifetime of tobacco chewing.

He told Bowie what Bill already knew—that the camp where the men would be held was in northern Nevada, just south of Reno near the old mining town of Virginia City. He said his cage was too full and much too inadequate for long-term incarceration, and these men had to be brought to trial before the people's court. It was Bowie's assignment to get them there. Bill Banneker, having been waiting there for him for two days, would go along to assist and direct him, and fly back to Indianapolis when the job was completed.

"What time can you be here in the morning?"

Bowie thought for a moment before saying, "About ten. They're supposed to start unloading me at seven, and I oughta be empty, checked out, and rolling by nine or nine thirty, at the latest. Make it 10:30 or 11:00 o'clock to allow for traffic."

"Good," Cochise said. I'll see that they all are bathed, shaved, and in their tuxedos by ten. Then I'll call our people up north and tell them to expect you a little after dark. It's going to take you nine hours. Bill knows how to sidetrack the only problem inspection station. Here's your two tickets for getting through the others." He handed Bowie two one-hundred-dollar bills and separate envelopes for each. "If there is any problem, tell 'em to call Smitty, but there won't be, because, when I know exactly what time you're leaving here, I'll know what time to tell them to expect you. Smitty will have everything covered at both stops."

"You hate these sunsabitches, don't you, Tonto," Bowie said more as a statement than a question.

Cochise pointed to his Medal of Honor on the wall, framed on faded green velvet and under glass with its accompanying certificate. "You see that," he said, not waiting for an answer. "That's nothing but a dried up horse turd if what I did to earn it represents these bastards back here," and he jerked his thumb toward the rear of the building as abruptly as an umpire signalling *You're Out!* His eyes widened, displaying his anger at the thought of them. "I make believe every one of 'em's name is Custer.

"They don't know what liberty means. They think freedom is being free to do whatever the goddamn government wants you to do. Give 'em a badge and a gun, and they think they're King Kong. They don't have any loyalty to anything but that government paycheck. One of them yesterday was crying and screaming when I was whippin' his ass, saying, 'I was just doing my job.' Yeah, that's what the Nazis said at the Nuremburg Trials, too. You watch these wimps when we parade their victims in front of them as witnesses. They'll wish they had never heard of the initials 'I.R.S.'

"Yeah, I hate 'em . . . because somebody told me I was fighting for freedom when I went over there to dodge bullets in the Korean snow, and freedom is what I am going to have, even if I have to die for it right here. Hell, they took the land from my grandfathers, now they want me to be a slave on it for them. Uh-uh, baby. I ain't filing no more tax forms, and I ain't collecting their sales tax, neither. I told the State of California tax boys to read the Thirteenth Amendment again, if they ever had the first time, because I ain't volunteering for their servitude. And if they want to set up a booth out there across the street, off my property, and collect sales taxes from any of my customers who are stupid enough to pay them, go ahead. But I don't work for them, and until they start paying me to, I'm not even considering it. You ought to see all the new customers I get every week, since word got around that I don't charge sales tax."

Bowie and Bill realized that they hadn't even begun to fight yet, but that they were on the right side. Cochise was picturing himself as had the colonists of 1775; fighting for liberty, principle, morality, and their very lives. Because the red-coated mercenaries had been committed to nothing more than a paycheck, they never had a chance of winning. After a few years, King George III had begun to figure this out.

But as long as there was one redcoat left alive and breathing on American soil, the life and liberty of every colonist had been in danger everyday. The mere wearing of the red uniform was a death sentence to be meted out by the freedom-loving colonists.

The carrying of an IRS badge signified the same to Cochise in
the 1980s. And here, over two hundred years later, there was
about to be another "King George" calling the shots for the
enemy, he reminded them, and there appeared to be no way that
Bush would lose the election. Red and Tonto had known the
name long before the world public ever heard it. They had worked
under Mr. Bush in Southeast Asia and Central America more
than a decade earlier before they learned the truth about the
intercontinental drug trade. There was no other slime dog on
earth that Cochise would have enjoyed carving to pieces more
than the world's top drug lord, George Bush.

At 11:15 the next morning, Bowie picked up Bill at the
Hertz office at the Orange County Airport, where he had checked
in the Buick, and the two were headed north on Interstate-Five
with the most unusual cargo Bowie had ever hauled. Cochise and
two helpers had already prepared the prisoners with handcuffs
and leg shackles when Bowie backed his rig next to the warehouse. The three of them had placed adhesive tape on the mouths
of each of the ten and chained them around the steel cross-
member on the wall of the trailor to prevent their moving-about
during the trip. Before they closed the door, Cochise told his
captives that they would be locked up for nine hours, and, if any
of them had bladder problems, they would just have to hold it or
go in their pants. He then turned to Bowie and, loud enough for
all to hear, said, "If any of them gives you any problems, drive
out into the desert, kick his brains out, and leave him for the
buzzards to eat." Bowie was loaded and gone within ten minutes,
and he was certain he would get no trouble out of these panic-
stricken prisoners.

After the doors were shut and Bowie was bidding his old
friend goodbye, he asked him if any of the victims could find
their way back to his place, should they ever escape.

"No," Cochise replied. They only saw the inside, just like
your guy. And I told them each individually that they had better
pray for my health and long life because if anything happens to
me, his wife and kids will disappear."

Probably would too, Bowie thought, as he shook his old
friend's hand and dived in behind the wheel of "Babe." The roar
of her engine drowned out the words of Cochise, as he yelled
"Good luck! See you in a few weeks."

"Seems like you know the old Indian a lot better than I do,"
Bill Banneker remarked after they were headed up the road
toward Bakersfield. "Is he really as bad-assed as he talks?"

"Worse," replied Bowie, without a moment's hesitation. "Most
of those guys from the company are trained to just kill whenever

the situation requires it, as quietly and quickly as the first opportunity allows. Not him. In those days of my past life, Tonto—which was all we ever knew him as—had the reputation of being the most feared of all. If he only *suspected* someone of being a snitch, and it didn't make any difference to him who it might be—an Asian cowboy drug-runner or an Air Force Colonel bagman—his warning was cutting an "S" in the left cheek of the suspect's ass and the pouring of salt into it. If suspicions were ever confirmed, the second time it was the right cheek too, and this time both were filled with acetone and ignited. The acetone alone in the bloodstream was enough to kill. The fire was just to make the death more agonizing."

"What a wonderful guy," Banneker remarked with a grin, ". . . to have on our side, I mean."

*   *   *   *   *

It was almost noon when the red phone on Spike Thorsten's desk was ringing for the fourth time. He emerged from his private bathroom and picked up. It was the private phone for which only twelve other people held the number, and these incoming calls did not go through the main switchboard.

"Ollie Pike," he barked into the receiver.

"Handy Dandy Don in K.C., returning your call."

"Yeah, and it's about time. Wherethehell 'ave you been?"

"Sorry, Boss." Handy's chipper voice sobered quickly. "I grabbed a day's vacation time on Friday and took the wife and kids over to Lake of the Ozarks for a long weekend and a much-belated holiday. I just got your message this morning. What's up?"

"The assessment on your man Freeman is what's up. Up over a million bucks now. Let's start thinking what we're going to do about it."

Don Handy gave an audible chuckle. "Ho-ho-ho. You will be delighted to know I wasn't loafing the whole weekend and that I have located the 'Miss Sarah.' She's ready for 'Plan C' whenever you are."

The "Miss Sarah" was the sixty foot house boat that had been Brock's gift to his wife on her fortieth birthday, and which the Freemans had always kept at Osage Beach on the lake. Although neither of them legally owned it anymore, Brock had felt, after he had become a federal "target," that it might be prudent to move the boat around a little. He had rented a space on the other side of the lake at Sunrise Beach in his father-in-law's name and moored it there for the past two summers.

"We can't confiscate it for taxes, but we can damned sure fix it so the DEA can get it," Handy smirked. That was the unwritten

"Plan C" for the OLLIE group: Plant the cocaine and call the locals. The DEA would take care of everything else. Spike might be able to make a deal with them going in so the "booty" would move over to the IRS's balance sheet instead of DEA's. He had done it before. DEA gets the headlines, but IRS gets the actual asset to improve their balance sheet for the quarterly report to the commissioner.

"What's it worth?" asked Thorsten.

"Oh, Three or four hundred thousand, maybe half a million. I haven't seen the inside yet, but some of the workers at the marina told me it is the most luxurious one out there. King-size bed in the master suite, two and a half baths, all the modern appliances in the kitchen, even a walk-around library."

"Can you get inside?"

"It should be no problem. A twenty-dollar bill would probably 'rent' the key from the marina's assistant manager for a half hour, or we can type up a letter of 'authorization' on Freeman's office stationery, which I just happen to have in his file, allowing us to have a look at it as 'prospective buyers.'"

"Yeah, do it. Use the letter; it's smoother, but be sure to retain it. And plant a heavy load, like a kilo or more. Let's sweat Freeman with some criminal charges. That'll run his legal bill up real quick. And keep me abreast of your progress," Spike said before hanging up pouring himself a glass of Chivas Regal.

* * * * *

Dr. Joe Day was in trouble with his friends and didn't know it. After the attacks by the IRS, Brock had begun to patch together a few pieces of his personal puzzle and could come up with one solution: Joe Day was an IRS plant. Brock had no proof but enough circumstantial evidence combined with his own conjecture to warn the others. They agreed with Mozzarella's suggestion to slowly extricate themselves from the inspection of Joe Day. If he showed up at the poker table, they would suddenly all decide to break up the game. If he appeared at the bar for a drink, conversation would halt. If he happened to be at a social function at which all the others were thrown together inadvertently—and this would happen somewhere every month or so because none of the wives were privy to their husband's suspicions—they were forewarned and behaved accordingly.

Joe was suddenly anathema, and now he was slowly coming to the realization that he had been found out. But he didn't dare ask any of his former buddies what the problem might be. He trembled at the thought of the correct answer.

THIRTEEN

Before a year had passed, Spike Thorsten had completed missions similar to the Kansas hit in or around Phoenix, San Diego, Denver, Sacramento, Seattle, Portland, Cheyenne, Atlanta, Birmingham, Austin, El Paso, and Santa Fe, in that order. The victims were always ruled as "accidental," "a suicide," or "a victim of a random shooting by persons unknown," but the message was always plain to his family and friends. The cases seldom got as far as a formal inquest and *never* went any further. A brief conversation with a local judge saw to that. While all had not gone perfectly, they had pulled off the first phase of Operation Loss Leader without any major repercussions. Two dozen high-profile leaders of the tax movement who had never seen a line of coke were serving from "2 to 5" in various federal penitentiaries for "possession." In addition someone had mysteriously firebombed and burned the Idaho house of IRS Whistleblower Paul J. DesFosses to the ground. Spike Thorsten's private reign of terror had begun.

On November 28, 1984, in a middle class suburb of Detroit, a day care center was raided by seven IRS agents. Some thirty children—including infants—were held hostage. Revenue agents pressured the children's parents into paying the IRS money which the parents normally would have paid to the day care center. Astonished and intimidated parents were informed that their children would not be released to them until the checks were written. The director of the day care center, Marilyn Derby, described it as "something out of a police state."

Congressman George Hanson of Idaho, author of *To Harass Our People*—an exposé of IRS atrocities—and another outspoken adversary of the collection tactics and utter existence of the IRS, was secretly jailed and hidden out under the assumed name of *Frederick Smith* in Alexandria, Virginia. He was forced to endure the indignity of wearing the same dirty overalls for ten smelly days. He would be charged with various trumped-up federal

violations and be in and out of jails all over the country for the
next decade.

Gordon Kahl, 63, had been tracked down and shot in the
back of the head in Arkansas. The remote farmhouse was torched
with gasoline by federal agents. Arthur Kirk, 49, was shot in his
yard by officers in Nebraska. Donald McGrath, 51, was shot and
killed in his car in front of his wife and son by officers in Minne-
sota. Their "crimes" were all identical. They had spoken out
against and had refused to pay tribute to Caesar's new monetary
policy. The federal government was laying down the ground
rules for its Mafioso tactics of enforcement. Its underlying, unwritten edict was, apparently, "Obey or Die."

The independent Coalition of Whistleblowers had also uncovered and made public *"The IRS's Strategic Plan for the United
States,* a 204-page, tightly-guarded document which contained
startling revelations about the IRS's intentions to:

- Prepare massive dossiers—called "taxpayer profiles"—
with detailed, personal, non-tax information on all American citizens

- Include in these dossiers a wide range of information not
gathered from taxpayer returns, including "behavioral data
from attitude surveys;"

- Establish a "task force" to work with other federal agencies—
including the Federal Deposit Insurance Corporation, The Federal Reserve Board, the Federal Home Loan Bank, the National Credit Union Administration, and the Office of the Comp-
troller of the Currency—in order to gain access to these agencies' investigative files and, presumably to gather all-encompassing information about credit card usage, banking deposits
and withdrawals, loan applications and payments, and other
financial transactions

- To "formalize federal/state liaison in each IRS district" in
order to gather additional, detailed information about citizens
and their private lives, including business licenses, professional
fees, property transactions, arrest records, traffic violations,
and memberships in groups.

Upon learning of the existence of the Coalition, Spike
Thorsten privately instructed his confederates in the various cities to add the names of all Whistleblowers to the OLLIE hit-list.

Meanwhile, Brock Freeman was called in for an audit on
both his personal and corporate returns for the last year he had
filed before establishing the off-shore trust. It was the year following the IRS's attempt to extract the extra $200,000 by chang-

ing his tax forms. Because the corporation was "creature of the state" and had no constitutional rights, he let Stan Potts handle everything—Brock didn't bother to attend the meeting—and it passed with flying colors. The IRS auditors had so little to question that Stan had decided before they were halfway finished that it was just another harassment—a fishing expedition in vain attempt to find an error. But it did take a full day of Stan's time and, therewith, four hundred of Brock's federal reserve note "dollars."

The personal audit Brock handled in his own way. He took along four friends from his poker group, including especially Mozzarella, who wanted to be in on the fun. They were all dressed in three-piece business suits appearing to be attorneys to the female auditor in charge. Each had a tape recorder under his arm. Brock marched in with a large, sealed box of receipts in his hands.

"Are you ready to get started, Mr. Freeman?" she said.

"Sure thing, Melissa." It was part of remaining in control. They call you "Mister," you call them by their first names. After all, they are public servants, he had told Mozarella who, as a prior victim, was enjoying it more than the others. Brock knew how to be friendly and courteous without being a subservient ass-kisser.

"But there are a couple of questions I would like to ask you first," he said.

"Certainly," she said. Go ahead."

"Question number one: If I voluntarily turn these books and records over to you, is there any way the government will use them against me in a criminal prosecution?"

It was straight out of Irwin Schiff's book, *How Anyone Can Stop Paying Income Taxes.* The Fourth Amendment protects private citizens against unlawful search and seizure, ". . . and no warrants shall issue without probable cause . . ." No government auditor could even touch that box without Brock's permission. And, without that permission, they would have to get a court order. But then again, because "no warrants shall issue without probable cause," no warrant could be obtained. If there was any probable cause, it was in the box, and no judge would issue a warrant on those dubious prospects. Judges call that "a fishing expedition." Brock had her on the ropes with his first punch, and they both knew it.

She didn't answer but whispered, "And what is your second question?" There had been nothing wrong with her voice a few moments earlier, but she had suddenly been attacked by a case of laryngitis and was as terrified as a baby bunny. Brock noticed but ignored it.

"Oh, it's even easier than the first. I would like to know if there is any law that requires me to turn over the books and records to you, or are you just asking me to volunteer them?"

It was obvious that Melissa had never before been caught in a predicament such as this. She gulped, started around the conference table, and seemed to be fighting off a seizure of apoplexy as she wobbled to the door and said, "I need to talk to my supervisor. I'll be right back." Brock and his "counselors" smiled at one another and put their recorders on "Pause."

"Schiff says 'give 'em about three minutes,'" Brock remarked to the wall after looking at his watch, never having taken a seat. "It looks like it's all going to script."

One hundred and fifty seven seconds later, Melissa came back through the door into the conference room. She was walking more confidently now and seemed greatly relieved. Even her voice, though not 100% yet, was stronger already.

"Mr. Freeman, Mr. Dunbar said to tell you that this audit is terminated."

Brock grinned. "That's fine, Melissa. Did he give you an answer to my two questions?"

"No, and he said I don't have to talk to you anymore. The audit is terminated."

"Wonderful. May I remind you that you didn't have to talk to me in the first place, nor I you. You invited me here, remember? But, tell me. Just what is your *next* move."

"Well, he did say we could get a subpoena to see your books and records," she retorted with a mild defiance, obviously finding it difficult to be antagonistic to such a polite and especially such a good-looking man.

Brock replied unflinchingly. "That's fine. You tell Mr. Dunbar to get his subpoena, and because that would be a court order and I am a law-abiding person, I will be there at the prescribed time and place; and I will still have my same two questions for you, him, and the judge. I am sure Mr. Dunbar abides by the law, too, doesn't he?"

Melissa didn't answer, but she never felt more relieved in her life. Now she could get back to the easy work of punching a calculator and computing additional taxes on anyone who would submit to her assumed authority. But Brock knew he had contracted into their jurisdiction and was at the mercy of the IRS. It was only a matter of waiting to find out if the other shoe would drop.

Six weeks later it did when Brock received a certified letter from the Internal Revenue Service and anxiously signed for it. Stan had warned him that they would not let him off so easy and that they would probably pull some more of their notorious shenanigans. They had. The one-page computer printout said that because he had "refused" an audit of his records for that particular tax year, they had disallowed *all* of his deductions and had assessed a tax of 60% on a gross earnings of $150,000. Penalties and interest had already begun accruing. With this on top of the previous arbitrary assessment, Brock now owed the government over a million fed notes.

"At least they didn't change the figures this time to four hundred and fifty thousand," he said to Stan Potts in his office that late afternoon in the late spring.

"This is unofficial advice, of course, but I think you should tell them to hang it in their friggin' ear," Stan replied, handing Brock a cold bottle of Heineken. "You are legally indigent now that all your former assets are owned by the trust. They can never collect it. It's a civil judgment, and they can't put you in jail for not being able to pay. They can't even collect from your estate after you're dead, because you won't have one. Fortunately, we don't have 'debtors prison' in this country yet, but they hold all the legal cards, and I can guarantee they will continue to harass you because of the roadblocks you have thrown up for them. If they prosecute you criminally and get a conviction, it will be blown all over the papers in every city in the country. If you get acquitted, there will not be a word."

Brock's letter back to the IRS was not nearly so blunt and crass as Stan had suggested, but he did point out—just for the record, if he ever needed it—that he had not "refused" an audit, and, in fact, it had been terminated by a certain Mr. Dunbar of their Kansas City office. He pointed out that he supposed that Mr. Dunbar's decision had been wholly based on the fact that he, Brock, had asked a couple of simple questions. Questions, incidentally, to which he had never received an answer. He then politely closed the letter with the fact that he was a "pauper" and did not see any way in the foreseeable future that he would be able to pay such a ridiculously high amount, especially when those who had been responsible knew it was an unfair assessment. He mailed the letter, never got a reply, and promptly forgot about it. Freeman felt like a "Free Man" who did not live in that jurisdiction anymore.

*   *   *   *   *

Somehow word of Brock Freeman's successful defiance reached the desk of Spike Thorsten in Washington. Brock later believed it had come from Dr. Joe Day, the poker-playing phony friend who was feeding information to Don Handy daily. In any case, Thorsten recognized the name immediately as one of the original targets of OLLIE which had to be "pigeon-holed" because of Don Handy's initial distaste for violence. But Thorsten knew that Handy had long overcome that problem. He had personally seen him use a high-powered rifle to blow away a black businessman on the southeast side of Kansas City, six months after the hit on Jenkins on the tractor. The two had gone out for drinks and a couple of Porterhouse steaks at the Hereford House an hour afterward. Don Handy had become one of Spike's most reliable confederates. There were twelve in a dozen different cities, but no one else knew the others, and no one else in each office had any knowledge of any of the operation except his own assignments. There were only one or two others he might have chosen ahead of Don Handy for any operation. Because the mission would take place in Kansas City and that was Handy's turf, Don was the only one Spike considered for the Freeman case. He dialed Handy's Overland Park office and left a message for him to call "Ollie Pike." Not even the receptionists and secretarial personnel in the offices across the country would have any record of any "Mr. Thorsten" ever calling these agents.

During the conversation with Handy's return call, Brock Freeman became the most recent target of the OLLIE Hit Squad.

FOURTEEN

Historically, the purpose of the grand jury has been to protect people against the abuse of government power. The founding fathers got the idea from the British and inserted it into the Bill of Rights: "No person shall be held to answer for a capital or otherwise infamous crime, unless on presentment or indictment of a Grand Jury." This was structured to interpose a shield between the individual and the state—forcing the state to show that its desire to prosecute somebody is based on public interest, not political whimsy. Before the state could drag a man out of his house and put him on trial, it had to convince his neighbors that the crime had been committed and that there was ample reason to suspect him. In order to protect the man from frivolous or malicious accusations, the grand jury was to meet in secret.

This skepticism about the motives of politicians and what later evolved into "law enforcement" personnel proved to be well founded by the 1980s, because, as it turned out, new generations of judicial wizards since the founding of the nation had managed to transform and corrupt this protective instrument into a tool of persecution and suppression by the state. The jurors, randomly selected from voter lists, heard only what the prosecutor wanted them to hear and thus often became rubber stamps for the state, thereby making a farce out of the whole procedure.

By the year 1995, following the Oklahoma City bombing, a grand juror would actually be removed by a federal judge for asking too many questions. When government prosecutors were instigating a cover-up, their judicial power was despotic.

The prosecutor was not required to tell the jury what an investigation was about or why he wanted a particular bit of testimony, and he needed not present any evidence or testimony that he knew existed in favor of the defendant. He could lie with impunity, knowing that a false or prejudicial statement, uttered while a witness is absent, could be stricken from the record. Courts had little or no control over the conduct of a prosecutor before a grand jury, and subpoenas were often issued for irrelevant records in order to conceal the true objective of the inquiry.

A grand jury witness had to face the prosecutor alone, without benefit of counsel, while his attorney waited outside. And if this witness exercised his Fifth Amendment right and refused to answer any questions, he could have immunity forced on him and be jailed for contempt until he decided to answer. Despite this immunity a person could be prosecuted anyway, if the evidence against him was obtained "independent" of his testimony.

As to the jurors themselves, rarely if ever, were their fundamental duties explained to them. They would never know, for example, that they could and should determine charges, call witnesses and ask questions— even of the accused; and that their power to investigate or indict was not limited to the accused person. Nor did they know that regardless of how fervently and emphatically they refused to indict an individual, the prosecutor could take his case to another, over and over; or if they indicted someone against his wishes, he could simply refuse to sign the true bill and end the matter right there.

<hr />

Brock and Sarah's silver wedding anniversary was falling on Thanksgiving Day in 1988, and Sarah had already begun planning for the celebration on Labor Day weekend. She decided, and prevailed over Brock, to have it in their big home on Ward Parkway rather than at the Mission Hills Country Club "the way everybody else does." On Thursday night Brock had told her to spare no expense because the company would pay for it. Sarah decided to do her serious planning on the houseboat at the lake over the long weekend. He had already placed an order for her surprise gift—a silver Rolls Royce to significantly commemorate the occasion.

Brent was a junior at K.U.; Maria a sophomore. It was difficult for the family to have many outings together anymore, with the various activities pulling each of them his or her own way, but they had managed to put together some plans for the last weekend before school started again.

After lunch on Friday, Sarah took the new BMW with Maria and three of her girlfriends, two were high school seniors, to Sunrise Beach, and Brent followed them in his new Corvette with his girlfriend, Susan. Brock had a real estate transaction to complete on Friday afternoon and was already obligated to play in the club "Four-Ball" golf tournament on Saturday morning with Mozzarella, Pottsie, and "Goldfinger," an OB-GYN who had been accepted into their inner poker circle after the unofficial banishment of Dr. Day. Dr. Goldman and Vince had been acquainted for some time, and Vince had sold him a truckload of furniture over the years for the doctor's home and office. Some of the others knew Goldfinger from seeing him on the golf course and when he had expressed an interest in joining their weekly poker club, no one had any objections. They needed another player. Except for the fact that his buddies could not replace him at such short notice, Brock would have cancelled the golf game and gone with his family on Friday, but he promised to get away before noon and complete the two and a half hour trip to join them by mid-afternoon.

Only Sarah missed him that first day as she lounged on the deck of the houseboat making her party plans for the anniversary. Brent took the girls out on the speedboat for three hours of skiing and boatriding and didn't return until dusk. While his mom prepared a salad and baked beans in the kitchen, Brent broiled a batch of hamburgers on the outside grill. Bone-tired, they all went to bed at 9:30—Maria with her mother in the master suite, the other four girls in the double beds in the other two bedrooms, and Brent on the couch in the front room with the television.

Brent had gone to sleep for a couple of hours with the TV on, awakened and tuned it to a late movie, and had fallen asleep again before it was over. At 6:45 A.M., half awake, he realized the TV was still on and at first thought the strange and muffled voices outside were coming from it. Suddenly, the room was filled with the explosion of a battering ram hitting the entrance door of the houseboat, closely followed by the crash of the door being ripped from its hinges with the second blow. In his semi-somnambulistic state, Brent stood in his jockey shorts in the middle of the room too stunned to speak, surrounded by a dozen heavily-armed men in blue jackets. He was immediately slammed against the wall and cuffed with his hands behind his back.

"We're agents of the United States Government, and we have a warrant to search the premises," announced the pompous and truculent man who appeared to be in charge. "How many other people are here?"

Brent's mind was racing. "Do you have a warrant to tear the place down?" he said calmly, facing the wall.

In a cruel display of hostility, the belligerent drug enforcement agent slammed Brent's head against the wall, cutting his forehead on the grooves of the paneling. "Don't get smart with me, boy, and answer me. How many people are here?"

Brent quickly calculated and said, "Six. Seven. My mother, my sister, and four friends. All girls. Please don't hurt them."

By this time four other agents had opened the two guest room doors to arouse the girls, and Sarah was already standing in her housecoat at the doorway of the master suite. "What is going on here, Brent?" she said.

The agent in charge marched toward her. "We are agents of the Drug Enforcement Agency and have a warrant to search your boat. What is your name?"

"I'm Sarah Freeman and we are here on a family outing. That is my son and these are my children's friends. We just came over here yesterday, and I can assure you no one in this group has been using drugs. I think you have made a mistake."

"Please have a seat on the couch, Mrs. Freeman, and have everyone else do the same. Where is your husband?"

"He's in Kansas City and will be arriving here this afternoon," she said taking her seat in a chair and signalling the others to sit down.

While the bewildered family and friends sat around, Brent still in handcuffs and underwear, the agents went through the charade of searching. In less than five minutes one of the older agents emerged from the master bathroom with a meatloaf-size package wrapped in plastic and sealed with adhesive tape. He handed it to his superior, who opened it, licked his finger and dipped it into the white powder, gave a silly smirk, and said, "I guess you don't know anything about this, do you, Mrs. Freeman?"

"No sir, I certainly do not. And if you have deduced that it is some kind of illegal substance, I can tell you it was brought here by someone other than the members of this party."

"Tell it to the judge, Mrs. Freeman. I am placing you all under arrest for possession of cocaine with intent to distribute." All seven people were first allowed to get dressed, then handcuffed, shackled, and loaded into three separate cars. Photographers and TV newsmen were conveniently on the scene to record it all on film for the nightly news and to accompany the next day's blazing headlines.

The two high school girls were horribly frightened and crying uncontrollably. Sarah asked to ride with them to calm them down but was refused. They rode together in the back seat of one car, Sarah and a furious Maria rode in the second, and Brent rode with Susan and the calmest of the girls—Maria's new college roommate from Denver—in the third. All had two agents in the front seat. Brent and the two girls thought the whole thing, excepting his headache, was hilarious and laughed much of the way to Jefferson City.

Everyone was allowed one phone call until they got an answer from a live person. Answering machines did not count against them. Knowing his dad was probably still on the golf course, Brent left messages on the office recorder and a more detailed one at their house in hopes that Brock would check one or both before leaving town. At 11:15 Sarah called the pro shop at the country club and learned from the golf pro that Brock was currently on the seventeenth hole and would be finished shortly. She told him to hold Brock there because she had to talk with him immediately and would call back at exactly 11:45. Her one call spent, Brent used his, and Brock answered.

"Dad! Mom's in jail," he barked the moment he heard Brock's voice. Somehow, the fact that he and his sister were in jail, too, was not as important to him right now as their mother being there.

His son had a great sense of humor, but something about the gravity of the boy's voice and his own intuition told Brock that this was no joke. "Has there been an accident, Son?"

Brent told him everything that happened as he remembered it. Now, they all were being processed into jail. Because it was a holiday weekend, their arraignment would not be until 9:30 Tuesday morning, and no bail could be set before then, when they could go before a magistrate. Meanwhile, he would be in the Jefferson City lockup and the six women would go to the female section of the county facility.

"Dad, it's a setup. Nobody had any drugs. Somebody planted that package before we got there, and I think they meant to get you. They kept asking about you and wondering why you weren't there and when you would come. Don't go to the boat, Dad, or don't come here, either. I'm afraid they want to arrest you, too. They seemed awful disappointed that you weren't here."

"Stay cool, Son; I'll be over there in three hours."

"Are you sure?"

"Yes, I'm sure. Take care of your mother and sister. I'm coming right away."

What Brent didn't understand and his father did was that, if Brock were indeed the main target, they had missed their chance. He could not be charged with anything concerning the drugs now. They could have held him with Sarah and the others had he been there, but he didn't own the boat anymore—the trust did—and he was nowhere near the so-called "possession." He also knew that one of the government's favorite tricks was to charge the wife along with the husband whenever feasible in order to exert more pressure. Another was to arrest them on a weekend to give them more time in jail before a lawful arraignment could be held. As far as he was concerned, they had succeeded on both counts. Even though they didn't have him in custody, they had Sarah, and this was just as disconcerting. More so.

Brock remembered that his old law school friend, Kenton Williams, a highly successful and competent criminal attorney from Topeka, who maintained an office in Kansas City as well, had been playing in the foursome ahead of him. He had never needed his services before but always knew in the back of his mind that Kenton would be whom he would call first, if and when he ever did. Brock spotted him ordering lunch in the bar, called him aside, and told him what he knew of the difficulty.

"Old buddy, I don't want to scare you, but you've got a problem," Williams said. *Lawyers always say that to people in distress,* Brock thought. It runs up the tab after they've successfully solved it. It was like being at the mercy of an auto mechanic when your car begins to make expensive noises a thousand miles from home.

"But your problem is not getting them sprung so much as it's a holiday weekend, and I don't know if we're going to be able to find a U.S. Magistrate at home. If we can, I can explain the extenuating circumstances and probably get him to set an emergency bond. Those guys are all pretty reasonable and not even the crankiest one would keep Sarah in jail with her children over the weekend, if he just knew about it."

"I know Ken, and I'm sure these assholes planned it that way." Williams was taken aback. He couldn't remember when he had ever heard his old pal use vile language, but he could see that Brock was getting angrier by the minute as the full realization of the whole scenario was setting in. "What can we do? I don't want Sarah and the kids staying in that jail for three days and nights. What U.S. Magistrate do you know?"

"I know them all, but, I told you, that's not the problem. There is no telling where any of them might be this weekend. Let me gobble down this sandwich, and we'll go to the office and start making some calls. Maybe we can get lucky."

"Okay," Brock said. "You go on, and I'll meet you there in an hour. I want to run home and shower and get changed so I can be ready to zoom over to Jeff City as soon as you can get a bail set. Oh, and I'd better call the parents of those other girls, too."

Twenty minutes later, Brock was showered and hastily getting dressed when Kenton Williams called to say they had gotten lucky. He had caught a magistrate at home who was sympathetic to the situation, who believed Williams' assessment of the quality of the people involved, and was willing to agree with Williams that a mistake could have been made. But, without knowing the prosecution's side of the story, he could not be very lenient with the amount. When he had learned of the Freeman's means, he set bond for each of them at $100,000.

Williams had pleaded that his client could certainly come up with that amount on any business day, but the banks were closed, too, and he had asked the judge to reconsider something more reasonable. Even Williams had been amazed that the magistrate had then relented not by reducing the bond but by changing it to $100,000 "own recognizance." This meant that Sarah and all the children could be released as soon as Brock would sign for them. It also meant that he would be liable for the "settling up" in the event any or all of them did not show up for arraignment and trial. Brock preferred it this way. He did not want the other parents to have to stand bail for what he considered his problem, and it might help smooth some ruffled feathers of those who would surely be more than a little bit incensed over learning that their child was in jail for nothing more than merely having been in the wrong place at the right time.

After calling the other parents, Brock was in the motorhome and on the way to Jefferson City by two o'clock. By six, they were all released, laughing about their experience, and ordering dinner in Shoney's restaurant. All except Sarah were laughing, that is.

The women's facility had been overcrowded, and she and Maria had been placed in a cell with only four beds and which already contained six people. Sarah and Maria were about to have to spend the night on the floor with two Jeff City prostitutes—one black, one Mexican. Maria, with typical school girl curiosity, had made friends with both and had been questioning them on the motivation that had driven them to the world's oldest profession. She was making the best of a bad situation, just as her father had always taught her, and thought all this might make for a great source of information for her next paper in psychology class. Sarah had had little interest at the time and even less now.

"Maria," she said, "if you tell them you were in jail with a bunch of prostitutes, you had better not mention your mother was with you, or you are going to pay your own way to college from now on. I'll guarantee you that." The whole ordeal had been about as exciting to her as a night on the town with Jerry Falwell. Brock and the others laughed heartily, and it seemed to relieve them all as they released the pent-up emotions. Brent commented about the sign on the small office he had seen across the street from the jailhouse when they had arrived in shackles that morning: "It's always *Spring*time at Jefferson Bonding. Call 314-634-1234.

After dinner, they sidetracked back to the lake to pick up the cars and headed for home. Sarah said nothing more about her humiliation when they went to bed, but she was more disturbed by it than Brock would immediately realize. But this was not the worst thing. She now harbored a fear that was more real than any emotional stress could ever be of what other people might think— the vulnerability of her children. Her son had had his head slammed against the wall by a grown man. Her daughter had been in jail. *These bastards could do it to anyone,* she realized. Her husband had only questioned the system and had shown up at a few seminars in various places of the country. Was this all it took these days to become an enemy of the State in the so-called Land of the Free? Lingering like a dull ache just beyond the edge of consciousness, the fear persisted.

*   *   *   *   *

Dr. Martin Goldman was out of town on Mondays and Tuesdays of every week, but his receptionist had been instructed to always say to callers at the clinic, "He is in surgery today. May I take your number and have him call you?" When he had first become friends with his new poker group, "Goldfinger" had told them the same story, and it really wasn't a lie. He was performing operations every Monday and Tuesday. The fact that he was in another state a thousand miles away was not important for anyone else to know.

*   *   *   *   *

The Tuesday hearing was routine and over in ten minutes. The youths were released on "O.R.," as before, but now as probable "witnesses only," as it was doubtful that the government could build a substantial case against any of them, and only Sarah, pending a grand jury indictment, would have to stand trial for "possession and planned distribution of a controlled substance"—namely 2.2 pounds of cocaine. Kenton Williams argued that there was no evidence of any drug use, drug distribution, or prior convictions, but the magistrate's hands were tied. The kilo of coke had been found on board a boat under the supervision of Mrs. Freeman, and if the grand jury chose to indict, he had no choice but to keep her under bond until trial. If the U.S. Attorney failed to get an indictment "within a reasonable length of time," Sarah would be released from the bond. Meanwhile, at least she would be under no further restraints by the court. It was cut and dried, and Williams knew it.

Brock wanted to vomit. Sarah did—in the ladies room immediately after the hearing. Maybe she would be under no legal restraints, but the emotional restraints were already devastating. What would her friends think? To the public an indictment was evidence of guilt. Heavens above, the simple arrest was already a permanent blight. She could never rectify this situation with her peers, and she knew it. She would become an outcast—a topic of the country club whisperers whenever she passed their bridge tables and was out of earshot. She knew they would always, as long as she lived, refer to her as "that lady who was arrested and jailed for cocaine distribution." She felt that her life was ruined forever.

All because of Brock and that damned patriotic stand he had taken. Their life had been so good when he had paid his taxes and behaved like everybody else. The point that he had broken no laws and had been attacked out of spite by the omnipotent U.S. Government, a certainty that they both knew to be true, did not compute with Sarah when it came to her sanity and the sanctity of her family. She knew that her life would never be the same again, and, over the subsequent weeks, it was not.

"Honey, please talk to me," he said to her at breakfast one morning a fortnight later. She had hardly spoken in two weeks, except for the necessities such as at mealtime when the children were there. "You can't let this get to you."

"Brock, I am miserable. Do you realize what you have done to me?"

"What *I* have done to you? Please tell me what *I* did. I am not the one who threw you in the slammer. Matter of fact, I'm the one who got you out, in case you've forgotten."

"But you are the one they wanted, and you know it," she said. "If it hadn't been for you waving that red flag at them, it never would have happened. Okay, Mr. Legal Eagle, you got us in this mess, how are you going to get us out?" She was starting to cry.

This thing had just gone too far where she was concerned. A guiltless bystander who had found her husband's ingenuous expedition toward learning the truth to be interesting and entertaining at best, Sarah was suddenly engulfed in a situation about which there was nothing amusing at all. She could go to jail for a long time, and the emotional baggage was becoming more than she could carry.

"Sarah, listen. Those weasels want to drive us apart. The U.S. Attorneys would want me to testify against you, or you against me, if it were possible. It's their ammunition. They want to steal our property. They want convictions, and that's all. They don't give a damn about integrity and propriety and truth. They only get ahead when they can hang another prosecutorial scalp on their belts. It's man's law that has replaced God's, and we must not succumb to it. Don't weaken, Honey, just stand by me. We are going to win this thing."

The tears were soon streaming down Brock's face, too. He loved her so, so much; but he, as any mortal man would, found it too difficult to tell her how much when she was attacking him— blaming him for her predicament. Subconsciously, he couldn't argue that he was at the heart of the maelstrom with her, but to be "the blame" was more than he was willing to take account for. He was a victim, just as she. Why couldn't she understand that? They were in this thing together.

"Because we can't win the God-damned thing, Brock. Don't you see that? Even if we win, we lose. Everybody thinks we're guilty, even if we are not. We are a blight on society."

"Honey, don't take the Lord's name in vain. I have never heard you do that. We are living in truth, under God's law. Don't let worldly legalisms distort your thinking. We mustn't care what people think, as long as *we* know we are living lawfully. We can show people the duplicity in the justice system and the courts by proving ourselves innocent at a trial. They have no case. Kenton says they may even back off and not even prosecute," he exaggerated, "because they know they can't get a conviction. Please release this thing. It's killing you. You must not let them whip you mentally. Don't you understand? If they can drive us apart, they have won. The slime-digging bastards will win by default! Sheeeit!" Brock slammed his left fist into the wall—smashing the sheetrock and bloodying his knuckles—and went storming out the door.

After he had cooled off and rehashed the confrontation in his mind, he realized that it was not the real threat of jail that was bothering Sarah, but the perceived hazard of damage to her reputation in the community. The mental torture of what her friends would think was a far more powerful force at this time in her life than the fear of being put in chains in a federal dungeon somewhere.

Sarah stopped crying. She realized how small she had been to attempt to turn her back on her best friend, lover, and confidant. Nothing was more important to Brock than his family, and he was right. She had done enough reading and absorbing through his conversations with her and others to be certain he was right. Of course he hadn't planned it this way. He had undoubtedly been the target of something that mere circumstances had caused to smash her. She vowed to stop feeling sorry for herself and get back on his team. She knew she had been framed, and if the bastards could send her to jail for nothing, then so be it, but she would not go down without a fight.

That night when they were alone before dinner, she apologized to her husband for being so upset and pledged her everlasting support. "I am scared to death, Brock," she said, "but I will follow whatever advice you and Ken give me. I know I'm just a pawn in the game, but you are my king." He smiled at her corny sincerity but knew it was not the time to make any facetious comment as he gave her a hug and kiss on the back of the neck.

"And you are my queen. I love you, Baby," he said with an assuring smile, "and we are going to win."

* * * * *

In the days and weeks that followed their conversation, Brock became angrier at the whole situation while Sarah slowly withdrew from her despondency and grew more sanguine. During the previous fortnight not only had she stopped going to civic and social functions altogether but was always "busy" enough with some contrived thing to cut short telephone calls from her best friends after only a minute or two. When Brock or the children would take a message for her, she would never return the calls. Soon her friends had seen the trend, taken it personally, and stopped calling her altogether. She had spent the early days of this turmoil crying, reading, watching television, and crying more. She could not forget that ugly headline in the *Kansas City Times* and the subsequent stories in the days that followed that horrible Labor Day weekend.

One night when Brock, having taken note of her depression, suggested that she get some counseling to ease her psychalgia, she screamed at him, "I don't need a damned shrink, I need a new life." Now she was so ashamed of herself for that, as she grew to realize she had almost let an outside influence destroy everything they had built together.

Sarah decided to work diligently to change all that. She would no longer address the problem subtly but meet it head on. She began by calling everyone she could think of, first apologizing for her recent behavior and then explaining the whole story. Upon reflection she had begun to believe that her friends really wouldn't run out on her but would be sympathetic to her cause, if they only knew the whole story, and she was right.

"A federal indictment is like a fatal disease," she told them. "Everybody wants to know whatcha got, but nobody wants to ask. Well, let me tell you . . ."

Instead of hiding it from the bridge club and the tennis league, she began announcing it to anyone who would listen, charging through the window of opportunity with no embarrassment. "They did this to me to get to my husband," she told her friends, "and if it can happen to me, it can happen to any of you. You had better wake up and begin to realize that the great United States government is not necessarily your friend and protector that we once thought it was."

It worked. Many of her friends responded by calling her every few days to get a progress report and to offer their support in any way they could. A few even took some of her literature to read, but she doubted if any of them could possibly discern the truth with a cursory examination. Maybe it would generate enough interest to make them or their husbands want to read more, as it had with Brock.

Meanwhile, Brock was so worried about what the future held for Sarah that he thought of going to a psychologist himself maybe just to garner a little advice and knowledge on how to best handle Sarah in her current state of confusion. *But I can hear him now,* Brock thought to himself: *Why don't you just pay your taxes?* There was just no simple way to make the uninitiated understand. The nation had been brainwashed long ago into believing that patriotic people must pay their income tax in order to support the country; or that a win by the Democrats will bring change next time. Educated, articulate, intelligent people still believed that the American people accomplished something by electing Reagan over the incompetent Carter, and the same disillusioned faction will be just as smug when they elect Bush over Dukakis. *Double-minded nitwits.* They hadn't read anything but the newspaper and *Time* magazine since college. Liberal versus conservative was nothing but subterfuge. Nothing changed after an election but the faces. There were no political solutions anymore. Senator Jacob K. Javits' administrative assistant, Harold Rosenthal, had boasted this fact to the world in a magazine interview shortly before he was murdered in 1976:

> "We continue to be amazed with the ease by which Christian Americans have fallen into our hands . . . naive Americans . . . We have taught them to submit to our every demand. Americans have not had a presidential choice since 1932. Roosevelt

was our man; every president since Roosevelt has been our man. We have put issue upon issue to the American people. Then we promote both sides of the issue as confusion reigns.

With their eyes fixed on the issues, they fail to see who is behind every scene. We toy with the American public as a cat toys with a mouse. The blood of the masses will flow as we wait for our day of world victory. The naive politicians in Washington are gullible, and most of them are not too bright. Money is more important than morality. We can accomplish anything with money . . . Politically, Americans hail the blessings of Democracy and never understand that through Democracy we gained control. Democracy is mob-rule which we control through their churches, our news media, and economic institutions. These religious puppets' stupidity is only exceeded by their cowardice, for they are ruled easily."

Brock had realized this to be true, but it was the most blatant admission he had ever seen in media print. But when he presented people with the suggestion that the American capture is so far advanced that political action has become a farce, they all fell back in disbelief. The idea that both sides or all sides could be managed by a single faction with controlled, phony opposition is ludicrous to any tax-paying, TV-watching, newspaper-reading American; and they would politely change the subject every time he tried to discuss it. This finally became so obvious to Brock that sometimes he would throw in an intentional barb just to be able to laugh back at them: "I notice you changed the subject without answering my question. But don't feel dumb. Nobody else can answer it either." It did little to win friends and influence people, but it made Brock feel better. In the early days he had been tolerant of their ignorance, but he no longer suffered fools gladly . . . or barely . . . or at all.

But when would some of his friends, anybody, start asking some intelligent questions? Can't they think? No, they cannot, he decided. If his friends could think, they would ask stimulating questions such as: Why must our sons go ten thousand miles to "fight communism" when all ten planks of the Communist Manifesto are already firmly in place in the United States, and anyone who resists it will be ridiculed and jailed by his neighbors? If people could think, they would wonder why the tons of currency that are shredded each year are not given to the American Cancer Society or sent to the starving Ethiopians, neither of whom would care that the currency is soiled or torn. Before voting in a jury room to send a fellow American to jail for not filing tax forms, they might even ask to see a copy of the nonexistent law requiring people to do so.

"So you paid fifty thousand in income taxes last year," Brock imagined himself saying to the next sucker he heard gloating about being so patriotic that he gladly paid his fare share, "just what do you think that funded? If the government can create all the money it wants with the push of a computer button, do you think they really need your 'tax dollars' to finance anything? Your money is worth no more to them than a handful of sand to a beachcomber." If nothing else, it was good therapy for Brock.

*   *   *   *   *

It was early in the afternoon when Brock got a call in his office from his attorney, Kenton Williams. "Brock, are you sitting down?"

"Uh-oh," Brock uttered, "What is it?"

"The Grand jury indicted Sarah. I just got a copy of it."

"Those low-living scoundrels," whispered Brock, referring not to the members on the grand jury panel, who only listen to the facts they get and decide whether the case is worthy of trial, but the IRS, DEA, and U.S. Attorney. Kenton knew exactly whom he meant.

"I've got a copy of it here," he said. They will probably serve her on Friday. Do you want to see it now?"

"Yeah. What's the precise charge?"

"Uh, let's see, 18 USC some odd. Here it is: "Possession with Intent to Distribute and 18 USC 371, Conspiracy . . . Whoa, wait-a-minute. Conspiracy? It takes two to conspire. What the hell is this . . . uh-hmmmm . . . Brock, you'd better let me read this whole thing. Can you come over today—anytime after 3:30?"

"Yeah. Everybody is taking off early here. I'll see you at four o'clock."

When Brock arrived at a minute after four, the receptionist sent him straight back to Kenton William's office.

"Here's the deal, Brock. They've indicted her on both counts, but you will see that nowhere does it say anything about any other individual who has conspired with her."

"Allegedly."

"Right. *Allegedly* conspired with her. All they're saying right now is 'unindicted co-conspirators.' That means anybody they can come up with later. So here's what they are up to. They've got the goods found on board, and it might as well be a ton as a kilo. They can get a life sentence with either. This will be the tough part to beat. The conspiracy charge puzzled me at first, but then I remembered how they tried to work it on me once before. They figure they've got the raw material for a simple conviction with those young girls. They will try to discover the weakest link and terrify her into rolling over on Sarah. Then they drop the Conspiracy on everyone but try to nail Sarah with a plea bargain for the Possession. I need to talk to them all, Brock. Can you get them to come in here on Friday? I need to find out if they have already been approached and, if not, warn them of what to expect when they are."

"What do you mean, 'Roll over on Sarah?' Sarah hasn't done anything for anybody to roll over for," Brock said angrily. "And she damn sure is not going to plead guilty to anything."

"Brock, wake up. You know U.S. Attorneys care only about convictions. I've told you how it is the way they move up the ladder, and there are a few hundred of them out there who all think they are going to be Attorney General of the United States some day. Once the stuff is planted, the possession trap is set. So, if they can bring enough pressure to bear on Sarah, by granting immunity to one of the girls in exchange for the testimony that she brought the drugs on board upon Sarah's instructions, then they will think they can get a guilty plea out of Sarah in exchange for, say, probation and community service, and they'll never have to go to trial. You and I have to decide whether or not we can convince a jury that it was planted."

"The bastards," Brock whispered. "Filthy sunsabitches. So either way, she ends up a convicted felon. She can either plead guilty to something she didn't do to maybe avoid jail; or she can fight it, spend a mint, and if she still loses, get life in prison."

Kenton nodded his head, raised his eyebrows, and resignedly uttered, "Emm-huh, but I think we can get that Conspiracy count dismissed at the front end. Either that or make them produce the parties right now that she allegedly conspired with. That's why I need to talk to the others as soon as possible."

"Just how much *are* we talking about to defend her, Ken?"

Williams didn't hesitate. He knew what the current traffic could bear, but he wasn't out to gig his friend. He quoted his standard criminal trial rates. "Fifty thousand. Twenty-five up front, and twenty-five more if and when we go to trial."

"I would pay ten times that if I had any guarantee you could get her off."

"I know you would, Brock, but you know there are no guarantees."

Brock, always the free enterpriser and motivator, thought for a moment and said, "Ken, I'll tell you what I'll do. To plead guilty to something you didn't do, is to tell a lie before God. I wouldn't do it, and I won't have my wife do it. I'll give you *twenty* thousand up front, *twenty* thousand when we go to trial, and *another* twenty thousand bonus if the jury says 'Not Guilty.' "

Williams liked the incentive. "You've got a deal. Let's go for it."

"Bring all the kids and Sarah with you at nine o'clock on Friday, and we'll get right to work on it."

Attorney Williams ran a copy of the indictment for Brock to take with him, but Brock had already decided not to tell Sarah the bad news until Thursday night. That way she would have enough time to be prepared for the visit by the marshals the next day but not have to worry about it all week. He told Kenton about the $100,000 Silver Anniversary gift for Sarah.

"Cancel it," ordered Kenton, calmly but with emphasis.

"What?" replied Brock, wondering if he had heard right.

"Brock, now just think like a lawyer for a moment. Sarah's going on trial for being a distributor of illegal drugs. The U.S. Attorney shows a picture to the jurors of her cruising around in a brand new chariot that cost more than the house that most of them live in. Then he brings in the salesman to verify how much you paid and when. You and I know it was on the up-and-up, but it will be one more thing to plant a doubt. I can't make you cancel it, but as your legal counsel, I'm telling you it's a mistake right now. Have you paid them for it yet?"

"Just a binder of fifteen thousand."

"My advice then is to either wait until this is over all together or get them to put that toward a less expensive car. I'm sure they will work with you. Get her another BMW or small Mercedes. That's expensive enough, but at least we can justify it from your lifestyle the past decade or more."

Brock knew that made sense and didn't argue. He called the sales manager at Patrician Motor Company and made an appointment to see him right away. He had done enough business with them in the past, the sales manager assured him, that some different arrangements could be made without Brock losing his deposit.

FIFTEEN

Sarah's trial had been a joke—a Halloween trick on the prosecutor and a treat for the defense. Knowing that the purported "evidence" had been planted and that the government had nothing else in his client's history to even suggest that such a preposterous accusation could be true, Kenton Williams had moved for a speedy trial. The judge had granted it for the last week of October. For two long days the judge and jury listened to law enforcement people and federal agents drone away on the witness stand with little or nothing concerning the particular guilt of Sarah Freeman.

Sarah had planned to take the stand and say that she hadn't even been on the boat all summer long—since Memorial Day weekend—and that numerous people at the marina could have access. Kenton Williams had already told the jury as much in his opening statement. He was certain Sarah would make an excellent witness and that the jury would believe her. Her testimony wasn't even necessary.

When the government finally rested on the morning of the third day, Williams moved for a Directed Verdict under Rule 29.

It is standard operating procedure for a defense attorney to ask for a Directed Verdict—a ruling by the judge that the jury not be subjected to any more discourse because the prosecution has failed to prove its case, and there is simply nothing against which to defend. It is always requested and almost never granted. Some judges may spend a whole career never honoring a motion for a Directed Verdict. Nevertheless, it is such a common motion, any experienced trial lawyer just awakened from a sound sleep can recite at a moment's notice the few sentences describing the "outrageous behavior of the prosecution" in the persecution of his poor client who has had his/her life interrupted by these ridiculous, ungrounded charges still not proven by the prosecutor.

But in Sarah's case it had been obvious to the judge that Kenton Williams was not just recounting empty words from memory for the court record. The judge called a 30-minute recess and invited Williams and the prosecutor for a confab around the conference table in his chambers. He told them of his intentions and invited the U.S. Attorney to show from the evidence why he should not grant the Rule 29 directed verdict. The prosecutor's half-hearted argument—indicating that even he was not convinced this case should ever have come to trial—was over in five minutes, and he had failed to point out to the judge anything the court may have missed. They re-entered the courtroom, and the judge rendered his verdict directing that Sarah Freeman be released from prosecution. It was as good as a "not guilty" from the jury. She could never be tried on the same charges again, and the jury was sent home, the case dismissed.

When the courtroom erupted in a cheer, most were too busy congratulating Sarah, Brock, and Kenton to notice how difficult it had been for the judge to suppress a smile as he left the bench. Before finalizing his verdict, he had even—on behalf of the U.S. Government—issued a small apology to "this kind lady" and an admonishment to the "bureaucratic cowboys whose zeal sometimes exceeds their authority."

Later Kenton Williams, in a bizarre attack of magnanimity for a lawyer, released Brock from his final $20,000 obligation because their agreement had been "when the jury says 'not guilty,'" and it had not been necessary to put on the defense and closing statement. Brock thanked him but gave him a check for $10,000 anyway to meet what was Williams' standard fee of $50,000 for a criminal trial. To say that both were satisfied would have been a gross understatement.

*   *   *   *   *

November came, and because of the family strife, Sarah had done nothing to follow through with the anniversary party plans on the Saturday night following Thanksgiving. However, Brock had decided to invite some of their closest friends for early evening cocktails and *hors d'oeuvres* on Thursday night, the actual anniversary date, and keep it as a surprise for her. Afterwards, he would take them all out to dinner at Crown Center or The Plaza or somewhere.

When secretly surprised in the past, Sarah had pretended to disdain the bushwhacking, but her radiant face had always betrayed her performance. She relished it! This time it would be a chance to see some of the old friends that she hadn't spoken to except by phone since the problem at the boat back at Labor Day, and it might give her a permanent lift from the ever present doldrums she had been fighting. It would at least break the ice and allow her to see in person that they still loved, cared, and believed in her. She needed to know that they did not believe she was a drug dealer and that they were not whispering behind her back. An indictment is always a permanent scar in the eyes of the public, regardless of the later verdict by the court.

Brock learned that all but one of the half dozen couples he wished to invite would be in town over the holiday when he began to call the wives on the Monday of Thanksgiving week. A light snowfall, the first of the season, began sprinkling the lawns and streets of Kansas City.

"Don't bring any gifts," he told them, "just your love and hugs for Sarah. She needs that more than anything. About five-ish." He had gotten a call later that morning from Patrician Motors informing him the other surprise for Sarah had arrived over the weekend. He told them he would be in later that day to complete all the financial arrangements and told the salesman to plan to deliver the silver BMW 735 at precisely five-thirty on Thanksgiving evening. Now he was wishing it could be the Rolls Royce again, but it had been important at the time to heed Kenton's advice about that.

Next was the problem of keeping the party a surprise for Sarah. He had warned all the couples not to let on, but he would have to come up with some ploy in order to get her spruced up and ready so that she not be caught in an embarrassing situation when their friends arrived. It merely being a holiday would not be enough to motivate her to dress up for a dinner out, in fact it was more reason not to. But it being their silver wedding anniversary was certainly reason enough. Brock told her on Tuesday of that week to plan to dress for a nice place for dinner on Thursday and to be ready at five. It worked. She was enthusiastic about it.

"Oh, Brock, can we go to The Plaza and watch them turn on the lights?"

Of course. In all the recent hecticity of his battered life, he had forgotten. The Plaza tree-lighting ceremony every Thanksgiving night had grown to be one of the most popular autumn activities in the Midwest. People trek from hundreds of miles around—out of Oklahoma, Kansas, Nebraska, Iowa, and Missouri to witness the spectacular event. At eight o'clock, following a certain measure of hoopla, office party imbibing, and anticipation, the switch is thrown, and the pitch dark explodes into a colorful array of decorations announcing the coming of Christmas, while over a quarter million awe-struck people watch and cheer. While all this had gone on only a few blocks from their house, they had been content to watch the festivities on television the last several years rather than fight the crowds. It would be an appropriate time to do it in person again.

"Great idea, Honey. I'll see if Bristol's is open that night and get our reservations there." She didn't hear him make the seven o'clock reservations later for twelve people instead of just two.

On his way home Wednesday evening, he stopped at his favorite deli and picked up the pre-arranged hors d'oeuvres. The lady assured him that, in the cool weather, he could leave the platters in the trunk of his car overnight, and it would be just as good as a refrigerator. *Good,* thought Brock with a smile. *I'll spring 'em on the crowd right after the initial surprise when Sarah is lamenting about not having anything ready to serve the guests.*

*   *   *   *   *

On the Wednesday morning following the national election, Bowie had dialed the private number of the phone on the office desk in the garage/body shop in Newport Beach. Whenever it rang, only one man was allowed to answer.

"Yeah," barked the gruff voice.

"Good morning. It's Mountain Red. You sound like your normal, caustic self. You must be reading the paper."

"Don't be springing those fifty cent words on me this early in the morning, Red. Yeah, matter of fact I am reading the front page right now. That's why I'm so goddammed happy. How are you doing?"

"Fine. I'm looking at a picture of George and Howdy-Doody here on the front page of the Knoxville paper, and I predict that Bush will be the most protected president in history."

"Oh, no doubt. But I'll go one more than that. I predict that you will see more people going to prison in the name of drugs than ever before. Not only in this country but worldwide. He will keep an iron hand on all of it, and I'll betcha' fifty bucks on something else."

"What's that?" replied Bowie.

"That Panamanian General. What's his name? Noriega?"

"Yeah."

"He's going down, Red. He's getting too damned big for his britches. Pretty soon we will pick up these two papers and see that he committed suicide or some shit like that. Only you and I and a handful of others will know the truth."

Bowie hadn't thought of that, but he knew his old pal was right. Nobody could screw around with the drug cartel. To try to take it over was tantamount to a declaration of war. It was a known fact amongst the Company men that the only people to go to jail in the United States for drug conspiracy were those who were in competition with the U.S. government. With the former head of the CIA now sitting in the White House, he would finally have enough firepower at his fingertips to instantly smash any intervention anywhere on earth.

*   *   *   *   *

Thanksgiving morning in the Freeman household was the same as at most of the others in America. The whole family slept late. Susan had spent the night in the guest room, and she and Brent were planning to take the four-hour drive to her parents house in St. Louis to visit for two nights before returning on Saturday. At 10:30, when they all were finally up, Brock informed them of the surprise in the wind and requested that they be back by five if they wanted to go out for a turkey dinner. They agreed to postpone their cross-state trip until Friday morning.

The three youngsters, Brent, Susan, and Maria, opted to spend the afternoon at the movies. Maria had been wanting to see *Who Framed Roger Rabbit*, but the other two wouldn't hear of it. After arguing over *Tucker* and *Moon over Parador*, they finally settled on *A Fish Called Wanda*, with the idea that they might even split up and see their first choices at the multi-screened theater before the afternoon was over. Shortly after noon the three rode away together in Susan's car leaving Brock to watch the Lions game and Sarah to decide what to wear to dinner that night.

It was mid-afternoon and the stadium clock on the television screen was ticking away the final seconds of the game when Sarah walked into the den in the new silver cocktail dress she had bought the day before. "How do I look?" she announced more than asked.

Brock was stunned. Her pretty face and model figure looked better than he had seen her in months. "Wow! Like a million bucks, Honey. You're beautiful." He stood, strode to her, and gave her a soft embrace, followed by a kiss on the cheek. "You look like you did the day I married you, except maybe . . . oh . . . five years older. Happy Anniversary, Sarah."

"And Happy Anniversary to you, too, Sweetie." She returned the kiss, this time on his lips. "Now, you had better think about getting ready, if we are going to leave at five-thirty."

"Emmm. Wait a minute," he said. "Let's do that again."

"Oh, Brock, I just put on my makeup and . . ."

Suddenly they were embraced and kissing again as if it were the first time, and for a moment they were both back on the sorority house dance floor listening to the Platters. The cocktail dress dropped to the floor, and they fell onto the sofa. "Brock, what about the kids?" she whispered in a half-hearted defense. "They'll be coming home any . . ."

"They're great kids," he replied without hesitation. "Let's make another one." They felt closer to each other than they had in months.

By four o'clock Brock had gone upstairs and begun to pick out something to wear to dinner. When he had turned on the hot shower to warm up the room and was grabbing a clean change of underwear from his dresser, he thought he heard the front doorbell ring. Knowing that it was too early to be his guests and that Sarah was downstairs to tend to it, he paid little attention and proceeded to shut the bathroom door and go about his business of cleaning up, shaving, and getting dressed. It was probably one of Brent's or Maria's friends. He grabbed his razor and stepped into the shower. The susurrous rustling of the spraying water from the shower head mixed with his own habitual singing in these surroundings would drown out the bedlam in his life about to come down in the front foyer.

The tall, uniformed marshal was standing on the porch when she opened the door. She noticed a dark gray Ford backed into the driveway at the end of their walkway with a man wearing sunglasses sitting behind the wheel. The visible exhaust emission told her that the motor was running.

He stared at her a moment before saying, "Mrs. Freeman?"

"Yes."

He appeared to be extremely nervous. "Are you Sarah Freeman?"

"Yes."

"I have some legal papers to serve on you."

"Again? What is it this time?"

The man reached into his blue quilted, Eisenhower-style jacket with the gold star sewn into the outside of the left breast pocket. Instead of gripping papers, his right hand emerged holding the longest handgun Sarah had ever seen. The western-style .22 Magnum with a silencer attached to the barrel quickly reminded her of a "Dirty Harry" movie she had seen once, and suddenly it was leveled only inches from her face. The explosion burned her lips, but she never had time to feel the sensation as the slug ripped away her front teeth, tore through her nasal cavity and the lower portion of her brain before exiting and smashing through the dining room mirror forty feet behind her and lodging in the wall. Sarah Freeman was dead before her body hit the hardwood floor of the front foyer.

The explosion was louder than the amateur assassin had hoped. A silencer on a revolver is only half effective, muffling only the noise emitting from the barrel, but the sound from the exploding cap in the chamber is still considerable. Noisier but cleaner. No shell is ejected from a revolver to be traced later.

He calmly closed the door, stuffed the pistol back inside his jacket, and carefully did not run but briskly walked to the waiting car and got in on the passenger's side. Spike Thorsten put it in gear and pulled away in an ordinary fashion. In a few seconds the gray Ford had disappeared around the corner of the driveway and had quietly blended into the boulevard traffic on Ward Parkway. As far as the two men could tell, no one of consequence had seen them. There had been an old woman walking a dog, but she had been far past the house before the incident and could not have heard anything. Once again, Spike apparently had pulled off the perfect crime. It served the bitch right for beating them in court. *Freeman might be so scared of us now that he'll pay off that big assessment just to get me out of his hair,* he thought. The deputy commissioner would be proud, if only Spike could tell him. Maybe someday he would.

* * * * *

It was after five o'clock when Brock heard the doorbell ring again, while he was still upstairs putting on the finishing touches of cologne. He knew who this must be and thought it would be fun if Sarah would answer it. "Honey, if that's for me, I'm on the way down," he yelled but got no reply.

The bell rang a second time as Brock paused at the top of the stairwell in front of the full-length mirror straightening his tie. "Sarah, are you going to get that?" he said hopefully from the second floor, but his voice echoed. He decided she must be gone to the cellar for something or maybe was in the downstairs bathroom, and he would have to get the door himself. Darn it all. He wanted her to answer it. With the Windsor knot still unfinished, he turned to descend the stairwell.

When he reached the bottom of the stairs and turned to answer the door, he saw her near the carpet on the hardwood floor in front of the double doors. Simultaneously, through the glass, he recognized Pottsie and Mozzarella and their wives impatiently standing on the front porch.

"C'mon, Freeman, give us a hot toddy. It's cold out here," one of them yelled just before Brock reached up and opened the door behind him while still kneeling over Sarah.

"My God," screamed one of the women. "What happened?"

The three men gently rolled over Sarah's dead body, exposing the bloody mess that had been made of her face. Her upper lip and front teeth had been blown away. The missing portion in the back of her head was the size of a golf ball. A large pool of sticky dark blood was drying on the hardwood floor where it had run onto the Persian rug in front of the doorway.

From that moment on, the seconds grew pristine. Suddenly, while Brock was still weeping and hugging the lifeless, already cold body of his beloved Sarah, people began to appear from everywhere. Brent, Maria, and Susan returned from the movies, and the other three invited couples were in a panic. If anyone even wondered if Brock had done this, they quickly suppressed the thought with their present knowledge that there was no way he ever could. Stan Potts quietly moved to the phone and called 911, vainly hoping it was not too late. Brent sat on the stairwell, silently stunned and hugging Susan. Maria was still screaming hysterically when the salesman from Patrician Motors cruised into the driveway in the gleaming silver BMW.

*   *   *   *   *

The large sanctuary of the Presbyterian Church on Glenwood was filled to capacity at 3:00 on Sunday afternoon, as the body of Sarah Prince Freeman lay in a closed casket draped and surrounded by more flowers than anyone could remember ever seeing there before. Her widowed mother and her sister's large families took up much of the front several pews. They had arrived on Friday night from Nebraska, California, and western Kansas.

It had taken a lifetime to store away the stamina and endurance that had bolstered Brock the last few months. Now his account was depleted. He sat ashen-faced through the funeral on Sunday afternoon as a rock unmoved. As the soloist sang "How Great Thou Art" and "Amazing Grace," two plainclothes detectives stood at separate aisles in the rear to scan the crowd, and outside a third was aiming a video camera at everyone who arrived and departed. The three would quietly continue their duties at the cemetery, but Brock paid little heed. He knew the people responsible for this would not be at Sarah's funeral. He was more concerned with trying to cope with condolences to a husband of a murdered wife—condolences no one knows exactly how to offer, and no one knows how to receive—and with consoling his children, especially his daughter. He had slept only in snatches since the murder, and all weekend long he had been experiencing a slight but perpetual pain in the depths of his brain—the kind of headache the alcoholic wears the morning after until he can locate his next drink. He knew what faction had murdered his wife, he just didn't know which individuals. But he would find out if it took him the rest of his life. They had taken away the light of his life, the keeper of his dreams.

The short ride to the cemetery seemed to take hours as Brock relived a quarter of a century in his mind. The trees stood gray, gaunt and bare, their dead leaves rustling under the hearse's tires ahead of them, reminding Brock that he was witnessing nature's funeral too—the passing of another year. He stepped on black walnuts among the brown leaves as they slowly and reluctantly walked to the gravesite. He was cried out, and when the sporadic attacks of grief would hit him once more, he would shake all over for a quick moment before suddenly regaining control again.

Maria had carried a long-stemmed rose. When everyone had finally left the graveside and the workers had lowered the casket, she kissed the flower and dropped it into the open crypt. Her tear ducts drained too, Maria stood there with her body silently shaking until Brock and Brent appeared by her side and eventually led her away. The sun peeked faintly through the dull gray clouds for a moment, then disappeared. When the final mourners turned from the gravesite and headed to their cars, no shadows followed them.

Then came the coroner's inquest on Monday which finally determined that Sarah had been murdered "by a person or persons unknown." Brock had never owned a weapon larger than the .22 rifle that he and Brent had occasionally used for rabbits, squirrels, and target shooting; and inspection by the sheriff's department showed that it had not been fired in a long time. In addition to that, since he was the only one in the house at the time of the murder, he had voluntarily submitted to a paraffin test before the investigating officers left the scene, to officially determine that he had not fired a weapon that day. In a few days he would pass a polygraph test without suspicion.

The initial autopsy showed that Sarah had been dead "since approximately 4:30 P.M." and had been killed by a medium caliber slug, likely a .38. The smashed lead dug from the dining room wall later was too mutilated for ballistics but the weight of it and the circumstances of the case suggested to them that it "probably had been fired from a .22 magnum weapon." Far more powerful than an ordinary .22, a .22 magnum has the hitting power of a .38. Brock didn't care what they determined. His Sarah was gone. *Charge me with murder if you want to,* he thought as he sat in the courtroom. *As a matter of fact, you had better put me away because, if you don't, I am going to hunt down all the low-living bastards who did this.* He knew who had to be responsible. They had already destroyed Sarah's life by playing with her mind, but, no, that wasn't enough. They had to murder her to get to him. Maybe the bullet was meant for him, but they were willing to settle for either of them. Maybe they thought killing Sarah would take the heart out of him. If that was their ploy, he had some hot news for them. They would pay. His personal *esprit de corps* level had not been at such feisty heights since the night so long ago when he had pummeled Butch Evans around the dance floor at The Stables.

Any silent speculation at the hearing about the likelihood of Brock being the killer of his wife went out the window when one of the Freeman neighbors testified that she had been walking her dog past their house when the gray Ford had paused outside. She had noticed it bore a "G-12" blue-on-white government license plate and had backed into the driveway after she had walked by. There were two men inside. She had heard what she thought was a holiday firecracker, but by that time she had walked almost a block or more down the street. When she returned a half hour later to see the commotion at the Freeman house, she realized that she may have some information and had reported all this to the Jackson County Sheriff's office. Brock was immediately exonerated at the inquest, but the murder investigation was later stymied by the mere fact that the woman had disappeared the following day. Brock had wanted to talk to her. Nobody ever knew that she had been hauled away to the federal hospital in Springfield for 120 days of "mental observation." She never returned. The case of Sarah Prince Freeman was officially logged on the books as "Murder . . . by a person or persons unknown."

*   *   *   *   *

On Monday evening, after everyone else had left the office on Shawnee Mission Parkway, Spike Thorsten poured a glass of straight scotch for himself and a tall Jack Daniels and water for his visitor. After they laughed for a few moments about the simplicity of the mission, Spike handed him an overstuffed, bulging letter-sized envelope.

"Here it is, Doc, as promised. Two hundred and fifty twenty-dollar bills. Too bad the main target couldn't have answered the door. You could have had twice this much." That had been the deal. $10,000 for Brock, $5,000 for any other family member. Only Don Handy, who had recruited the gynecologist for undercover work months before, knew of the arrangement. He had sat unnoticed in the back of the courtroom that morning and observed the proceedings. Handy had personally handled the transfer of the bank funds in the late afternoon and had given the cash to Spike for the payoff.

The distinguished gentleman who wore a pencil-thin mustache and an expensive three-piece suit nodded and smiled as he stuffed the envelope into his inside coat pocket without opening it. He said nothing more about the subject before gulping down a large and final portion of his drink.

"What time is your flight?" he said to Spike.

"8:45 on Northwest. I haven't much time for celebrating, Doc."

"Okay. Drink up, and I'll have you at KCI by eight," replied the doctor.

SIXTEEN

The older man offered the younger another tidbit from historical data:

"History shows that from the beginning of time most governments have been corrupt and the pattern has remained constant for five thousand years. The rulers of a nation—be they pharaohs, kings, emperors, or those who have gained power through election—all soon begin to serve their own interests and that of their chosen friends and family members, and always at the expense of those whom they govern. This theft and corruption always expands to despotic tyranny beyond the previous generation's comprehension as the people are enslaved by those who were permitted to exercise leadership. It evolves as naturally as night following day.

"When the covenant between free people and their government is broken and statutes are passed that fly in the face of supposed constitutional restraints, the people become cynical and contemptuous, and a large percentage silently drift toward non-compliance. A smaller percentage often take on a larger battle and accomplish much more, as evidenced by the French resistance in Paris prior to and during World War II."

March had been by far the most productive month in the short history of the underground resistance. Following one of the boldest sweeps yet, three Assistant United States Attorneys in one night in Portland found themselves gagged and handcuffed and lying in the back of a panel truck headed for a temporary jail cell. They had been arrested right at the front doors of their homes. One had been mowing his lawn, stranding the power mower with the engine still running when they pulled away from his house. Four IRS agents from various offices in the SeaTac metro area disappeared from the streets without a trace in the middle of one workday, and the next week a dozen more quit their jobs. IRS audits were at a standstill. The district directors of the three cities were in a panic, conferring only among themselves and their superiors in Washington D. C. Then the district director in Spokane disappeared on his way home one evening. His new Cadillac was found a week later

on a deserted mountain road near Missoula, Montana, stripped and
burned out.

Federal District Judge Jeremiah Forrestal of San Francisco, re-
morsefully cognizant of the ominous role he had played for years by
sending innocent husbands and fathers to jail and thereby destroying
families, blew his brains out in his U.S. Courthouse office. There was no
question that it was suicide. He had left a twenty-page handwritten
letter, confessing his sins and begging for forgiveness from God and all
the families. It was obvious that he had researched his files before pains-
takingly citing each case in a letter that must have taken several days to
write. He had requested that it be published in the San Francisco
Chronicle, but the U.S. Attorney made sure that no reporter ever saw it.

<hr />

Bowie Crockett's "Baby Needs Shoes" was rolling at 70 m.p.h.
down I-5 out of Oregon at the California state line. Bill Banneker
was at his side. In the rear trailer were chained twenty-eight IRS
personnel, three Assistant U.S. Attorneys, and one U.S. District
Judge from Seattle—the only black man in the group. The Oregon and Washington patriots had also done their jobs well. The
coup de grace for the federal judge had come when he put an
attorney, who was defending a "tax protestor," in jail for contempt over a weekend for asking the wrong questions of the
court. Several months later, on his way to the courthouse early
one morning, the judge's car was side-swiped by a van, and he
was "arrested" by three local patriots and taken to the secret
lockup in Tacoma. He had been there for nearly two weeks when
Crockett and Banneker made their pickup and hauled him away
to Virginia City. Bowie and Bill had begun this latest mission the
day before by making pickups in Spokane, Tacoma, and Portland. This morning they had collected their final six prisoners in
Grant's Pass and begun to travel south.

"Oh, another day, another dollar," chimed Bowie.

"Don't worry, Bro', there are plenty of dollars available to
pay you now. You just keep on arranging your schedule in order
to do this once a month. I'll take care of the rest."

Bowie knew that Bill had sold some of his real estate holdings and had placed the funds in a private non-interest-bearing
account to fund this operation. Banks are restricted by law from
requiring social security or federal I.D. numbers on such accounts.

Mr. Roark was taking care of the considerable expense of the
operation of the camp and occasional runs by Cochise's team

from southern California and Arizona. Bowie had agreed to make monthly runs for minimal expenses and equipment depreciation only, with Bill bringing forward the cash. This was their fourth trip—all out of western states—and next month would be their longest; their first from east of the Mississippi, out of Buffalo, New York. There would be over forty in their trailer for the cross-country run the following month, according to the estimates they had learned through telephone conversations the previous week. The forty had already been identified by their victims. They would be tried, convicted, and turned into hunting fodder in the compound in Nevada. The underground freedom fighters around the country were retaliating to the OLLIE activities with humiliating counterpunches.

*   *   *   *   *

Meanwhile, Cochise had discovered a new and secret means of telephone communication. In 1987, responding to a newspaper advertisement, he had walked into an electronics and appliance store in Anaheim to get a demonstration of "the newest, most modern, and least expensive tool of communication." This dealer was one of the first in southern California to handle cellular telephones, and Cochise was about to stumble upon just how inexpensive this method could be—although it would not be exactly what the manufacturer and dealer had intended.

Cochise patiently listened to the twenty-minute presentation and watched a ten-minute video about the upcoming plans of the industry. Within five years, a customer would be able to travel from coast to coast on the nation's interstate system and use this instrument almost without interruption of service. It was the coming thing, and while all that sounded good to Cochise, he really was more interested right now in establishing a more efficient system of communication between his shop and the wrecker drivers out on the various jobs. The old fashioned two-way radio just wouldn't reach out far enough in the expanded Los Angeles area, and for years the CB had been too crowded for even local conversation.

He purchased one Mitsubishi cellular phone with the idea of getting three more in a week or so if he was happy with what he got. He signed up for the service and understood that it would be the next day before it would be activated because it was already past six o'clock in the evening.

That night after supper he began to fool around with his new toy as he read the instruction manual. When he hit the "Power" switch he saw the horizontal hyphenated line extend almost all the way across the screen, indicating that he was near a carrier tower. It also printed out the word "Roaming," but that meant nothing to him.

He dialed his brother's number in New Mexico, just to see what would happen, and was amazed to hear his sister-in-law answer on the second ring. He talked to them both for a few minutes before hanging up and asking himself, "*Now I wonder who the hell is going to get that bill?*" He decided to try again. This time he called an old friend in the 503 Area near Portland and again it went through.

Having fun now and beating the system with what appeared to be free calls, he dialed another friend in Phoenix, but this time, after incessant ringing, a recorded message came on from Orange County Cellular telling him that his was not an authorized number and to "please check with your home carrier for roaming instructions." No other calls could be completed.

The next day Cochise went back to see his salesman, explaining what had happened and asking for clarification of exactly what he had done.

"Oh, forgot to tell you," chuckled the young salesman. "That's one of the glitches in the system." He went on to explain that cellular service, in order to operate nationwide with the least hindrance to the user, had built in a computerized Roaming system.

"So even though you are registered for service in Orange County, you can travel to Bakersfield, Las Vegas, or any other sizable city and have automatic service. The computer recognizes your number as being not from its area and immediately switches you into the "Roam" mode. You can then dial your number, long distance or local, and it goes through first and connects you before searching the computer for your billing number. That's where the glitch comes in. There was no billing number for you because your unit wasn't activated yet."

Cochise thought he understood so far but had to know more details.

"So why did it quit? I called New Mexico and Oregon, but then I couldn't get through to Arizona."

The salesman went on. "You probably talked twenty minutes or so, didn't you?"

"Yeah, matter of fact that's about right on. Ten minutes or so for each call."

"Sure. The computer spent about 15 to 30 minutes scanning for a billing location on that first call to New Mexico before it came to the rude awakening that this was a brand new phone that had not been activated yet. Probably sometime in the middle of your second call, it shut down your number. It couldn't shut down the call you were on—you could have talked for hours—but it could prevent any future calls until you get your phone activated. The sequential numbers in this phone can never be used again until your service is activated. The computer will reject it now. It is the same security system that prevents anyone else from stealing your unit and using it for very long. As soon as you report it stolen, the thief will be stopped in a matter of minutes. But don't worry about that. The professionals already know that there is no point in stealing cell phones because nobody else can use them anyway, so there's no market for them."

"No, I'm not worried about thieves, but tell me more about this roam system. Did I get two free calls?"

"Yep, but you won't get any more. Besides, your service will be activated today, so you will soon be legal."

"Where did the long distance bill go?"

"Into Never-Never Land. It bounces around for a day and then lands in the 'Unbillable' slot. You were like the old time railroad hobo grabbing a ride on a train that was already up and going where he wanted to go anyway. We understand that the cellular companies get hundreds of them every month from curious people just like you, but it's cheaper to just swallow it than try to collect the four or five dollar bill the new customer ran up before getting shut down. Besides, they've got your business now, so there is no need to muddy the water. They just build it into their price as part of their standard overhead."

Driving back to the shop in Newport that day, Cochise began to think. *A glitch in the system . . . up to a half an hour for the computer to detect . . . can't unplug the call you are already on . . . could have talked for hours . . . the Roam system is everywhere the cellular service is . . . it can be used anywhere in the country and nobody gets a bill . . . into Never-Never Land.*

That evening he went to see a close and trusted friend, one who just happened to be a wizard at electronics and, in recent years, had taken a part time job teaching a course in computer technology at Orange County Community College. He told his friend everything and then proposed a few questions:

What if we had a phone that was so programmed as to have the ability to change the numbers within each time it got knocked out? Wouldn't the computer read it as a brand new phone each time? Wouldn't we then have free phone calls to any area code in the United States? Was such an idea feasible or would the rigging make it cost prohibitive?

The answers to the final three questions were Yes, Yes, and Definitely Not. He believed he could do it.

"And wouldn't the calls be untraceable?" Cochise asked. "It seems to me like they are lost forever."

"Maybe so," replied his friend. "Let me do a little research. Give me a few days."

A week later, the system was not only up and running but Cochise and his friend had begun a very lucrative business in black market cellular phones. Cochise put up the money for the raw materials, the computer virtuoso molded the new chips and did the rigging, and they began to sell the units for $3,000 apiece. Not a bad deal for people who were already spending several hundred a month for cellular and long distance service.

In the game of Spy vs. Spy on the field of industrial espionage, a company is almost always prepared to counter the latest chess move by its adversary. *"If they do that, then we'll do this."* Around the same time that Cochise was stumbling onto his remarkable discovery, drug runners in Miami came up with different, less ingenious and definitely more criminal, idea. They would have one of their own go in and sign up for cellular service and purchase a phone. Then, the gang would order ten or more from another company and re-program the phones for each participant to match the legitimate one. The cellular companies dubbed these as "Clone Phones." A massive bill of $25,000 or more would often be run up over the next ninety day period before the cellular company would realize that their customer had disappeared and they were never going to be paid.

However, there was a federal law on the books with which they could prosecute this kind of flagrant fraud. Section 1029 had been added to Title 18 of the United States Code as part of the "Counterfeit Access Device and Computer Fraud and Abuse Act of 1984," which was incorporated into the Comprehensive Crime Control Act of 1984. This was originally designed to frustrate telephone and credit card fraud. As capsulated by the *Department of Justice Manual,* the legislative history reflects that "Congress intended that prosecutions for the use of 'unauthorized access devices' be directed to activity involving a criminal or an organized crime ring that traffics in fraudulent credit cards."

In paragraph (e)(1) of Section 1029, the term "access device" meant any card, plate, code, account number, or other means of account access that can be used . . . to initiate a transfer of funds." The law fit for the prosecution of the users of the "Clone Phones" but the courts would later rule that the free-riding "Hobo Phone" did not initiate a transfer of funds—no account had been accessed, nothing had been stolen from any identifiable individual—and, therefore the law did not fit the alleged crime. It would be years before the 18 USC 1029 would be amended to include the free-riding hoboes, and this would be long after Cochise and Bowie would have any more need for the system. Meanwhile, every call they made to each other and elsewhere could in no way be traced.

*   *   *   *   *

In another hour Crockett and Banneker would be swinging southeast in northern California at Mount Shasta on State Road 89 toward Susanville before picking up U.S. 395 into Reno. This was the shortest route "as the crow flies" but a tedious one through the mountains on the two-lane roads. They figured to be unloading at the private prison outside of Virginia City shortly after nightfall. Although the trip on the two-lane road was only about 250 miles to Reno, and shorter in distance than by staying on the interstate, it would take more time. Still, they felt it was prudent.

After they had finished a lunchtime hamburger and fries in Mount Shasta, they gave the prisoners a drink of water and were off again. The slower pace had cut down on the noise level and given the two friends a chance to converse a little more easily than they had been able to do on the interstate.

"Raoul will be happy with this new meat," said Crockett. "Have you got any special plans for our first Black American?"

Bowie, don't desecrate my heritage by calling that first class, gold-plated, nigger son of a bitch 'American.' He don't qualify to be 'black' or 'American.' He's a low-livin' nigger." Bill Banneker was a literate man but, while in the heat of passion, his grammar tended to slip into the Ebonic vernacular.

Bowie thought he knew what his black friend meant, but he wanted him to clarify it anyway. Besides that, he enjoyed riling him. "What's the difference?" he asked.

"I'll tell you the difference, and most racist honkies just don't understand it. They want to couple us all together with the only distinguishing characteristic being black skin, and that ain't it, Man. Lemmee tell you an example. Do you remember in Watts back in '65, that guy, that truck driver who got caught in the middle of the mess in those riots. They pulled him out of his truck and near 'bout beat the poor guy to death? Remember him?"

"Sure I do."

"Well, see, those were gyat-dyam niggers doin' that. Low-livin' savages acting like they still slept under trees in the jungle. Now if *you* try to explain this, you'll get labelled as a racist too, but my black brothers agree with me every time. It's the niggers that are robbing and killing the good black people, too. Anyway, do you remember what happened next in that story?"

"No, what?" said Bowie.

"I thought you wouldn't remember because the national media only reported it the first day. There was a couple who lived just a few blocks away from that intersection and, watching the whole mess on television, realized where it was. Husband and wife both jumped in their car and drove over and picked up that unconscious white man and hauled him to the hospital before those crazy apes could kill him; and they would have, too. That couple was black, Bowie. They ain't niggers and never will be. They are black and American, the kind of honest and law-abiding people that every American, white or black, should be proud to have living in their neighborhoods or next door. Most of us don't want your women or whatever else you got. The niggers do; we don't. We just want to be left alone to pursue our own dreams, man. But if you can drink out of that water fountain or piss in that urinal, then I can too. That's what our struggle of the sixties was about, Bowie. And I think most of white America has agreed with that now. Most have accepted the black people not as a necessary evil or obstacle in their lives but as ordinary humans who just want to get along. It's the gyat-dyam niggers they are still objecting to, and they always will. I do, too. I love you, man, and I love Stella, too, but I don't want her or any other white woman. I believe in racial purity as much as those Aryan Nation boys do, and I don't chase white women just like they don't go after black ones. Niggers do, but not me. The niggers of today make my row a little tougher to hoe tomorrow.

In the midst of the stress of Bill's ardor, Bowie couldn't resist another jab at his friend. "Is that why my uncle always said that N-double-A-C-P really stood for 'Niggers Ain't Actin' like Colored People?' "

Bill had to laugh. "I never heard that one, but it's still pretty accurate today," he said. "But when we use the derogatory term, let us not forget them red-neck "white niggers" out there who can't see beyond my skin color. If people would define the term 'nigger' as a low class, sorry, good-for-nothin', poor excuse for a human being who might be white, yellow, red, or black; then I have no argument about it; because that's my perception of a nigger, too, and I don't intend to ever be one. But somehow society has grouped only black people into this definition and made all of us "niggers." That's the unfair part, and that's why we resent it. How would you like it if I called your wife "Whore Bitch" every time I referred to her or had some belittling name or comment about you each time I introduced you to someone? 'Yeah, Tyrone, I'd like for you to meet my good friend here, Bad Breath Bowie! He's about the biggest asshole you'll ever meet. He doesn't bathe or brush his teeth, he doesn't work, he ain't got one damn thing to recommend him. He just a third-class piece of shit.' How would you like to start off every new relationship of your life, business and social, on the defensive like that?"

Bowie looked straight ahead at the road and only nodded his head without comment or reply. Bill caught the acknowledgment and continued.

"This is the unfair disadvantage that black people must overcome everyday. That of proving that he or she has risen above the nigger status. There are millions of us out here who are living each day with the goal in mind of climbing out of that pit, and when we call one another 'nigger,' it is an altogether different situation. We're a brotherhood who have been struggling together, and oftentimes it is no more than the jovial impetus we use to remind one another that the struggle ain't over. And sometimes we're serious. When a brother gets drunk and starts acting a fool and talking about cuttin' up somebody or robbin' a store, we'll tell him: 'Hey, man, quit acting like a stupid-ass nigger!'"

"Hey, no kidding?" Bowie said. "That's what we say, too! But, you know, I do remember that family now," and we sure didn't hear much about them after that. But if they ever want to move to Tennessee, they can live next door to me anytime."

He was sincere, but he wasn't sure that he hadn't sounded patronizing to his black friend. If he had, Bill ignored it because he wasn't quite finished yet with his diatribe. But Bowie temporarily interrupted that with a cellular phone call to Cochise, more to test out once again his new toy than anything else, but he did want to give an update and let him know that they were running on schedule. Bill then proceeded as if there had been no interlude.

"Someday, Americans will have to realize that government-forced integration of the races will never work because the large majority of both blacks and whites prefer to be among themselves. Take a look at the overall situation. In the sixties, the federal agents infiltrated both the Civil Rights Movement and the KKK to fan the flames of hate between the races. When I was growing up, we didn't hate 'Whitey.' We just wanted the freedom to do what Whitey did. Now after a quarter century of forced integration, the hate is far more widespread than it ever was before. The amalgamation of the races doesn't work because it's

unnatural. Blacks and whites will never get along until we separate again—get our own nation or group of states. As long as we
are meshed together, it will always be politically expedient for
government to use one against the other. A 'racism' charge is
always cheap shot, from either side. Any discussion of it will
always be characterized by angry finger-pointing, accusations of
wicked prejudice, outbreaks of civil disorder and violence, and
irrational and unsubstantiated caricatures of the races themselves.
Nope, we will both be better off apart but as friendly neighbors
in separate locales.

"Okay, now meanwhile, let's understand, this uppity nigger
we got back here don't qualify to be one of us. Just because his
folks found enough money to send him to college and law school
and then Reagan appointed him to a federal judgeship to satisfy
some Equal Opportunity bullshit doesn't elevate him from
"nigger" status. Only his own behavior can do that, and he has
flunked the test. He had higher standards to meet and didn't
make it. I'm gonna personally flog his ass when we get there
tonight so he can't claim any white racism. And I'm going to
privately take responsibility for his education and explain to him
everything I just told you. With his head so full of legalisms, it
will take several lessons to sort it out, I am sure, but it is about
time he learned a little bit about the real law and the dispensing
of *lawful* punishment. The White man discovered the Cross by
way of the Bible, but the Black man discovered the Bible by way
of the Cross."

SEVENTEEN

In his notes the young writer had written something he had been wanting to ask all evening, and he had found his opening.

"Did you really threaten the Secretary of Treasury with crashing your Lear Jet into the Capitol Building in Washington?" he asked.

"That's not quite accurate. That's the way rumors start. It wasn't a Lear. It was a 747, and it wasn't the Capitol, it was the IRS offices; but I'm not ready to get into that yet, son. Let's take first things first. How about another glass of wine?"

"Okay."

As the older man stood and poured from the carafe and looked out the window, he saw the snow falling in bundles, stacking onto anything that would grab it. "I don't think you'll be wanting to drive across town in this mess," he said. "You may have to sleep here tonight."

"I don't mind, if you don't mind. That will give us more time to talk. What about Larry McDonald, the Georgia congressman. Did you really find him in that Russian prison? How did you manage that?"

"Slow down, Young Turk," the older man chortled. "We're a long way off from that yet. Don't you want to write this in the order that it happened? There's a lot more I want to tell you about Crockett and Banneker, a couple of the toughest and slickest dudes since G. Gordon Liddy."

❦

Six weeks had passed since the brutal murder of Sarah, the police had no clues, and Brock suspected that they had already shelved it in the "Unsolved" file. But Sarah was still with him, in a ghastly dying sprawl on the floor of his foyer, perpetually etched into the walls of his mind. The eye records. The eye takes vivid, unforgettable pictures. Sarah was on her side, eyes half open in the grey-bronze of the emptied face, one open hand outflung, all of her shrunken and dwindled by the lake of blood in which she lay. She wasn't bouncing out the door, racquet in hand, in her cute white tennis frock anymore; neither was she out in the kitchen singing and mixing up some new exotic recipes. Nor would she ever be. She was dead. The bastards had closed her account forever. This time it had not been an unknown farmer in rural Kansas or a faceless patriot in Phoenix. It was, still inconceivably, his precious sweetheart Sarah. He sat in his big chair in the library in the Ward Parkway mansion with the writing tablet on his lap and clenched a pen until his wrist ached like an infected tooth.

It couldn't happen to him, but it did. Now they had taken one of his, and he intended to have more than just a word or two with the account closers. He had made enough defensive maneuvers in the past to protect his things, his "toys," all the crap he had accumulated since early in their marriage and could have replaced again with time. But he had unwittingly left vulnerable his most prized possession, and the enemy had struck like a bolt out of the blue and stolen it forever. There was little worth defending anymore. His children were away from him in college, and if something happened to him, they were well taken care of. It was time to go to war under the battle flag of Sarah.

Some old philosopher had said—Brock had read it somewhere—that there are but two real motivating factors in life, love and revenge; and Brock had them both going at once. He had never been and would never be one of the so-called normal people who tend not to get as much out of life as they should, but just exist from day to day. Life for them is one big yawn. There are always a few times in life when a man's got to do what a man's got to do, but most don't do it. Brock would.

At first, with the Christmas holidays coming up, he had been content to let the cops work on it without his intervention. Now, after no action whatsoever from the professionals, he had decided to solve it himself. While previously in his life he had shunned the idea of murdering his enemies, it was now time to declare "Holy War." He had begun his own "hit list"—with no definite plans for those on the list—beginning with local dentist Joe Day and closely followed by other chief suspects in the murder of Sarah and the financial attack on himself. The second line said, "Local IRS Contact." The third read: "Local's Boss In Washington," with "???" beside each. It wasn't much to start with, but it was a start. Somehow, someday, he would track down everyone involved in the slightest way with the murder of Sarah. It was his new obsession. Meanwhile, the fifty bucks an hour he had invested in Independence private detective and old friend Frank Flowers had proven to be very productive after only a half day's billing.

Flowers was older than Brock and had garnered over thirty years experience as a P.I. after spending a short tenure as a Kansas City cop. "For the peanuts they paid me, it wasn't worth it," he was always quick to say. "I had more fights on the street in three years than I've had in thirty doing private work." The four-inch slash mark on his left tricep—compliments of a doped-up, knife-wielding Black Panther—laid further claim to the veracity of his statement. Most working P.I.s had paid their investigative dues in law enforcement at one level or another. Once a cop, always a cop, and former policemen—even many who were not P.I.s and worked in totally unrelated fields—strapped on their weapons as naturally as they strapped on their wrist watches. To be without a piece, even with a humdrum paper shuffle in the downtown records building, was unthinkable. It would have been easier to catch the Pope swimming nude in a pool full of nuns than to find Frank Flowers without his gun.

When Brock had come in that day, Frank was alone wearing his normal office attire, a pullover golf shirt and casual slacks from J.C. Penny, and looking for some important papers in the cluttered disarray of his desk and table. His pudgy pot belly hung over his belt, and from his mouth protruded the stub of a half-burned cigar. He mumbled something about the filing incompetence of his bumbling secretary who couldn't type and was always sassing him back. "If she weren't so nice to the kids, I'd divorce her," he said, flashing an animated grin without removing the cigar.

Frank Flowers worked alone almost exclusively and could find out more sitting behind his desk and computer with telephone in hand than most investigators could out beating the bushes. With a name and a social security number, he could learn the life history of anybody in America in less time than it took to watch the evening news. Without the number he could still do it, but it took a little longer. And it cost more. He also had contacts upon contacts—a must for a P.I.—with many favors owed him. Dozens of cops, government clerks, bank tellers, and personnel directors from various corporations knew that a very nice Christmas gift would be arriving each year from Frank Flowers. As an old-time John Bircher since the early days of the society, he harbored a special enmity for the "American Gestapo." He knew they operated with impunity outside of the law and had wondered for years if they would ever stoop to murder in order to prolong and preserve their stranglehold on the people. Anxious to help after learning the gory details of Sarah's case, he said, "We need to teach them some manners."

"They've had Joe Day on a string for three years or more," he reported to Brock the next morning. "After they waved a little cash in front of his face, he was hooked. Now they've got an 'Evasion' charge they're holding over him. He has sold out to them lock, stock, and barrel."

"Just as I thought," replied Brock. "Did you find out who his contact is at IRS?"

"Yep. I found Day's ex-secretary who still has her feathers ruffled because he fired her a month ago, and she left with some interesting copies of correspondence. One is an affidavit to the grand jury attesting to the fact that an informant by the name of Dr. Joe Day supplied them with information on one Vince Jaekel of KayCee Kan, which resulted in an IRS raid on his furniture store and office. It is signed by a CID boy named Don Handy. The lady tells me that Handy has been to the office several times over the last couple years and always talked with Day with the door shut."

"Is that H-A-N-D-E-Y?" Brock asked while scribbling in a small notebook.

"No 'E'. H-A-N-D-Y."

"Good job, Francis. That's our boy for sure. Vince Jaekel is my close friend, and he played golf and poker with Joe Day. If Don Handy worked against Vince, we can bet he was involved with Sarah's case, too. Joe Day would have been his snitch against all of us. Have you got any particulars on this Handy?" Brock was scratching out the question marks on line two of his list and penciling in "Don Handy" as they spoke. Frank Flowers had earned his pay. He had Handy's home address, his wife's name, the ages of his children, and the church and schools they attended.

A week later he presented Brock with a sheet documenting Handy's daily habits, including the Quick-Stop Mart where he got a newspaper and a mug of coffee-to-go each morning at 7:30, and his favorite watering hole with the nude dancers on 75th Street. If this was his secret habit, maybe they could catch him dunking his donut in someone else's coffee. And if they were lucky enough to get pictures, it should provide enough leverage for whatever information they might need out of him later.

That evening as Brock was pondering Flowers' three-page report and attempting to formulate a plan in his mind, the phone rang in the library. Bowie Crockett was on the other end in St. Louis. He would be in Kansas City by midnight and would have the whole morning free the next day while the warehouse men unloaded and reloaded his trailer. The two made plans to have breakfast together at Chubby's on Broadway.

By the time the Yellow Cab came rolling to a stop at eight o'clock, Brock had already decided to bring Bowie into his confidence. He had to trust somebody. Remembering the Chattanooga saga, Brock knew he would have no worries with Crockett. He had appeared to thrive on this sort of intrigue, and this thing was too big to handle alone—at least some parts of it were. Bowie Crockett was a Godsend.

As Bowie sat in the corner booth, his massive body consuming most of the bench built for two, Brock told him the whole story. Bowie had heard of the murder via the patriot grapevine a week after it happened and had called Brock in early December to express his condolences, but this was the first inkling he had had that the "Gyatdam, scum-sucking Feds" had been behind it. He was livid. Yes, he would help. Of course he would. He would be a proud and enthusiastic participant, one who would hurt from the inside out for the rest of his life if he missed this golden opportunity. He assured Brock that they could bring Bill Banneker into their confidence too, with no worries about breach of security.

They made some plans. Bowie would make his run back to St. Louis, complete his contract, leave his truck, and fly back to KCI the next afternoon at Brock's expense. He wanted nothing for his services other than his expenses covered. The sheer pleasure he would derive from the mission would be worth more than any monetary payment. Following a call to TWA, they chose the flight number and time. Because of Brock's need to remain separated from the action from here on, it was decided that Bowie would rent a car at the airport. Perfect. Thanks to Bill Banneker, Bowie had obtained a second I.D. from which he had procured a bank account and, by establishing good credit, a Visa card a little later.

As the sun was setting the next day over the flat land west of the airport twenty miles north of Kansas City, "Thomas Paine" was stuffing the Hertz papers into the glove compartment of the Lincoln as he turned onto the northbound exit on I-29. After a short jaunt northwest he swung back south on I-435 toward the Kansas side of the city. The 75th Street exit was another half hour away. Before leaving the airport he had called Brock's car phone to confirm that their quarry was where they expected him to be, all the time speaking in hesitant, code-like phrases so as not to alert anyone else who might be listening. Brock confirmed that the fish was in the correct pond. Bowie already knew what the car looked like and its Kansas tag number. The rest would be mere child's play for him—especially with a pansy like Don Handy. And there was no hurry. It was just after seven.

Handy's habit was to always stay until 8:30 before being drunk enough to go home for supper at nine and bed by ten. It was the only way he could sleep nights.

A few minutes before eight o'clock Bowie wheeled the big Lincoln into the parking lot of the Silver Slipper. The flashing neon sign on the roof of the building depicted a large-busted woman in an evening gown sipping champagne. As expected, he found the green Ford he was seeking in the shadows of the rear lot and a parking place in the adjacent row between his target and the night club. He pulled in, facing the Ford. When he entered the club, Frank Flowers was standing in the foyer and greeted him at the door with, "Hello, Tom."

"Frank?"

"Right. Brock said that I would have no trouble recognizing you."

"Yep. It's pretty hard for me to hide in a crowd."

"How about a beer?"

"No, thanks, not yet. I've got work to do. Where is he?"

Frank pointed out Don Handy sitting by himself at the bar, engrossed with the show going on in front and above him. There was a vacant seat next to him and Bowie proceeded toward it. Frank bid him goodbye and good luck and went out the door. The music stopped just as Bowie sat down, while the deejay changed a record.

"Whoo-wee. These ladies get better looking ever' time I come in heah," Bowie whooped as he sat down next to Don Handy, who was feeling pretty friendly himself after three double scotches.

"Where did you come in from, Big Guy? Texas?" Handy asked with a friendly smile.

It was exactly the type of reception Bowie had hoped for— friendly and unsuspecting. *Come into my home, said the spider to the fly,* Crockett thought to himself briefly before replying. "Naw, man, ah'm from West Virginia, and we ain't got nuthin' like this around Mullens. "Ah'm Tom Paine," he said sticking out his hand and flashing a big smile.

"Welcome to Kansas City. I'm Don Handy. What kind of business you in?"

"Sales. Farm equipment. I'll be here all week. What about you?"

"I'm an accountant," lied Handy, but Bowie wasn't surprised. All the CID personnel have a cover story, the lying dogs. He knew the last thing Handy would admit was that he was with the IRS. None will admit it. A new blast of music interrupted the conversation before it could go any further, as a new girl on stage diverted Handy's concentration.

They carried on casual conversation during the next couple of interludes the way strangers always do when they first meet, but when the record was over the next time, Bowie asked Handy where in the area he might get a good Kansas City steak.

"Where are you staying?" Handy inquired.

"The Ramada on I-35." Bowie had been ready with his own cover story.

"Well, let's see. The best places are downtown, but the Longbranch is right up here at the 87th Street exit—right across the highway from your Ramada matter of fact. The next exit up. You can't miss it on your right when you pull off. The Longbranch Saloon. Lou Pinella's place. You know, the Yankee manager? Well, he's never in there, but their steaks are about as good as any around."

Bowie looked at his watch and saw it was 8:20. He did not want Handy to leave first. "Good. Thanks a lot. I baleeve I'll giv'em a try. Nice to meetcha, Don."

"You bet. Nice to meet you, too, Tom."

Pretty tolerable sunuvabitch, Bowie thought, *when he ain't hiding behind that phony badge and tormenting folks.*

He emerged from the noisy building into the muggy night and walked to the rear parking lot. He unlocked the driver's door, popped the latch under the left dashboard, walked to the front, and pulled up the hood of the Lincoln. If he was running true to form, Don Handy should be out very shortly. Bowie fooled around with his head stuck under the hood pretending to be attempting to fix something. All the while his eyes were peering through the space in front of the windshield watching the building. He had to wait longer than he had hoped, but at 8:37 he spotted Don Handy whistling as he strolled toward his car parked in the rear row. His chosen route was the space right beside Bowie's car! About the time he got within earshot—near the rear of the Lincoln—Bowie began to curse gently as he unsnapped the distributor wires.

"Cheap ass piece of Ford shit!" he mumbled, pretending not to see anyone as Handy was walking by,

"Tom, what's the trouble?" Don innocently asked when he saw who it was.

Bowie backed out as if he were surprised to see him. "Oh, hey, Don. Sheeit! I just paid Hertz forty-five bucks a day for this hunk of tin and it won't even start."

"Is it the battery?"

"Naw. It turns over fine. It just won't kick off. It acts like it's flooded."

Handy leaped at the chance to help. "No, it's not flooded. It's fuel injection. It's probably water in the fuel line. That's a common problem in our climate. I know what it needs. You have to blow the fuel past the vapor problem."

"I never heard of that where I come from. Would you mind doing it for me?"

"Well, I'm running a little late, but okay, sure; it shouldn't take long."

Don reluctantly sat in the driver's seat, slammed down the accelerator, and began to grind the ignition. Bowie kept up the charade by allowing him about a half minute before waving him to stop. "Wait! Hold it a second," he said, before hooking up the distributor cap once again. "Now try it," he yelled.

The Lincoln belched and in three seconds was purring like a kitten. As Bowie slammed the hood and walked toward the driver's door, Don was sitting behind the wheel and proudly saying, "You see, Tom, you have to burn that vapor out of the way. The flood of fuel washes it to the rear and enough gas gets through to fire the engine off. It'll happen again in a day or two though, so you'll have to . . ."

Bowie's giant right hand was around Handy's throat and about to break it like a pretzel as his left reached into the inside coat pocket and removed the snub-nosed .38 from Handy's shoulder holster. Twice he slammed the gun into the startled face before the captive agent collapsed and was pushed into the opposite seat. Bowie shoved him over, patted him down and handcuffed him, slid behind the wheel, and calmly moved the big Lincoln out of the lot and onto the street. Handy was only semi-conscious and whimpering as they pulled onto I-35 toward the city. Bowie had no patience with the enemy.

"Shutup, Scumbag, and you won't get hurt—too much. And stay down on the seat."

"Are you going to rob me?" whined Handy.

"Yeah, and then I'm gonna rape ya. And if you don't shut up, I'm gonna hit you so hard it's gonna kill your whole family."

Handy started to cry.

They drove north at 55 m.p.h. for ten minutes to the Broadway Street exit downtown, and Bowie peeled off to the right. He headed south on Broadway for two blocks and turned right again on Fifteenth Street, continuing for four blocks before stopping in front of an old warehouse at the corner of Madison. He recognized Brock's Mercedes parked and facing him on the other side of the street a half block away. He slapped Handy hard across the face with a backhand and told him, "Get up, Shithead, and don't give me any trouble." He grabbed Handy's loosened tie

near the collar and pulled him across to the driver's side as easy
as one would pick up a pillow. Once outside, he lifted him to his
feet with his one hand still around the necktie. "March, Shitbag.
You are a prisoner of war," Bowie whispered in his ear. Handy
obeyed by rote. He had no idea where he was or if he was dead
or dreaming.

When they climbed the steps and knocked, Brock opened
the door and locked it behind them. The inside walls of the old
warehouse were stacked to the ceiling with every kind of junk
imaginable from old refrigerators and small appliances to pianos
and lawnmower engines. In the center of the room dangled a
long light cord with a single 60-watt bulb. Crockett and Handy
followed him, and Brock pulled on the chain for light and placed
a metal fold-up chair directly under it. The interrogation of the
prisoner was about to begin. Bowie stood intimidatingly against
the wall as Brock began to speak.

"Are you Don Handy?"

The prisoner said nothing but only glared into space. The
dark blood had dried on his cheeks and lips. Bowie told Brock to
wait a minute and left the room. In the bathroom he found a
half-filled gallon bucket with a dried mop stashed inside and
propped against the wall behind the door. He could hear Brock
attempting to catechize Handy from the other room, but no
answers were forthcoming. He removed the mop, urinated in the
bucket, and added some cold water from the sink, before returning to the big warehouse room and splashing the squalid contents into Don Handy's bewildered face. Then he smashed him
over the head with the empty bucket, knocking him to the floor.

Sputtering, shaking like a wet dog, and coughing, Handy
looked up at Bowie and said, "Who are you?" He was on a trip
through a sewer in a glass bottom boat.

"I'll ask the questions," Brock barked. "This the last time I'll
ask you. Is your name Don Handy?"

Handy quickly acquiesced. "Yes."

Brock first asked him for perfunctory information such as his
office address, and Handy told him about the semi-concealed
CID offices on Shawnee Mission Parkway, which the two inquisi-
tors already knew to be true. It was on the second floor of the
Cellular One building, with no signs outside to say so.

"Do you know Joe Day? Doctor Joe Day?" Brock asked, and
Bowie added, "And don't lie, Shitbag, or I'll beat your brains
out."

Handy believed him. "Yes," he quickly spit out.

Brock continued. "Did you use him as an informant against
Vince Jaekel?"

"Yes," Handy admitted.

"Do you know who I am?"

"Yes, you are Brock Freeman."

"Did you kill my wife?"

Don Handy's demeanor suddenly soared from frightened to totally terrified. "Hell no!" he whined.

"Who were the two guys in the government car who backed into my driveway that day?"

Handy looked into Brock's eyes with a pleading glare. "Please don't make me tell you that. They will kill me."

Bowie interjected, "Maybe they will and maybe they won't, but we damn sure are gonna' kill you if you don't tell us. So you'd better come across now and take your chances with them later."

Handy stared at them again, this time for a full minute, obviously wrestling with himself. Brock waited. Following the closing line of a sale, the first guy who speaks loses. Finally the prisoner said, "The man who went to the door was Dr. Marty Goldman. He did the shooting. That's all I can tell you. I cannot tell you who the other man was who drove the car."

Bowie picked up the bucket and smashed it across Handy's face, knocking him off the chair again. "You are not going to die quickly, Prick," he said as he reached for an axe he had found lying on the warehouse floor. If Brock had not known that Bowie was on his side and intentionally overacting, he would have run out the door himself, as Bowie went into a maniacal frenzy and began to bellow.

"We are going to cut off your fingers first, then your hands, then your toes, then your feet, then your arms, and then your legs, you piece of scumbag shit. Then I'm gonna remove your head and send it to your wife and kids. Do you understand?" Bowie was screaming with more hate than Brock had ever imagined a human could harbor. Without further warning he then slammed the axe blade through the middle of Handy's right hand, severing four fingers cleanly onto the concrete floor. Blood spurted as from a garden hose. Brock winced but somehow maintained his macho demeanor. Don Handy went into a mix of semi-shock and hysterics when he saw his body parts on the floor and the blood pumping from his half a hand.

"SPIKE THORSTEN! SPIKE THORSTEN!!" he screamed. "S. Pike Thorsten is the head of a Service hit team secretly called OLLIE—It stands for Operation Loss Leader. He's in Washington. I don't know what the 'S' in his name stands for. I don't know where he lives. I only have his phone number. Please don't hurt me anymore. I'll tell you everything I know."

While Bowie calmly extracted the super-secret Thorsten phone number from a petrified Don Handy, Brock installed a crude tourniquet to stop the bleeding and soaked the fingerless right hand in alcohol before wrapping it in a towel. With a phone call to Cochise in Newport Beach they learned that another transfer team traveling from Chicago to Nevada could pick up their new prisoner and any others they might have by the end of the week. In a few days, Don Handy would be just another hunter's frightened and running prey in the large compound near Virginia City. Meanwhile, he would stay in the warehouse awaiting their arrival. They wrapped his legs with a logging chain and padlocked it around the sink pipe, leaving him on the bathroom floor with the door nailed shut.

As Brock headed up Broadway toward Ward Parkway and home, he realized that somehow he had teamed up with what must be the Number 1, gold-plated bad-ass in all of America to help him stalk the killers of his beloved Sarah. "I'd rather have him on my side than Attilla," he whispered to himself.

* * * * *

It was almost noon on Friday when Spike Thorsten's secretary knocked on his office door with the day's mail delivery. She had been instructed long ago not to open any mail addressed to the code name of "Ollie Pike" or anything else that came with Thorsten's name on it. This day he received two progress reports from part of his field team—Atlanta and Sacramento—and a small package in a plain brown wrapper.

He opened and read the envelopes first, always excited to learn of the successes by his team against the "inventory," as he liked to refer to the millions of tax filers. He grinned and even felt a shrill thrill in his abdomen as he read the enclosed news clipping from the *Sacramento Bee* of a family near Placerville who had been burned out when the father refused to leave their small farmhouse which had been previously confiscated by the IRS. The report from Atlanta exhibited snapshots of various homes and businesses in the area which had been captured without incident during the last month's activities.

As Spike tore the brown paper off the package and noticed the red box with black letters saying *Titleist,* he wondered who in the world would be sending him a dozen golf balls. But then the bulge in the box told him it was something else. He opened the flap and saw a red wire twisty securing a transparent plastic bag, which he slid out of the box. Suddenly he realized he was holding a neatly wrapped package of human fingers.

"Take the prints," said the typewritten card enclosed.

"Jaheezus!" he screamed and slung it to the carpet. He stared at it on the floor for a half minute before recovering his composure enough to call the FBI. Two agents arrived within the hour and took the plastic container and contents to the FBI lab. On Monday afternoon they called him back to report that their fingerprint department had determined that the prints belonged to the IRS's own CID agent, Donald R. Handy of Kansas City. They had already ascertained that Handy had been missing since the previous Tuesday night. Except for Thorsten's, there were no other prints on the cardboard box or plastic bag.

*   *   *   *   *

Bill Banneker looked the part. No one could doubt that the wiry black man in the steely grey workshirt and blue dungarees carrying the bucketful of mops and brooms was who he purported to be. After he entered the lobby of Cellular One building on Shawnee Mission Parkway, he marched straight to the officious, snuff-dipping white man—who was shouting instructions to his maintenance crew—and assumed his most subservient attitude for the role. He set the tools on the floor and took a deep breath.

"Howya do, suh. I's Sam. I bleebe I woiked foy ya one day last yeah."

The boss glared at him. "Sam who?"

"Sam Adams, yassuh."

"Who sent you?"

"Labor Power. Miz Johnson called me 'bout fo' clock, said ya'll was shote of hep."

"Nobody told me you was coming, but she's right. We need you. You remember our procedure?"

"Yassuh, sho' do. Clean da' toilets and mop da' batroom floze. Den vacum da' offices, dust de shelves, and don't touch nuthin' on nobody's dest. And don't do nuthin' outa da' odenary wittout axin' you fust. Ha-hah! I know dat's raat." Sam was grinning his best white-toothed smile.

"You got it, Sam," the white man smiled back, exposing his snuff-stained, almost tan teeth. "Get the supplies you need out of the closet there between the restrooms. That's Rosie there working the east end offices, you take the west end after you finish the restroom area. I'm taking the rest of the crew to the Burnham Building. We should have it knocked out and be back here by ten. Whatever you haven't done, we'll finish up together. Any questions?"

"Nawsuh."

"Get on with it then. Your clock has already started," the boss said and headed out the front door to the parking lot.

Banneker scooped up his implements and headed for the restrooms. As he opened the closet door, he noticed the back stairwell which his concealed map already had told him would lead to the second floor and the temporary IRS offices which housed the CID files. He looked over his other shoulder to see that Rosie was out of sight and took a quick sprint up the stairs to the next level. As he was told it would be, the door was unlocked. The inside doors were never locked until the maintenance crew left late at night. He scrambled back downstairs quietly and put on his work gloves. If he was going to have to feign working, it was going to be with a mop and broom, not on his hands and knees scrubbing the filthy toilets, that was for damned sure. He began to sweep the tile floor in the men's room.

Thirty minutes later Rosie had disappeared into the eastern core of the office cubicles, and Bill strolled outside in the chilly Kansas air and lit a cigarette. After a couple of unobserved drags, he set the burning butt on a ledge and stepped to his pickup truck. After pulling on his work gloves and plucking a blasting cap from the glove box, he lifted a five-gallon canister of propane gas from the floorboard on the passenger side of the cab. Returning to the entrance way and pausing at the door to take one more drag off the cigarette and be sure he was unobserved, he wasted only five seconds. He re-entered through the double doors, turned toward the restrooms, and headed up the back stairwell to the second floor offices of the IRS/CID. He chose the office with the most file cabinets, knowing that it would make little difference if he had not selected the precise one, flipped the switch on the overhead fluorescent lights, and set the canister under the lone desk. He quickly scribbled down the number listed on the telephone. Then the tedious work began.

Removing a small screwdriver from his pocket, Bill quickly detached the casing from the phone, and turned the set over to have a look. Bowie had instructed him that with the older models the detonation method was to break a wooden match to the measured size, tape it to the metal ringer in a direct bullseye from the small clapper; thereby converting it into a pestle, poised and ready. But these units with bells and strikers had not been manufactured for a decade or more, and the IRS offices probably used the newer models. No problem. The modern units were easier to utilize for this operation anyway, and he had the older model in the van, if he needed it. A quick examination told him where he stood, and he pulled the low-voltage blasting cap from his shirt pocket and wired it into the ring circuit wires in the phone. He replaced the screws in the casing, set the phone on the floor, and finally reached under the desk and loosened the handle on the propane canister. A barely audible sibilant sound began to discharge into the air. He exited the room, intentionally leaving the lights on to serve as an ignition backup should his phone call fail. Propane gas is heavier than air and hovers near the floor. However, twenty pounds of it would pack a small room and eventually reach the ceiling—requiring half an hour or less, he surmised.

He sneaked back down the stairway, peeked to be sure Rosie was not in the lobby, entered, and began to pick up his tools. He calmly strolled out the door, threw his things in the back of the pickup, and slowly drove away. His main concern was Rosie, but he knew that she had no business on the second floor and the explosion would blow out and up rather than down to the area where she was. She might need a change of underwear in a little while, but she shouldn't be hurt.

He traveled west on Shawnee Mission Parkway toward I-35. Fifteen minutes should be sufficient time for the lower couple of feet in the room to be saturated with the gas, he thought, and stopped at a fast food outlet and ordered a burger and a coke from the drive-up window to go.

Although he had neglected to check it precisely on his watch, by the time he pulled into the Drury Inn near the entrance to I-35, a good quarter hour had passed since releasing the fuel handle. He moved slowly to allow plenty of time as he removed his work shirt and put on a white one with a necktie. The dark sport coat stashed on the seat was a close enough match to the blue work pants for him to appear dapper enough for this short mission, and he emerged from the truck and walked into the main lobby. To his left was a sign indicating restrooms and telephones. He deposited a quarter, dialed the number he had written down in the office, and thought he heard a distant thunder clap as the phone rang once, then stopped. He hung up the receiver to return to his truck and, while walking across the asphalt parking lot, wondered if his assumption of "mission accomplished" was correct. The phone had rung but once, and it definitely did not look like rain in any direction. He looked to the east but could see no red glow over the lights. He was tempted to drive back down Shawnee Mission Parkway to confirm what he believed to be true, but the better angels of his nature told him to stay away. Besides, Brock and Bowie had promised to present him with a snapshot as a memento. Instead, Bill Banneker pulled out of the motel and headed west to the interstate and turned north toward the city and Brock's office to park the truck and wait.

Meanwhile, Brock and Bowie and been waiting for the fireworks in the parked BMW at the post office at the far north end of the strip shopping center a furlong or more away from the Cellular One building. They had watched Banneker walk to his pickup truck, load up and drive away. They had assumed that, if everything went right, they had only another twenty minutes or so to wait. They had checked their watches at the time to note that it was 8:47 P.M. At 9:08 the explosion rocked the area, and they turned to see the upper portion of the Cellular One Building erupting like a volcano. Brick and concrete chips sprinkled the parking lot where they sat. Bowie grabbed the camera from the backseat, and the two walked in front of the strip of stores toward the flaming building. The last cubicle on the south end was a small boutique, and he stood in front of it while he excitedly photographed the beautiful scene of the IRS records disintegrating into smoke and ash.

They hung around for a few minutes to see the firetrucks arrive and watched the futile attempts by the firemen to stop the raging inferno. It was obvious that the building was going to be a total loss from the second floor up, and the firemen from the additional trucks that arrived a short time later pursuing a vain attempt at saving the Cellular One offices on the ground floor. After mingling for a few minutes in the throng of motorists who had stopped to watch, Brock and Bowie slowly pulled onto Metcalf Avenue and headed the BMW north toward Brock's real estate office where Bill Banneker was waiting in the pickup.

Bowie greeted him with, "Good job, Bill," when they all three emerged from their vehicles a few minutes later, a little after 10:00 P.M.

"Mission accomplished?" Banneker replied with a query.

"Mission accomplished," grinned Bowie, handing him the Polaroid snapshots. "It looked like something out of a movie . . . Like Atlanta in "Gone With The Wind." Bill hadn't felt such a rush of adrenaline since he and Sam Prescott had bashed the IRS auditor's Dodge back in Indianapolis.

"I hate we had to treat Cellular One so roughly though," lamented Brock. "They were innocent bystanders who never did anything except rent out their offices.

"But to the wrong people," replied Banneker. "Casualties of war. Besides, I think it's a pretty fair payback for aiding and abetting the enemy. Maybe with enough of these office hits, everybody will eventually be afraid to rent to the bastards."

"You've got a point there. C'mon inside. We've got to talk. We've got places to go and people to see."

EIGHTEEN

The FBI Agents had been swarming around the Washington IRS headquarters for days. If the human fingers that were sent through USPS had stirred them up, the bombing in Kansas City had put them into a frenzy. They knew they might have a jurisdictional problem in that the explosion took place on private and not federal property, but they would bluff their way through that as they always did. If nobody ever questioned what the FBI was doing in a state case such as with the murder of Martin Luther King in Tennessee, there should be no problem here, either. Besides, federal property and records were destroyed, and that should secure the jurisdiction.

Back in D.C. they were grilling Spike Thorsten incessantly, believing that he knew more than he was telling them. After all, Don Handy, the IRS/CID agent who was missing and whose fingers they now had on ice, had an office in the burned-out building. They had every reason to believe that the two crimes—only days apart—were tied together, but Thorsten was reticent as a rock and of little help to them. In their favor, they had managed to keep a lid on the media. Not the first blurb about Handy had appeared anywhere.

Spike kept remembering the words of the commissioner. *You are on your own, Thorsten . . . The Service will disavow any knowledge of your activities . . . We've never heard of Operation Loss Leader.* Spike just hoped the commissioner wouldn't crack. No, he wouldn't. Spike was certain he wouldn't. The boss had too much to lose. *"The buck stops with you,"* he had said. *". . . and if your people screw up and get caught . . ."* but Spike's people had not screwed up. No OLLIE man had been caught doing anything. He didn't know what had happened to Handy, but even that had in no way compromised their secret operation, as far as he knew. Yes, the burden was on Spike's back, all right, but he could handle it. He and the commissioner were the only ones the Fibbies could talk to, and if the boss still intended to "disavow any knowledge" if confronted, he certainly wouldn't volunteer anything. So, if Spike didn't say too much, the investigators couldn't find out anything. *The buck stops with me.*

It was mid-morning when Spike stepped out of the IRS building and strode down the sidewalk. He turned at the corner and casually looked behind him to be sure he wasn't followed. At the newsstand on the next corner he bought a newspaper and asked the old man for a roll of his quarters, handing him a ten dollar bill. He walked several more blocks in a different direction before choosing a phone booth outside a pharmacy. He removed the list from his wallet and spent the next hour calling all eleven of his remaining team members in eleven different cities, pausing only to enter the pharmacy for another ten bucks in quarters.

He told each about the unknown fate of one of their own without mentioning his name, referring to him only as "our man in Kansas City," and asking if any of the others had experienced any trouble. None had. He concluded each brief conversation with the admonition that they should continue operations as scheduled but not call him on the private line until further notice, except for a dire emergency, in which case they were not to discuss OLLIE in any way. Spike assured each that he would be in touch with more regularity than before, but that it would not be from his office phone. He began his walk back to the office as puzzled as when he had left.

What in the hell had happened to Don Handy? he wondered. Handy was the only team member attacked so far, but still there was that mystifying sweep of those twenty-two in Orange County, California, of which nobody ever found a trace. They had disappeared into the mist like journalists in Argentina. And the half dozen in the northwest, and now the half dozen more in Chicago, the one in Springfield, two in St. Louis, and one in Jeff City. And there were many more singular incidents in places like Ocala, Florida; Waxahatchie, Texas; and Poughkeepsie, New York. What the hell was going on? With these kinds of rising numbers, they wouldn't be able to keep a lid on this much longer. As soon as a wife got wind that her husband's disappearance was not an isolated case, all hell would break loose.

Spike decided that Handy must have suffered the same fate as the others, and he realized with some relief that, if it were true, at least OLLIE had not been compromised. *Where were they?* If they were dead, where were the bodies? And if they were still alive, how in the hell do you hide that many people without some detection. Maybe they have some sympathetic sheriff somewhere who is providing them with a jailhouse. *Probably with that son of a bitch in Arizona would be a good place to start looking,* he thought.

There was one particular Arizona sheriff who had mounted great opposition against the use of local law enforcement officers to enforce the Brady Bill, which the sheriff had considered to be the next giant step toward gun confiscation. More recently he had been speaking to the Arizona State Legislature about state enforcement of the tenth Amendment which, if put into action, would prevent IRS agents from visiting anyone in the state without first clearing it through the local sheriff's office. The prospects of success had everyone from the commissioner on down to the newest agent horrified at the potential ramifications of that. Yes, not only would that Arizona sheriff be cooperating with an underground movement like this, he might even be *leading* it. Thorsten decided to have his team man in Tucson take a week to stalk the sheriff's moves and see if they could uncover anything of interest.

*   *   *   *   *

Crockett, Banneker, and Freeman drank coffee in the office that night, rehashing the relative ease of their successes—considering the spontaneity of each—and planning more. For two hours they talked. Bowie and Bill were anxious to proceed with more, to "put the fear of God in them." Brock was more restrained. It was his own lifelong fear of God, that Biblical grounding of growing up in the church, that had him more bridled than the others, and they talked a little about it.

Bowie said, "I've read the Bible a few times too, and still do. But have you read any of the new editions lately? That's not God's Word. The slick bastards have re-written the Rulebook. Now that the churches are teaching everybody to 'obey the government,' they've got Christians so screwed-up that nobody knows what God's Law is anymore. It is them and us who have permitted the government to act in our name and in our behalf in a criminal fashion. I, for one, am through cooperating with them. Look, I believe in God Almighty and His only Son, Jesus Christ who was conceived by the Holy Spirit, born of the Virgin Mary, suffered under Pontius Pilate, died, descended, ascended and all that . . . rose again and sitteth on the Right Hand . . . I believe all that, man. And because I believe it, I have to believe that to take up the sword and shield to defend Truth would be a Godly stand, and one that He will protect. If that goes against the grain of the current bullshit Christian tradition, then all the little wimps out there who would sit back and be content to be swallowed up into a hell on earth . . . well, let 'em bow down and worship Caesar, but he and they can just kiss my ass!"

Banneker glanced at Brock and saw a squint of incredulity before facing Bowie again. "That's quite a testimonial, Bro," he said. "You should go on the speaker's circuit for the churches around the country. Maybe if you didn't sugarcoat it so much, we could even get Pat Robertson and Jerry Falwell to make you a regular on their TV shows. Or maybe Reverend Ike. SHAZAM! And now we is proud to present Pastor Bowie Crockett, that baaad mutha' from the East Tennessee Diocese of da' Butt-Kickers for Jesus with his message for todaaay, 'If You Don't Love da' Lawd, You Can Kiss My Ass.' "

Brock had been sitting on the sofa, and when he heard the last exchange, he exploded in wild laughter, spilling half a cup of coffee on his pants as he writhed and shook. Banneker had provided some much-needed comic relief. After they all stopped snickering and agreed to the point that at least they were at war, Brock took the conversation back to the subject at hand.

"We're batting a thousand, Boys, and no one can do that forever. We've got to be careful," he said. "The more we rain down on them, the tighter their security will get."

"That's why we need to strike fast," said Banneker, "before they can get organized and get more funding for protection. Half of those morons still have their names and addresses in the phone books. We can hit 'em right on their doorsteps."

"Dang right," growled the imposing Bowie Crockett, sitting on the carpet and sipping his coffee while leaning against the wall. "Raoul told me himself that they were busting at the seams out there in Virginia City. He said Mr. Roark is talking about executing some of the worst offenders right after trial and not even giving them a chance at running in the woods. They don't need any more sporting targets out there right now. I say we take 'em out wherever they are."

Brock could not participate in that sort of thing and told them so. If they wanted to do it, fine, but he was not interested in taking out anybody except those who had assassinated his wife; and those turncoats such as Joe Day who had been instrumental in helping organize it. Don Handy had spilled his guts about the whole OLLIE trip, that he had seen Spike Thorsten write something on a list and replace it in his wallet. Handy had believed at the time that it was a list of those involved with the IRS Hit Squad in various cities in the country.

"I say we go to Washington and pick up Spike Thorsten and find that list in his billfold. Then if you guys want to declare war on the Hit Squad, I'll be with you. But to just indiscriminately take out anyone who happens to work for the IRS is more than I want to be involved with. I guess I am saying that I will kill if I have to in war, but to butcher innocent people who don't even know that they are on the wrong side in a war is too much. We couldn't get away with it for very long anyway, and when we were finally killed, the government-controlled news media would make us look like radical fools. No, we must work covertly and knock out the enemy in his most vulnerable positions. I know there is a thin line here, but I hope you understand me. I cannot make those families husbandless and fatherless just because he held that job. Now give me the guy who killed Sarah, and I'll cut him up one square inch at a time. I've got no problem with retaliating against those who did it to me, but I only want to assume the role of defender, not aggressor. Does that make sense?"

Even the strongest Christians have a breaking point when it comes to turning the other cheek.

"It makes perfect sense to me," replied Bowie, "but I just happen not to share the same consideration for the scum-suckers. Look, ole buddy, I'll help you take care of your problem any way you want to handle it. But please pardon me, if, in my spare time, I wander off the beaten path occasionally to participate in a little extracurricular entertainment . . ."

"Yeah, me too," interrupted Bill Banneker. "I have to agree with Brock that the clerks and auditors are innocent workers who don't have any idea what master plan they are involved with. The soldiers in their army are the gun-toters, and that is every man and woman in the Criminal Investigation Division. I see no cause for restraint in a war against them."

". . . and I say if we are at war," continued Crockett, "then we are at war with every one of the bastards. The more we take out, the more the next son of a bitch will think before he joins up with them. You can't stop the rooster from crowing once the sun is up. Well, the sun is up."

Banneker interjected again with, "You got that right! They are all the enemy. Your daddy didn't ask what their rank was when he fired at 'em in the South Pacific," he directed at Brock. "And the colonists took 'em out if they were wearing a red coat. Period. The enemy is the enemy, I say. They are either with us or against us, and, as long as they carry IRS credentials, they are wearing the red coats. But I do agree that our primary targets must be the CID and not the beancounters."

Brock knew he had two tough confederates, and he was glad they were on his side. He didn't want to lose them. "Just how much impact do you two think you can have against an army that is in the thousands?"

"A helluva lot more than you think, Bro," Banneker said, "and don't forget, we are not alone. We are not just *two*. There are a few thousand of us around the country just as dedicated. Maybe not organized yet, but just as dedicated. The bureaucrats try to put the fear in us by sending people to jail and blowing it all over the news. We'll put the fear in them by blowing away their cohorts from the earth."

The room went quiet for a half minute while Brock pondered that declaration. Would they *ever* get organized he wondered. Probably not, but it might be better if they didn't. They just might be more effective if they remained in guerilla warfare unrelated to any leadership. *The Unorganized Militia, but suddenly on the offensive rather than just maintaining the ordinary defensive mode.* Some of them might be captured, even killed, but this fashion of warfare would make it impossible for the enemy to ever round up the masses. He knew from history that it was this unsophisticated technique that had finally driven the British out of the colonies two centuries ago. It had stopped Sherman from ever burning Montgomery, and it had been responsible for the death of thousands of American soldiers in Vietnam. How can one defend against an unknown enemy? Brock knew that his confederates had a viable plan for what they wanted to do. He just did not wish to be in that war. But there was one war that he had to win—for Brent and Maria, and especially for Sarah—and the mode of attack had to be exactly what they had discussed. There was no other choice. To be organized with outsiders was to court eventual disaster by infiltration.

"Okay," he relented. "You guys help me do what I've got to do. It will help satisfy your inner needs as well. If we can take out this Hit Squad, we can deal a major blow to the opposition. I will finance it. Anything else you want to do meantime or afterwards is your business. I don't even want to know about it, but if I happen to find out about any of it, I promise you my lips are sealed. I will go to jail for life or even to the gas chamber before I will ever mention your names to the enemy. Can you give me the same pledge?"

"Damn right," they both said in unison, as if they had been reading from a script. A tighter bond than the earlier undeclared one had been formed. There was newer madness in this driving obsession.

"Okay. Here's what we do. Now that we've got Thorsten's private number . . ."

*   *   *   *   *

The *Cessna Citation* came thundering onto the strip at Hyde Field near Clinton, Maryland, three miles southwest of Andrews Air Force Base. The sun was sinking with no warmth in the western sky as the three businessmen, two white and one black, with briefcases in hand, got off and unobtrusively entered the terminal and requested a taxi for the Henley Park Hotel, a mile north of the Federal Triangle. Clean shaven with spit-shined shoes, they appeared as though their satchels might have contained government proposals and contracts. The last thing anyone would have imagined was the truth, that the bags actually contained handcuffs, rope, and firearms—Bill's Uzi, Bowie's Colt .357 Magnum, and Brock's Smith and Wesson, 14-shot, .9mm semi-automatic pistol.

While in the cab, they small-talked about their proposed visit to see the senator from Ohio and little else. The cab driver was typically reticent and if ever questioned, would remember little of his three passengers. He hauled a dozen of these colorless frumps everyday and was long ago bored stiff with their big shot conversations.

The Henley Park was originally constructed as an apartment building in 1918 and recently converted to a small hotel, offering a bit of Britain in the antediluvian neighborhood near the Washington Convention Center. From their sidewalk open-air markets the costermongers hawked their fruits and vegetables with the same pert and cheeky banter that Brock remembered hearing on the streets of London when he had taken Sarah and the children there for a holiday just two summers before. Once inside the Tudor architecture and surrounded by the Edwardian decor, Brock and Bowie took a seat in the cozy sitting room with the working fireplace which could well have been transplanted from an English country house. It was a perfect location. Both their target and the car rental agency would be only a short bus ride away tomorrow.

Bill Banneker stepped to the front desk while the others unassumingly relaxed on the lobby sofa with the magazines and newspapers. The smiling bellman with the amusing British accent had already placed the one small suitcase each had been carrying on the dollie in preparation for pushing it to the elevator.

"Good evening, Ma'm, I'm Frank Hamer from Dallas. I believe you're holding my reservation for a two bedroom suite."

"Was it guaranteed, Mr. Hamer?" said the attractive brunette behind the counter whose name-tag announced that she was "Donna."

"Yes ma'm. Two days ago. I have the confirmation number in my briefcase, if you need it."

"Not necessary, Mr. Hamer," she replied after three seconds of dialing the computer. "I have it right here. For two nights. Is that correct?"

"It is. But we may need it for a third. I'll let you know."

"And how many people?"

"Two," he lied. What the hell. Keep 'em confused. A suite is a suite is a suite. They're going to charge us an arm and a leg as it is.

"Fine. Just fill in the particulars, sign here, please and give me your credit card for confirmation." She zipped it through the slot on the small card-checking machine on the countertop.

"Frank Hamer" completed the form by giving a contrived address on Mockingbird Lane in Dallas, the zip code which he had already ascertained to be correct, and his signature. The pleasant lady returned his credit card, handed him two card keys and added, "Mr. Hamer, you will be in three-nineteen. Please, if you can, let us know before noon tomorrow whether or not you will be staying the third day. The Orioles are in town this weekend, and we usually sell out on Saturday and Sunday when they are. More people stay in Washington than in Baltimore."

"Thanks for the tip, Donna. I'll do my best."

"Thank-*you*, sir. Your bellman will show you to your suite."

"By the way, how much am I paying?"

"Three seventy-five, sir, plus tax."

"Thank-you," Bill said once more, hoping Brock would not get an attack of apoplexy at the news.

Bill and the bellman took the elevator to the third floor of the high-rise, chatting discursively about the weather and the Redskins chances to repeat. Once inside the suite, he thanked him, tipped him with three bucks, and dialed the switchboard from the living room telephone.

"Please page Mr. Tom Paine; I believe he is in the lobby."

A minute later Bowie greeted him on a house phone.

"We are in 319," said Bill. "C'mon up."

"Three, one, nine," Bowie repeated. "We're on the way."

Bowie strolled back to the lobby couch and told Brock the instructions. Brock, never looking up from his newspaper, grunted an "Em-hmmm," and tarried a few extra minutes behind Bowie before taking the elevator to the third floor and gently rapping on the door of 319.

The suite had all the comforts of home and a few more luxuries. There was a king-size bed in one bedroom and two queen sizes in the other. The living room had a sofa, love seat, soft chair, dinner and card tables, and a wet bar. The kitchenette in the corner had a small refrigerator, microwave oven, and drawers and shelves full of silverware and crockery. They flipped coins in a short game of "Odd Man Out," and Brock won the king-size bed. Bill thought he should have had it in the first place because he was paying for all this, but Brock was wanting to surrender it to Bowie because of his size. Their light-hearted argument could only be settled one way, Bill decided. "Let the gods of chance tell us."

After he was relegated to the room he was to share with Bill, Bowie was heard to mutter, "I'd rather sleep on top of a queen than a king any day, but don't be going to bed with no dollar in your hand, Boy." Banneker smiled and ignored him.

"Hey, Bill, by the way," Brock inquired, who is this Mr. Hamer, and where did you get his credit card? I heard the lady at the desk call you "Mr. Hamer."

"A hero of mine. Captain Frank Hamer of the Texas Rangers during the depression years. He had been retired for a couple of years when they asked him to come back and track down Bonnie Parker and Clyde Barrow. He got 'em finally in Arcadia, Louisiana and shot 'em to pieces. I read his story last year in an old *Readers Digest* I found in a box of books I picked up at an antique store in Indianapolis."

"So how did you get his credit card?"

"C'mon, Man, join the real world of sleuthing. This is not *his* credit card. He never heard of a stinking credit card. He'd be a hundred and something now if he were still alive. I just admired the guy when I read about him and decided his name would make a nice alias. The rest was easy. It took a little time, but I got a driver's license and a voter registration card. After I established and used the bank account for a few months, all the credit card companies were busting a gut to issue me one of their cards. I have been building this I.D. for a year or more now, and it's clean. I've only used it when I've needed it to rent a car or something, and I've always paid the bills on time. I've got several different ones, but I decided Frank Hamer's was the appropriate one to use for this mission."

"Not that it matters, but isn't that against the law?"

"No, as a matter of fact it is not unlawful under the common law to go by any name you want, as long as you don't use it to defraud someone. The feds would like for it to be illegal under their admiralty jurisdiction, and I am sure they can dream up some statute to fit it. But, remember, I am not in that jurisdiction. Under the common law, you are who you say you are."

"Okay. Let's get settled in here, guys," Brock said to his two jocular confederates. "We've got work to do. Meeting time is in ten minutes right here around this table. Who wants coffee?"

When there were no other takers, Brock boiled some water and fixed himself a cup of decaf from one of the packets he found in the drawer. Once around the table, they tossed around the few remaining ideas that had not been settled concerning the capture and execution of Spike Thorsten.

"Can you believe we are doing this?" Brock lamented. Just a year or two earlier, he would have sent for the guys in the white coats if someone had suggested that he would be here now with these guys plotting the mass murder of a dozen or more people. But he, and the others as well, knew he wasn't having second thoughts—only making a comment. He had never been more fervently dedicated to a project in his life. He knew there was no other way. While nothing less than the murder of his Sarah could have ever gotten him here, regardless, he was here, and the Hit Squad had been discovered and had to be stopped. Now it was a mission from which there could be no retreat.

"Life takes strange twists, Bro'," Bill mused. "Now think about it. Who woulda' thought just five years ago that there would come a day when I would have more money than John Connally, higher morals than Jim Bakker and Jimmy Swaggart put together, and more women in my life than Rock Hudson?"

"And more honor and integrity than that two-faced, baby-raping President of the United States," added the big laughing redhead. He loathed the former chief of the Central Intelligence Agency. Although they had never met, he knew of the mind control experiments and activities of MK-Ultra's Project Monarch—how they used child-abused women to do their dirty work and be their messengers. George Bush had more skeletons in his closet, too, and Bowie knew it and could prove it; if there were ever a court of law where the evidence could be fairly presented. But because there was never likely to be such a thing in his lifetime, all he could do was frustratingly curse about it.

"C'mon guys, let's get back to the subject at hand," Brock interjected. "We've got some serious work here."

The plan was to somehow lure Thorsten out of his office and into their trap. The best way to do that was to gain his trust, and the best way to gain his trust was to use what they knew about him from Don Handy's terrified confession—the most important of which was the number of the private phone which rang on

Thorsten's desk. An even more valuable piece of information than Thorsten himself after the capture would be that list of the Hit Squad members around the country which Handy had said Spike carried in his wallet. But they could not be certain that he still did, or ever did. They didn't think that Handy had had any reason to make that up, so it was likely true that Thorsten had it on him that day in Kansas City. But did he *always* carry it in his wallet? Maybe so, maybe not. But then if he didn't always carry it on his person, why would he have had it with him in Kansas City? The three men were satisfied that it was because he needed it with him at all times in order to be in constant contact with his team whenever necessary, and it was too damned long to memorize. If he was to be in contact, he would have to have it with him. Therefore, it was axiomatic that the odds were in their favor that Thorsten would also have it in his wallet tomorrow. There was simply no other logical place for him to keep it for quick access. He traveled too much. It would have been neither practical nor prudent for him to be calling his office every time he needed the number of one of the team members.

The next facet of the plan for group discussion was what to do with Thorsten after they had extracted the necessary information and, more imminent right now, where to do it. Kansas City was out. The spotlight of attention was too intense in that locale right now. Bowie had a friend in Philadelphia, Mississippi, who owned a lake house on Barnett Reservoir near Brandon. His family used it only on weekends during the summer and fall and seldom at all otherwise. He had given Bowie permission to use it whenever they were not there and had shown him under which flower pot to find the concealed key.

Brock vetoed that plan but followed with the idea that they may use it later in the year. Besides, the weekend was looming around the corner, and they didn't need to be interrupted on this trip by a picnicking family taking advantage of the sunshine and a day off.

They decided instead to take Mr. Thorsten to Indianapolis. Bill had a shop in his cellar that would be perfect for their plan—secluded in the country on fifty acres.

"Now what is our cover story with Thorsten?" Brock threw to the committee. "How do we get him voluntarily into the plane and keep him content for a two-hour flight?"

"Because he is going to see Handy," said Bill.

"Under what pretense?"

Bill had been thinking about this for days and was anxious to spring his ideas to his two accomplices. He told them that he would assume the name of one of their captives from Orange County or Chicago. They had a black one from each area. Thorsten was undoubtedly aware of all the missing agents and could check it readily, but he couldn't do much else except take their word for everything after that because of the secrecy of the OLLIE operation. Whom could he talk to?

Banneker's cover story would be that he and Handy had escaped from their attackers and had been hiding in a farmhouse. Handy was too sick and mutilated to travel, was alive but barely. Banneker had wanted to call the cops, but Handy wouldn't let him. He had given Banneker the private number of Thorsten's "Red Phone" along with the code name "Ollie Pike." Nobody else could know that! Handy had given him explicit instructions to talk to no one else but Spike. Thorsten would have to buy their story, and again, because of the secrecy of the mission, he would not be able to take anybody else with them. Thorsten alone would be able to get Handy out of there, with Banneker's help, of course.

"It'll work, Brock," interjected Bowie. "If I can just restrain myself from strangling the son of a bitch before we get airborne, it'll work."

"What about my jet plane? How do we explain that?"

Bill jumped back in. "Oh, you are a sympathetic friend of mine from Indianapolis who offered your help. Of course I didn't tell you the whole story. You can be my buddy, Sam Prescott, who owns a big equipment business in Indianapolis. No, better yet, you are his brother, Bob. You don't look anything like him, but it won't make any difference anyway because Thorsten won't meet you until we're ready to take off, and he will have no way of checking you out. My car is already parked and waiting for us in the airport lot when we arrive."

Brock thought on it for a half minute while trying to cover every base. "Handy knew what I looked like. It would have been a simple matter for them to have gotten a dozen shots of me outside of the courthouse the day of the inquest—or anywhere else before or since. We know they've had me under surveillance. What if he has already sent my picture to Thorsten?"

"That's possible," replied Bill. "So we'll have you already in the pilot's seat warming up the engines when we board with him. I'll get on first, Thorsten next, and Bowie will be right behind him. If he recognizes you and tries anything funny, Crockett can put him in the famous Mountain Red hammerlock. We'll watch him close.

"What about Bowie? What's his story?"

" 'Tom Paine' works for you and traveled with us, that's all. He is Sam Prescott's lackey. Maybe even his bodyguard."

"Okay," said Brock, "let's do it. Get Raoul on your magic phone in Virginia City and find out which one of those black guys out there looks the most like you."

"Hell, Brock," Bowie couldn't resist saying, "Raoul cain't tell. You know all them black dudes look alike."

"Kiss my ass, Honkie," retorted Banneker.

"Okay," Brock laughed, "but find out which one you are closest to in size and age, and we just won't give Thorsten any time to check any photo records once we make contact with him."

"That'll work," said Crockett. He fired up his magic cellular and dialed the 702 area and the number in Virginia City for Raoul and delivered his message. Raoul promised to get back with them before the night was over. Bowie reminded him that they were three hours ahead of him and their night would be over much sooner than his. Raoul then said he would be back to them in two hours. With their system, the call was untraceable.

"Let's go find some dinner. I'm hungry enough to eat a dozen live lizards."

"Okay, anywhere but in the motel dining room you want to go, and any place we can walk to," admonished Brock. "No cabs except back to the airport tomorrow and no phone calls from this room—local or long distance. None, zilch, nada."

They asked at the desk, walked, and found a small diner three blocks away.

"Eat heartily, men," Brock told them. "We won't have the time for any breakfast in the morning."

Bill Banneker slept in his suit coat that night.

NINETEEN

The red phone on Spike Thorsten's desk rang five times at 7:45 A.M., and no one answered. Bill tried it again at eight with the same result. "Lazy ass, good-for-nothing bureaucrat," he muttered to the others on the sidewalk outside the phone booth. "He's probably on the golf course or in the congressional sauna room getting a rubdown." Bowie sat behind the wheel in the rental car curbside next to the phone booth. Brock leaned on the fender outside.

At 8:10 Bill tried again with no success but ten minutes later hit the jackpot. The phone was picked up on the third ring.

"Yeah," growled the unfriendly voice on the other end of the line. Bill signalled the "A-okay" sign with his thumb and forefinger to the others outside the glass-enclosed booth and went into his story.

"Mr. Pike? Ollie Pike?" he said in a harried tone.

"Yes. Who's calling?

"Mr. Pike, you don't know me, but please don't hang up. This is an emergency. My name is George Anderson, and I'm with the Service in Chicago. You may be aware that I've been missing since August 20th. I was kidnapped. I am calling for your friend Don Handy. He said you were the only one who could help him. He and I were confined together along with six others, and Don and I managed to escape. I wanted to . . ."

Thorsten interrupted with, "Where is he?"

"He's safe for now, but he's going to die if we don't get back to him real quick. He's got water, and I left him enough food for a couple of days. I wanted to call the police, but he wouldn't let me, and he said that I couldn't tell anyone but you where he is. He said he was on a different detail than I had ever heard of, and he couldn't tell me any more. He said the onliest way I could help him was by contacting you, that you would know what to do."

"Yeah, that's right, but where in the hell is he, Anderson?"

"That's another thing he told me, Mr. Pike. Don't be talking long about it on this phone. He said to just tell enough that you would know I was telling the truth and then hang up and meetcha' somewhere. He said the fact that I had this number and could tell you the name 'Ollie Pike' was enough of the private code for you to trust me. He told me that if you had any doubts, I was to use the word 'OLLIE' by itself, and you would understand. Do you trust me, Mr. Pike?"

"Okay, yes, I believe you. Where are you?" Spike said, and then cursed to himself that he had never installed the caller I.D. on the Red Phone. Since his number was known by only a dozen men, it never seemed necessary. But he wished he could check this guy out right now while they talked.

"I'm on Tenth Street across from Ford's Theater. There's a small diner just north of the Peterson House, you know where they took Lincoln after he got shot? Well, right next door is a diner where we can meet. I'm gonna' go 'head and have me some breakfast. I been up all night travelin' to see you. But I ain't got any money. Can you pay for it?"

"Yes, of course, and I know where it is. It's only a five minute cab ride. I'll be there in ten or fifteen at the most."

"Yessir, I have a car, so you won't need yours, but be sure to come alone, Mr. Pike. Don told me not to talk to you with anyone else around."

"Don't worry, I'll be alone. See ya shortly."

Bill stepped out of the booth with both his thumbs up. "We got him. He said he'd be here in ten minutes. Right now, you can bet, he's checking that computer for George Anderson's particulars."

"Good," said Bowie. If he gets here that fast, we'll know he didn't have time to get wired up."

Bill considered that for a moment, discerning the meaning, and said, "No, I don't think we have to worry about that. He went for it hook, line, and sinker. Now I've just got to convince him to get on that plane with us."

Brock caught a cab for the airport in Clinton to prepare for takeoff. Bill walked the half block to the designated diner to have breakfast, and Bowie drove and parked the newly rented car in a choice parking space he had found, and walked a minute behind Banneker to stand near the door of the diner to wait for Thorsten's arrival.

Ten minutes later the Yellow Cab stopped in the parking zone at 516 tenth Street NW in front of the Petersen House where President Lincoln's blood on the pillow case had been viewed by a few million curious and slightly morbid visitors since he died there in 1865. Crockett already presumed that the most deranged and bloodthirsty of all was arriving now and emerging from this taxi. If this was his man, he would not enter the Petersen House, Crockett surmised, but would come toward him next door at the diner. When the man did just that and paused to take a last drag off a cigarette before flipping it in the gutter and walking by him toward the diner's door, Bowie said, "Mr. Pike?"

Spike Thorsten was six feet tall, fifty pounds overweight, and, today at least, had an ashen look about him. He stopped and stared for a moment, wondering who this giant white man was who not only knew his super-private cryptonym but appeared to know something more about his business. "Yes," he half-whispered. "Who are you?"

"I'm Tom, Mr. Pike. Don't worry 'bout me, I'm just helping out Mr. Anderson—helped get him here last night. I'll be your driver and will be looking after you both. He's at the third table on your left as you go in."

"Thank you, Tom."

Thorsten spotted Bill Banneker immediately after entering the diner and stepped toward the table. Bill had caught his eye and signalled a look of recognition when Thorsten first appeared inside the door. Swallowing a mouthful of scrambled eggs, Banneker was already standing with his hand extended. He had purposefully installed a serious and sober expression on his face as Thorsten approached him.

"Anderson?"

"Hello, Mr. Pike, I'm George Anderson. I'm so glad you came. I thought you might be afraid to show up."

"Hello, George. No. If you can help me find Don Handy, I have to know how. I was afraid he was dead."

"No sir! He's not dead, but he's damn near it. We've got to help him."

"And what about the gorilla at the door?"

"That's our bodyguard, Tom, and he has been a great help to me. He was out renting the car while I was trying to call you."

"May I see some I.D.?" Thorsten said officiously.

Bill had expected this and was ready.

"I don't have a thing. They took it all from me. Meanest bunch of rednecks I've ever met. They cut off Handy's fingers . . ."

"Which hand?"

"Uh," . . . *Uh oh, He's testing me. Just stay in character and I'll be okay. I'm George Anderson from Chicago* . . . "uh, his right, and he told me they threatened to slowly cut off more and more body parts until he talked, and they probably would have sooner or later. But he didn't tell them anything, as far as I know. You can be proud of him Mr. Pike, but they damn near killed him before he passed out."

Thorsten knew that wasn't quite true. Only Handy—nobody else—could have given them enough information to know where to send those fingers, but he didn't deem it necessary to mention this to Anderson, at least not at this time.

"What's your wife's name, Anderson?"

"Mildred. I have two sons, George, Jr. and Troy. We live at 10548 South Mason in Chicago."

"What's your badge number?"

"564." Banneker had done his homework after talking with Raoul the night before.

"Good enough. Okay," Thorsten said, looking up from notes he was writing down on his pocket tablet. "Where is Handy now?" He seemed satisfied that the information was adequate for an accurate I.D.

"In the cellar of a farmhouse near Indianapolis. We slipped away during the night and walked about two miles to this occupied but vacant farmhouse. The people must be out of town, and we have no way of knowing when they might return. I found some food in the refrigerator upstairs and left him a jug of drinking water, but he's a dying man without a lot of time left. We've got to get back there and get him out. And he won't leave with anybody but you. He refuses to call the sheriff and won't go to a local hospital, either. He said you were the only man in the world who could solve his problem, and that's why I am here. You the only man in the world. Period. That's what he said."

"When did you leave him?"

"It was just about this time last night." Banneker looked at the clock on the wall and saw it was straight up nine o'clock. "He's been alone for twelve hours now."

He went on to tell Thorsten that his wealthy friend in Indianapolis had dispatched a jet plane and a pilot along with his bodyguard, Tom Paine, who was waiting out front with the rental car to take them to the airport. They had slept a few hours in lounge chairs at the airport terminal waiting for Thorsten's office to open. Their pilot had slept in the plane and was waiting for them to make the return trip. Neither of them had any knowledge of why they were in Washington except that their boss had told them to bring "George" there for an appointment and to fly him back when he was ready. Bill Banneker was putting on the acting performance of his life.

Then he moved in to close the sale. "Is there any reason why you can't leave right now? We've got to get Don out of there and to some medical attention as soon as possible."

"You're right. I can leave right now if your friend will let us use his plane to fly Don back here. Can you impose on him for another trip? I can arrange to reimburse his expenses later."

"Yes, I am sure we can do that. No problem."

"Good, because I want to put Don in a hospital back here with our own doctors to look after him. How long a flight is it, about two hours?"

He means Bethesda, where perfectly healthy but disobedient men walk in for "treatment" and are rolled out on a gurney and placed in a hearse a few days later. Some have been known to "jump" out of the upper story windows. The son of a bitch wants to kill him at Bethesda, Banneker figured.

"A little less. We can be back this evenin', maybe before the work day is over," Banneker assured him with confidence.

"Fine. Finish eating, Anderson, while I tell my office not to expect me any more today. Then I'll be ready to ride. We need to get going. I'll get your breakfast."

"Good," Banneker replied, " 'Cause, like I told ja, I ain't got any money, anyway. I was countin' on Tom to pay for this if you didn't show up."

Bill did not feel good about allowing Thorsten to make a call, but he did as he was told. Much as he wanted to remain in charge, he was, after all, playing the part of a lackey. Thorsten had not thought to learn the name of Sam Prescott or his company name, so he could not run a check on the plane or anything of value anyway. Once they were airborne, it would be all over for Spike Thorsten. As Banneker rushed down the last of his toast and coffee, he heard Thorsten on the phone at the nearby cashier's counter say, "Jeanie, I'll be out all day and cannot be reached. I'll call you after lunch for any messages," and watched him hang up the phone.

Beautiful. The fat bastard didn't tell her anything. We've got him.

*   *   *   *   *

Bowie turned in the rental car while the other two used the bathroom facilities in the lobby of the small airport. They boarded the *Citation* in the pre-planned manner without incident. When Bill introduced their pilot as only "Bob," Brock said hello without turning full face toward their quarry. Bowie was poised and ready in back of him, but Thorsten showed no reaction. He had no interest, either, in the pilot remembering what he looked like and paid little attention.

It was a little after noon, C.D.T., when Brock was talking with the Indianapolis tower for final clearance and lowering his flaps for landing. The flight had gone smoothly in great weather all the way. In order to appear more as the company pilot to Thorsten and participate less in any conversation, he had sat in the cockpit alone. The other three had remained in the back where the conversation had remained at a minimum. With Bowie nearby, Thorsten couldn't ask "George Anderson" many questions about Handy, and that is the way they wanted it. Except for explaining that they had left their car at the airport and it was a forty minute ride to the farmhouse from there—the airport was southwest and they had to drive northeast just beyond Noblesville—they did not discuss the main subject at hand. Instead, Banneker tried to keep the dialogue light with casual chat about his beloved Chicago Bears' chances against the Super Bowl Champion Redskins in the fall. Thorsten, after airing his dislike for Bear Head Coach Mike Ditka, was more eager to read the morning paper, which had suited Banneker and Crockett just fine. They both took notice of the bulge in Spike's coat produced by the pistol and shoulder holster underneath but said nothing.

As Thorsten was stepping down the ladder ramp onto the tarmac behind Brock, Bill, still on the plane behind him, slipped his car keys and parking receipt into Bowie's hand and whispered the instructions as to where to locate the automobile. "Don't forget, it's your car," he said, "George doesn't have one."

"I was wondering when you would think of that," Bowie whispered back in a sportive taunt.

By the time Brock had completed his business with the terminal manager for the parking of the plane, and all had had a bathroom stop, Bowie was pulling up out front in Banneker's fancy Buick station wagon. He had removed the magnetic real estate signs from the front doors and stashed them behind the backseat under a blanket. Freeman rode in front with Crockett. Banneker and Spike Thorsten got in the back seat. Forty minutes later they arrived at his house in the country and, with the other two following closely behind, Banneker led Thorsten toward the cellar door. Heinrich was barking from his pen, taking nips out of the silence in the evening air.

"I hope he's still all right," Bill bluffed one last time. "He sure will be glad to see us, especially you, Mr. Pike."

As they descended the cellar stairs, Bill called Don's name loudly several times and got no answer. Before Thorsten had time to ask any questions, Bowie was down the stairs two at a time and was placing him in a hammerlock. Bill spun around and reached into Thorsten's coat and removed the Beretta .380 automatic. Then he reached to the rear pants pocket and took his wallet. Thorsten turned white as Bill began to look at the driver's license confirming that Spratlin P. Thorsten was their prisoner.

At the other side of the semi-furnished basement was a pool table, a quarter slot machine, and a large old photograph of Bill's parents suspended in an archaic frame above the fireplace. They looked like the black version of Grant Wood's "American Gothic."

"Spratlin!?" Bowie exclaimed upon hearing the announcement. Is that what the 'S' stands for in his name? Gyat dyam, lardass," he exclaimed, turning toward Thorsten, "no wonder you don't tell anybody what it is. Sprat-lin," he repeated slowly, almost spitting it. "Cheeeit."

"Mr. Thorsten," Bill announced with histrionic aplomb, "like the newspapers headlined when the first black astronaut went into space, 'The Jig is Up.' You are a prisoner of war. You may cooperate readily and painlessly, or you may undergo the worst torture you have ever imagined, after which you will be eager to cooperate anyway, I guarantee it."

With that, Bowie released his hold momentarily before hammering the back of Spike's head with a right hand shot that sent him sprawling across the concrete floor. As Thorsten lay there counting the stars in his eyes, Bowie placed his big foot on the back of his neck while Bill removed his suit coat, tore off his shirt, and placed handcuffs around his wrists behind him. Then they rolled him over and removed his shoes, then his pants. In his high socks they found a small dagger in a sheath strapped to his right calf, which was the purpose of the exercise.

"Are you carrying any other weapons?" Banneker demanded.

"No," came the docile, muffled reply from the floor.

Bowie removed his foot and reached one hand down to the handcuff chain between Thorsten's wrists and lifted him off the floor from the rear by his arms. Spike screamed with both pain and terror as Crockett walked, lifted, and planted him in a sitting position on the large metal carpenter's table in Banneker's workshop.

"Listen, Meathead," Bowie was yelling in his face. "Handy is still alive because he told us everything we wanted to know and didn't lie to us. But he is still in custody, and we are still maintaining the option. You cooperate, and you get the same fair treatment. Bullshit us and you'll die with your nuts in your mouth. Do I make myself clear?"

"Yes, yes, no problem," he whimpered. "I'll tell you whatever you want to know, just don't hurt me."

Bowie was calmly cleaning his nails with the dagger point. "And your stories better match up, because anything we need to check with Handy, we can, in about thirty minutes. And you both will get a fair trial. Yours is beginning right now, with you on the witness stand first."

Unlike the first confrontation with Handy when Brock had taken charge, he now was letting his two confederates carry on the interrogation of the prisoner. He was anxious to know the details of what had happened at his house the previous Thanksgiving but already had learned the basics from Handy. Any unanswered questions as to the particulars he might be wondering about they would squeeze out of him in due time. Meanwhile, the team of Banneker and Crockett became the prosecution attorneys. They fatuously informed Thorsten of his right to counsel and offered their pilot, "who has been to law school," as his court-appointed attorney.

"Mister Spike Thorsten," Bill then said dramatically, "I would like to introduce you to Mister Brock Freeman . . ."

Spike's eyes enlarged in a look of holy terror as the recognition of the name hit him like a hammer.

". . . Mister Freeman is from the prestigious Kansas City law firm of Dewey, Cheatham, and Howe, and will exert all his best efforts in an attempt to pull a magic rabbit from his hatful of legal tricks in order to save your ass, I mean your life. We must maintain the proper courtroom decorum here.

Thorsten politely refused with a "No, thank you."

"Then let the record show," announced Banneker, with a grin, "that the defendant has waived his right to counsel and is appearing *pro se* as his own attorney. Didn't you ever hear the legal adage, Mr. Thorsten, that he who acts as his own lawyer has a fool for a client?"

"Yeah," Spike replied, playing along with their foolishness, "but somehow I don't believe this man will be acting in my own best interests."

"Oh," added Bowie. "You mean our court-appointed attorney might be slightly biased and just a wee bit beholden to the prosecution. Just like federal court back home, ain't it, Spike? Good, because we want you to feel right at home here. Okay, Mr. Freeman, if he doesn't want you, I guess you can join us at the prosecutor's table."

They dragged up three card table chairs and sat in front of Spike to begin the inquisition, and during the next hour they asked everything they could think of concerning Spike Thorsten's tenure with the IRS. They learned the details of the multiple rapes that had gotten him kicked out of the FBI, his years in Texas, the creative plots that had quickly elevated him to an executive office in Washington, and the creation of the OLLIE assassination team in recent years.

Finally, they were ready for the *coup de grace*. Banneker took the initiative.

"Spike, you have told us some very interesting things we did not know about your history. But you should also be aware that Don Handy has told us some things about you that you don't know we know. And if your stories don't match, one of you is going to die today. Lying is a capital offense in this court. It carries the death penalty. Once again, just like your friends in federal court, we make our own rules. You have not been placed under oath because we don't administer any goddam oaths in our court. You are under the threat of death. Tell the truth or die. Now, tell this court, how many people are involved in Operation Loss Leader?"

Thorsten glared at them for ten seconds before resignedly offering, "Twelve. Thirteen including myself."

"And who are they, and where?"

The afternoon heat was starting to overcome the damp coolness that had permeated the cellar when they first entered. For this and other reasons, Thorsten was beginning to perspire. He twisted his head to wipe his face on the shoulder of his tee shirt, his hands still cuffed behind his back. His grotesque pot belly hung over the elastic waist band of his boxer shorts. He paused, obviously mentally squirming to find a way to avoid answering this question. Then he hit on what might be the only way.

"Uhh . . . I don't think I could tell you all that from memory without, you know, referring to my computer records in my office."

"Well, try, Fat ass."

"Emmm, there's Don Handy, of course, in Kansas City, Jack Savage in Portland, and . . . oh yeah, uhh, Murdoch in Phoenix. Henry, I think is his first name."

Brock was busily flipping pages of a steno pad and scribbling down the names and cities.

"Who else? said Banneker.

Thorsten pondered some more before saying, "Leonard Burr is our man in Atlanta and Lance Purvis in San Diego. That's all I can think of off-hand."

"Don't you keep a list anywhere else like in your wallet here?"
"No."

"How can you maintain contact when you are out of the office.?"

"I only call them when I am in the office. On the off-chance that I might need to contact one of them when I am out, I can just call Jeanie, my secretary, and she can look up the numbers for me."

Damn! Bill thought. *The lardass must be telling the truth. He knows we're going to check his wallet.* He had a sinking feeling at the thought that they had missed the bonanza list of all the team members. He rose with the wallet in hand and stepped to the table beside Thorsten and began to riffle the dozens of cards and papers he found inside all the leather pockets, while continuing to interrogate the prisoner.

"Let me jog your memory a little, Spike. How about Boston? Do you have a team man in Boston?

"No. Nobody in Boston."

"Miami?"

"No."

"Cleveland?"

"No.

"Detroit?"

"Nope."

"All right. Let's try out west. Los Angeles or San Francisco?

"No."

"You mentioned Portland. How about Seattle?"

"Uhh, yes." Thorsten knew he was backed in a corner. "There *is* a guy in Seattle. Vito something or 'nother. It's a long Italian name I always have to look up on the computer. Never could remember how to pronounce it."

Of course. Most of the tax protestor movements had sprung up out west, so it was normal that most of the IRS's covert operation would be concentrated there. And by admitting to the city without divulging any names, Thorsten had not really told them anything.

"Okay. Now, while I finish checking out these papers, I want you to think very carefully about something very important, and Mr. Freeman is very interested in your answer to this one."

Thorsten looked up at Banneker, wanting to say *What's that?* but not daring to. He stubbornly waited. Bill glared back sober-faced as did the other two still sitting in the chairs in front of them. Finally Banneker dropped the bombshell Thorsten had to have known was coming sooner or later.

"Where did you spend last Thanksgiving?"

"Oh, hell, I don't know."

"Well, think about it."

Spike began to perspire more. He sat and stared into space but did not answer.

"Were you with your family?"

"I'm sure I was. We're always together for holidays, but I can't remember where we were last year."

"Let me help you. Do you know a Kansas City gynecologist by the name Dr. Martin Goldman?"

Thorsten stared into space again. His eyes began to glaze and he began to whimper. He emitted a weak, childish shriek. He wasn't wailing and blubbering but silently whimpering as a youngster who had just gotten the news that his favorite dog had died. Then he lowered his head and began to cry harder and shake all over. The other three knew he was about to crack, and waited. Banneker paused, not out of sympathy or respect, but to pounce on his prey at the proper moment. A full minute later he re-phrased the question.

"Spike, I believe you were about to tell us about your relationship with Dr. Marty Goldman."

"He did it, guys; I didn't," Thorsten retorted.

"Did what, Spike?"

"He shot Mrs. Freeman."

"How do you know? Were you there?"

"No, I wasn't there. Don Handy told me."

"How would he know. Was he there?"

"Yes," Spike lied. "He drove the car."

"Where were you?"

"I was in Kansas City, but I wasn't at Mr. Freeman's house. I was back at the Overland Park office when they returned and told me about it. Handy has had the collar on Goldman for a year or two now. It's not the first work Goldman did for Handy. I know he killed a farmer out in Kansas, too."

"What do you mean *he's had the collar on him?*"

"Goldman got way behind on his tax payments, owed us several hundred thousand. After Handy began his investigation, he discovered all kinds of money-laundering shit and evidence of evasion, and he was about to prosecute Goldman criminally when they came to an agreement. The doc could do some things for the service in exchange for not having to go to jail for a few years."

Brock was out of his seat and incensed. "You mean like murder?! You bastards trap innocent people into doing your killing for you? Is that what you are saying? Is this what you do all over the country?"

Thorsten lowered his head again and half whispered, "It has happened before and in other places, yes."

"How many other places?"

"I don't know exactly."

"Lots or a few?"

Spike admitted hesitatingly, "Lots."

Bill Banneker had finished going through Spike's wallet, finding nothing more interesting than phone numbers of several of his girl friends—identified by first name only. Bill beckoned the other three to the side of the room where they could talk quietly, while keeping an eye on the pathetic Spike Thorsten who was still seated on the carpenter's table in his underwear with his hands cuffed behind his back.

They agreed that Spike was holding out on them concerning the other names of his Hit Squad, and it was obvious that either he or Handy had lied about who drove the car on Thanksgiving night. Bowie thought it was Thorsten and that he was lying right now to save his own ass. But Handy had had the same heat put on him a few weeks ago, Banneker pointed out, and could have been lying at that time to save himself. Brock just listened and reserved judgment for later but offered that this technical point was not as important right now as was extracting the rest of the names somehow from Thorsten.

"Damn!" whispered Banneker. "I was sure that what you had told me about Handy having seen the list in Spike's wallet was going to mean he still had it there."

"Me too," said Bowie. "But it obviously ain't on him today."

"Listen, he's afraid to lie to us," Brock proposed. "All we have to do is hit correctly on some other cities where he has a man, and that will serve to remind him of the name. He's covering up about not knowing who they are, but let's play his silly game."

They were spared the trouble. Strolling back to their quarry, Brock noticed one of Spike's cordovan shoes that Bill had thrown aside earlier. The inner sole was hanging loose at the heel. He picked up the shoe and dislodged the inner sole. He noticed that it was the modern, watery cushion type designed for more comfort. He picked up the other shoe and did the same. When he removed the second inner sole, out popped a sheet of paper neatly folded letter-style to fit the length of the shoe. Upon unfolding it he found it was exactly what he had anticipated it to be—the coveted list of twelve names and phone numbers in twelve different cities. He quickly recognized the few correct names that Thorsten had already given them—Lance Purvis in the 619 area code, Henry Murdoch at 602, Jack Savage at 503, and the long, unpronounceable Italian name at 206. Spike, busied at the moment by the attention of Banneker and Crockett, had not seen what Brock had just found.

Brock marched over to join the others and, holding the sheet of paper behind his back, said, "Let me interrupt you gentlemen for a moment. Spike, can you think of any other names of your team members in any other places around the country?"

"No, Mr. Freeman, I'm sorry, I can't without my computer printout."

"And you say you have not ever made such a printout to carry with you when you are away from the office, is that right?"

"Right. I just haven't had any reason to need it."

"And just what is this," Brock said as he swung his hand back in front of him, clutching the paper, "your Christmas list?"

"Where in hell did you find that, Brock?" Bowie exclaimed, snatching it from Brock's hand before Spike could answer. Bill ran around the two of them to have a look. Spike Thorsten was hoisted by his own petard.

"The lying pig had it in his shoe. So we must assume, because he is a proven liar, that he also lied about driving the car on Thanksgiving. I think it is time for the jury to convene, gentlemen."

"Who the hell is the jury," asked Thorsten, dumbfounded.

"We are, you flabby piece of pig shit," barked Crockett, "and today we're gonna' allow you to sit in the jury room. Proceedings are starting right now. Okay, who wants to be foreman?"

Banneker said, "We don't need a foreman, Mr. Crockett; let's just vote. I think the evidence is clear that the defendant has lied to us in blatant disregard for the rules of this court. I also feel that he is guilty of Conspiracy to Murder, in that he probably was the driver of the car on the night Dr. Martin Goldman killed Sarah Freeman. I am now convinced that he lied about that, and that Don Handy told you the truth."

Before Bowie could reply, Brock said, "Okay, Mr. Banneker. Point well taken. How do you vote, Mr. Crockett?"

"Guilty as charged, and I think we should execute the son of a bitch twice. Once for each count. How about you, Mr. Freeman?"

Bill Banneker was incredulous. "How are you going to kill the son of a bitch twice, Bowie?" he wanted to know.

"Easy. First we take a *lloonnnggg* time to kill him. So long that he wishes he was dead. We could hang him up by his ankles right over there, paint a target on his back, and play darts. Then we put him out of his misery about three days from now after he spends his final night in an ant bed. Just the way his government trained us in the CIA. C'mon, Brock. How do you vote?"

"Guilty!"

The terrified Spike Thorsten was sweating again, this time as if a spigot had been left on in his innards. Banneker turned to him and said, "Mr. Ollie Pike Asshole Thorsten, this court has found you guilty of Lying and Conspiracy to Murder, not necessarily in that order, and sentences you to death. Execution is to be carried out immediately. Pray that God takes care of your soul, 'cause yo' ass is mine."

Bowie hammered Spike in the stomach with a right as hard as Brock had ever seen anyone hit. Crockett's fist disappeared all the way up to the forearm. As Spike pirouetted on his ass from the table edge, about to topple onto the floor, Bill punched him in the face, knocking him backwards, before Bowie caught him, flipped him over on his stomach and slammed him lengthwise onto the table. Spike's hands were clasped tightly behind his back, and his chin hung off the end of the metal table. Bill placed a wastebasket on the floor at the end of the table while Bowie held the convict in place. Brock pulled a third time on the chainsaw rope before the motor roared into action. He adjusted the throttle and handed the clamoring machine to Bill.

"You may have the pleasure, Mr. Banneker," he told him. "Dr. Goldman is mine." He handed the roaring piece of machinery to Bill.

In one final instinctive reaction, the horrified captive made a vain and feeble attempt to roll off the table. Bowie knocked him back down with a hard slap to the back of his head and held him above the waist. Three seconds later Spike Thorsten's head had tumbled off and his hollow neck was pouring blood into the wastebasket—first splattering, then sluggishly dripping into the wide-open eyes of his former face.

TWENTY

The three men worked past dark that evening cleaning up the cellar. Following old instructions learned from his early CIA days in Central America, Bowie used a vast array of electric tools to remove the remaining appendages from Thorsten's body. He washed the severed arms, legs, and trunk; installed them in several plastic bags, and placed them in Dawe's deep freezer along side Spike Thorsten's head. The finger tips were cut off, ground up in a meat grinder, and washed down the kitchen disposal along with the heart, lungs, kidneys, liver, and intestines.

Bill had recently paved a new driveway but had not poured the front sidewalk yet, although the crevice was dug and the forms had been laid. Without disclosing his proposed location, he silently admitted to himself that he would take sadistic pleasure in knowing that whenever the feds might come to his door looking for Spike Thorsten, they would walk on top of him en route. The three had already made other plans for disposition of the head—an immediate unanimous decision following a suggestion by Brock.

Although Bowie was the only one who seemed to desire something to eat that evening, the other two knew that they needed to do so before retiring for the night. They drove to a small restaurant in the town of Anderson where Bowie had a large sirloin with baked potato and all the trimmings. The other two ate salad only, trying to ignore their big friend's carnivorous indulgence.

Back at the house later, they uncorked a bottle of paisano and deliberated their plans for the rest of the hit team and Marty Goldman. Brock removed the list from his pocket, and Bill and Bowie each made a handwritten copy of it. After a little discussion it was concluded that they would assign Lance Purvis of San Diego and Henry Murdoch of Phoenix to their Orange County confederates under the direction of Cochise. Jack Savage in Portland and Vito whatever-his-name-is—even after writing it out one letter at a time, they still couldn't agree on the pronuncia-

tion—in Seattle could be captured and/or killed by their own
team in the Pacific Northwest. That would leave nine, including
Dr. Goldman, for the three of them to handle themselves—three
each.

"What about Joe Day, Brock," asked Bowie. "Don't we want
him, too?"

Brock thought a moment. "He has certainly earned it, hasn't
he. But I think we should hold off. Let him sweat awhile. After we
take out Goldman, it has got to have a wonderful emotional
effect on him."

They chose carefully. Brock had the *Citation* and didn't care
about the proximity of those he was left with as long as he had
Goldman, so he gave the others their choices. Bowie picked
Austin, El Paso, and Santa Fe because they were often on his
trucking route. Banneker didn't really care where he had to go
either, as long as the entire job was completed full-scale. He
thought that Brock should work Cheyenne, Wyoming, only because a black man might be a little too conspicuous in that locale
where so few of them lived. And with Denver the logical place to
land the *Citation* for the Cheyenne operation, Brock, with a little
luck, could "kill two birds" in one trip. Bill was content to take
Atlanta, Birmingham, and Sacramento. Brock agreed. He also
reminded the two that he would not be able to fund the remain-
der of the operation totally, but he was offering a $1,000 incen-
tive bonus to whoever could take out one of the Hit Squad members first; and before he got Dr. Goldman. "And guys," he admonished, "be careful. You are too important to get knocked out
of the game before we're finished. Do you realize that we are the
only people on earth who know who these people are. The members don't even know each other. And except for Cochise, I can't
think of anyone else that we could trust enough to bring in as a
substitute for any of us. We are it. So let's play it safe and do it
right, okay?"

The next morning Bill drove his two compatriots to the
airport and bid them adieu. They had agreed to correspond at
home only by FAX with instructions to respond as to what time
the other could be at his "Branch Office" telephone. Brock would
FAX to each his own new phone number which he would acquire
soon. There was a phone bank in the Main Street Branch of the
Kansas City Library at 48th and Main on the other side of Nichols
Plaza from his office. He would first need to ascertain the various
numbers and be sure that they were equipped to receive incoming calls.

Bill watched the sparkling white jet take off into the morning
sun, bank south and then west as it set course for St. Louis. Brock

would drop Bowie off there, in order that he pick up his "Babe" and head for Tennessee. Before getting in his car, Bill spotted a drive-up telephone in the parking lot and remembered something that needed tending to which had been important enough for him to have written himself a note the night before as a reminder.

He removed a book of matches from his pocket, took note of the number thereon, and dialed 800-222-8474. After three rings a male voice briefly said, "Please hold," and gave Bill no chance to argue before forcing him to do just that.

A minute later the cheerful voice came back on and said, "Good Morning! Henley Park Hotel reservations. How may I help you?"

Bill said, "Good morning. Is Donna working the front desk this morning?"

"Yessir, I believe she is. Let me connect you."

The phone crackled twice. "Front desk. Good morning."

"Hi. Is this Donna?".

"Yes, it is."

"Hi, Donna. This is Frank Hamer from Dallas, Texas. I'm in 319. You asked me to let you know if I would be needing it the third night, and I don't."

"Fine, Mr. Hamer, no problem. We have a waiting list."

"Good. Listen, Donna, I am tied up with business meetings all morning, and I won't be able to get back there today. But if you will just run that through on my card—I don't believe I had any other charges—I won't need your receipt."

"Hang on, let me check here," she said, as he heard the computer keys thumping in the background. "Yes sir, Mr. Hamer, that is correct. You have two nights only at $375 plus ten per cent tax which will be seventy-five dollars, bringing your total to eight twenty-five even. We will be happy to mail you this receipt."

"It really isn't necessary. My credit card receipt will suffice. Just throw it away and keep your overhead down."

"I am sure the management will appreciate that, sir," the chipper Donna chuckled. "Twenty two cents is twenty two cents!"

"Thanks, Donna. I enjoyed my stay and look forward to seeing you on my next trip. Bye now."

"Thank you, Mr. Hamer. Goodbye."

Bill would FAX the credit card billing to Brock for reimbursement when it came in the next month. Another four hundred bucks for the second night was a cheap price to pay for an alibi, should they ever need it, but there was no point in paying for the third.

*   *   *   *   *

Jean Darwin had not been concerned when her boss failed to
call her the previous Thursday afternoon as he had promised.
He often failed to do that. Even when she did not hear from him
on Friday, it had not been great cause for alarm. But now it was
late Monday morning, and she still had not heard a word. While
she was contemplating the ramifications of disturbing him at
home—a preconceived no-no—the phone on her desk rang. It
was Mrs. Thorsten.

"Jean, do you know where in the hell Spike is?"

"No, ma'm, I do not. I was just about to call you. He's got a
million messages on his desk, and he hasn't checked in with me
since last week. If you don't know where he is either, I don't
know what to think."

The two women tossed it around for a few minutes with Mrs.
Thorsten threatening to call the FBI, or Missing Persons at DCPD,
or somebody. Jean asked her to wait until she could talk to the
deputy commissioner.

"Mrs. Thorsten, he's been working on some highly confidential cases lately," Jean said. "It's so classified, he hasn't even told
me anything about it. Let me check with the hierarchy upstairs,
and I will call you later today. They may know something they
haven't bothered to tell me. Wouldn't be the first time around
here."

She dialed the deputy commissioner's office upstairs. He was
out until after lunch. "This is Jean Darwin, Mr. Thorsten's secretary downstairs. Would you please have him call me as soon as he
gets in. It is very important. Thank-you."

She was hesitant to call Mrs. Thorsten back with nothing
other than a delay and decided to do nothing else but wait. It was
at about this same time that Bill Banneker was leaving the UPS
Shipping Center in Louisville, Kentucky, removing his work gloves
as he walked across the parking lot, having just sent a one-foot
square package via "Two-Day Air" to:

The IRS Commissioner
1111 Constitution Avenue
Washington, D.C.

United Parcel Service guaranteed delivery by 10:30 on
Wednesday morning.

*   *   *   *   *

Brock had done a lot of thinking between St. Louis, after
dropping off Bowie, and landing in Kansas City fifty minutes

later. He didn't know Marty Goldman well, but he knew that Goldfinger loved money. He struck on an idea and decided to drop in at the weekly poker game next Friday when Marty would be there. It would take a titanic effort to remain nonchalant while sitting and socializing in the same room with the jackal who so cold-bloodedly shot his wife in the face, but Brock would manage it. He would have all week to plan his strategy.

Bowie had been thinking, too, during the ten-hour drive back to his home outside of Bluff City, Tennessee. He would not have a lot of time to waste on his runs out West. There were always deadlines to meet. He would have to spend a few hours each in Austin, El Paso, and Santa Fe doing a little reconnaissance work before laying his final plans, but meanwhile, he thought it would be a good idea to bone up again on his latent demolition talents. It might be the best way to collect that thousand-dollar bonus.

On Wednesday morning the lobby receptionist at IRS Headquarters looked suspiciously at the unusual package the man in the brown work uniform had just dropped on her counter top. She said nothing as she took the pen and clipboard from his hands, but she already knew she was not going to send this box upstairs right away. IRS gets packages everyday, lots of them. Most are addressed to the commissioner, almost all of them are flat—in varying degrees of size and weight—and contain legal briefs. While this one looked as if it contained a bowling ball, it was not as heavy. Could it be a bomb? Rather than send it to the mail room for opening and correct routing, she called her supervisor and asked that he come down to the front desk, explaining her trepidation. He gave the box a once-over inspection and called the bomb squad. When the dogs sniffed it, they went berserk.

It was in an open field two hours later that they finally removed the transparent bag containing a Virginia driver's license and the head of Spratlin P. Thorsten. The eyes were still wide open and staring in terror. They immediately called the FBI and turned everything over to them for investigation. They in turn called the commissioner to come over to their lab for possible identification. The commissioner passed the job on to his #1 Deputy.

On the previous Monday afternoon, the deputy commissioner had returned Jean Darwin's call and, upon learning of her consternation about Spike, had asked that she call Mrs. Thorsten and put her mind at ease with something.

"I don't want to alarm her, Jean," he had told her, "but

Spike was doing some very dangerous and highly classified investigative work, and I don't even know where. Please buy us some
time. Just tell her that he is undercover and will return soon.
That's all we can do right now." Now, two days later, his greatest
fears were about to be realized.

He recoiled in horror as he identified the terrified face as
that of his former right-hand man. He would spend the rest of
the day undergoing intense questioning by the FBI, denying any
knowledge of any dangerous work Spike might have been doing,
and saying over and over that he knew of no one who would want
to harm his chief of CID, *other than, generally, of course, everybody
in the United States.*

At this time back home in Indiana, Bill Banneker was skill-
fully using his masonry tools to put the final proud touches on
the new sidewalk in front of his house.

*   *   *   *   *

Brock had the goods on "Goldfinger" and he knew it. The
fact that Goldman did not have any idea that he was aware of it
gave Brock the upper hand in setting his trap, whatever he
finally decided that trap would be. He would like to just march
into the OB-GYN's office and shoot him through the mouth, just
as the bastard had done to Sarah, but he knew that wouldn't be
prudent. Effective but stupid. Nor could he report what he knew
to the police and have Goldman prosecuted through the normal
channels. His only eyewitness was chopped into a few dozen
pieces, and the only other with first hand knowledge, Don
Handy—locked in a cage in Nevada—was hardly in any position
to testify either. Brock would have to administer old fashioned
Western justice himself while closely adhering to the three S's of
sweet success—Silent, Swift, and Secretive. He was willing to bend
a little on the Swift part. Not only did he need to wait to seize the
opportune moment in order to preserve these final two ingredients of a successful operation, he wanted to see Goldman squirm—
maybe in a boiling cauldron—while Brock informed him of why
he was dying. He fantasized about tying Goldman to a desert tree
and whipping him with sandy cactus trunks in the blistering
Arizona sun. Boiling him in excrement. Everything he could
imagine was too good for Goldfinger.

He went to the Main Street branch of the public library at
48th and Main and headed around to his right for the vestibule
near the restrooms where the phone bank was located. He was
disappointed to notice the sticker on each of the three phones
informing the user that in order to protect the serenity of the

surroundings, the phones were fixed so as not to ring. In other words, no call backs were possible in here. Figured. Nobody wants bells ringing in the quietude of a library. He exited the front doors and turned north on Main and walked to the stoplight in the mid-morning sunlight of early autumn.

September was his favorite month in Kansas City, even better than April, when the early spring temperatures were still chilly and the rainfall more plentiful. But late April had all the great smells of the new blossoms, while the September air was permeated with the aroma of burning leaves. So he reckoned it was nearly a toss-up, but he definitely knew that in April and September there was no place on earth he would rather be than where "everything is up to date," and he began to whistle the tune from "Oklahoma," recalling with a wisp of melancholy that it had been one of Sarah's favorites from childhood. She had happily sung it over and over as she unloaded dishes and placed furniture that day they were moving into their first house in Kansas City, just a few hundred yards across the Plaza from where he now walked.

He crossed the street at the light, continued north past the public tennis courts, and turned left at 47th, circling back around the courts again. On his right across the street was the popular Mexican restaurant, Tijuana Annie's, and remembering the telephone bank on the lower level, he believed he had found what he was seeking. He entered, turned right, descended the staircase to the restroom area, and took down the phone number of his new branch office. It would be less than a five minute drive from both his house in one direction and from his office in the other.

Ten days later a one-page FAX was received on Brock's private line in his library at home. It carried instructions at the top reminding Brock it was "For your eyes only" and to "destroy after initial reading." The typed message said only, "You know where to send the G." It was signed by "Tom Paine" and followed at the bottom of the page by a copy of a small news clipping.

Mysterious Car-Bombing Has Investigators Baffled

The investigation is continuing in the mid-day car explosion in downtown Austin last Friday. It has been definitely tagged by FBI spokesmen as "a car-bombing by a person or persons unknown," but federal arson investigators have no leads.

Austin resident Hagood Stinson, 40, a federal employee, was killed instantly as he attempted to start his car after having lunch in a popular downtown restaurant. The sheriff's department and federal authorities are checking into Stinson's background to determine what private activi-

*ties he might have been involved in that would have provoked his
murder. A spokesman suggested a reward may be offered at a later date
if the current investigation continues to produce no leads.*

Brock suppressed a grin as he read the story, removed the
list from his wallet, and drew a line through "Hagood Stinson,
Austin" and the telephone number. He immediately replaced the
sheet into the FAX machine and sent it to Bill Banneker in
Indiana, with no comment. Then he destroyed the original. Nor
was it wise to carry the list on his person, he realized, and concealed it instead in a book on his library shelf.

But Bill would not receive the FAXed information for two
more days. Having decided to take care of the first of his problems the farthest away, he was in Sacramento tending to business, unaware of Bowie's successful mission. His target was Special Agent Dan Thorpe, a man who had appeared to Banneker,
following a day of recon, as being about fifty pounds out of his
weight class and probably too agile to take on face to face. Thorpe
was 6'3" and over 225 pounds. Banneker would have to resort to
a surprise attack.

He watched Thorpe leave the CID office at 5:15 in the afternoon and tracked him east on the four-lane. When the agent's
car pulled down the ramp on the Zinfandel Street exit at Rancho
Cordova, Bill followed and pulled into the left lane next to him.
The two cars in front of Thorpe turned right and before he could
pull up, Bill buzzed down the electric window on the passenger
side as if to ask directions. When Thorpe lowered his window in
response, Banneker raised the Uzi and gave him an automatic
burst of 9mm lead to the face. Thorpe was slammed over by the
impact, rose slowly, then slumped into the right hand seat, as his
car crept out into traffic under the light. In his rearview mirror
Banneker spotted another car pulling onto the exit from the
interstate but still a hundred yards or more back. He turned left,
took another left back up the ramp, and headed back to Sacramento. Even though he was sure he had not been observed, he
checked in the rental car downtown instead of keeping it overnight. Remembering Brock's admonition about exercising all cau-
tion, he decided it would be better to take a cab to the airport the
next day. He returned to the Sheraton to have dinner and maintain a low profile, confident that he had a bonus coming.

The next morning at the airport, while waiting for his flight
to Indianapolis via Chicago, Bill picked up a *Sacramento Bee* and
saw the short blurb on the second page of the front section.

Man Killed In Drive-By Shooting

Dan Thorpe, 37, of Rancho Cordova was killed in an apparent drive-by shooting on the Zinfandel Street ramp at U.S. 50 early last evening. No other details were available at press time and no suspects were in custody. Sacramento County Sheriff's Department is investigating the incident.

He was not surprised to see that there was no mention of Dan Thorpe's occupation.

When Bill returned to his home in the country, he found the FAX sheet in his machine from two days before. Bowie had beaten him and had won the thousand, fair and square, damn it all. First he FAXed the clipping from the *Sacramento Bee* to Brock to allow him to scratch one more from the list, then he sent a typed message to Bowie along with the clipping.

Congratulations, Honkie! You have won the first inning but not the game. I bet you the thousand that I complete my whole mission before you do yours. RSVP.
Frank H. (formerly of Dallas)
p.s. Big Birmingham B-B-Q coming within week.

When Bowie arrived back in Tennessee a few days later, he fired back the following retort, before leaving again for another run West.

You are on for five hundred, Loser. Daddy taught me if I don't gamble all my winnings, I would always be ahead, but you had better move faster this time. We had so much fun at the last one we had a Texas-size orgasm. Long live pyromania! Can't wait to see another bonfire. Watch for the big cookouts in El Paso and Santa Fe very soon.
Tom and Shoeless Babe—
on the road

Over the course of the next month, the second Texas rub-out went as smoothly for Bowie as the previous one in Austin. Only Santa Fe remained for him to win his bet and secure bragging rights over his buddy.

Meanwhile, Bill had discovered that his Birmingham target was a bachelor living alone. Because no one else would be there to be harmed, Banneker decided to burn him out by drilling a three-quarter inch hole in the bedroom wall during the afternoon. He went dressed in his work blues to appear as a gas company employee and completed the simple task in ten minutes. Then he returned at 4:30 A.M. with a cannister of propane, quietly inserted the hose into the hole, and released the handle.

When the radio/alarm clock went off at 5:30, the target was incinerated.

Bill immediately left Birmingham and went east in his black van on I-20 to Atlanta, racing to complete the job before Bowie could finish Santa Fe. He stopped at Denny's near Charley Brown Airport west of town and called the telephone operator to learn that the 441 exchange he was seeking was in Duluth, on the northeast side of the city. He circled the city on I-285 past Smyrna, Sandy Springs, and Chamblee before heading north on I-85, and stopped at the Falcon Inn near Buford. "Adam Samuels" checked into room 100 at poolside, paying with a fifty-dollar bill. A brief look at the desk clerk's city directory told him that the house he was seeking was on Scott's Mill Run just off U.S. 23 in Duluth. He watched some of the early TV shows and fell asleep before the eleven o'clock news.

At 6:30 the next morning he was parked down the hill in the 3500 block of Scott's Mill Run.

A minute after seven, Leonard Burr emerged from his house with a briefcase and got into a tan, late model, Plymouth Voyager van. He backed out of the driveway and headed north up the hill. Bill started the engine on his Chevy van and began to trail him from his position down the hill, having guessed correctly which way his target would leave for work. He did not count on Burr picking up a fellow worker en route, however, which presented an unforeseen problem.

Bill was not into the wholesale killing of just anybody who happened to work for the IRS and might get in the way. Following the office conversation with his two confederates on the subject, he still felt the same about all of them being part of the enemy but had silently agreed to heed Brock's advice and not take out any non-team members unless absolutely necessary. The CID assassination team he could eliminate with a clear conscience, but he was certain this second individual was not part of that— and if their security was still as tight as it had been, this man could not even be aware of any murder team inside the IRS, much less be guilty of working with the bastards. This guy was probably just some minion beancounter hitching a ride to work and who didn't even know Jimmy Carter wasn't still president. Bill felt it would be better to do only recon this morning and wait to hit Burr when he was alone. The Atlanta mission would have to be placed on hold for a few hours, maybe a day.

*   *   *   *   *

Brock entered the glass door with the correct number on it in the town square across from the Independence Courthouse and climbed the stairs to the second floor offices. Down the hallway in the rear was a small office that announced *FRANK FLOWERS—PRIVATE INVESTIGATOR* in four-inch lettering. *Please enter,* it said in smaller letters over the door handle. Brock followed instructions and found Frank leaning back in his swivel chair, with his feet propped up on his cluttered desk, and with the perpetual phone receiver stuck in his ear. He smiled and motioned for Brock to sit down while he quickly terminated the call.

The windowless office was plain with no pictures on the lime green walls. It was obvious that the bookshelves had not felt a dustcloth in weeks. The telephone that Flowers was placing back on the cradle was the antiquated rotary dial type.

"Brock! My man who pays in cash," he said. "Great to see you. Have you made any progress?"

"You bet we have. I know who killed Sarah," Brock said, not wasting any time with getting to the point.

"Who?"

"Frank, I knew you would ask me that, and I have decided it is better for you that I not tell you. I trust you, but it is something that you don't need to know right now. It would be excess baggage that you need not carry. You will know soon enough, and someday I'll tell you the whole story. But I do need your assistance again."

"You name it. By the way, did you know that your buddy Don Handy is missing?"

"No. Where did you hear that?"

"Well, us Columbos have a grapevine like every other business. I got a call from a friend in southern California about a skip-tracing case he was looking for a little help on. He mentioned that he had heard that around twenty or more IRS agents out of Orange County are missing. Somehow, he had gotten hold of a list and it showed several missing in other areas too. Naturally, I asked him if there were any from Kansas City. He ran down the list and read me the name of Donald Handy of Overland Park," but I told him I had never heard of him. You don't know anything about this, do you?"

"Of course not," Brock smiled, "but it couldn't happen to a nicer group of people."

"Yeah, I'll bet you don't. Strangest thing. The date on the sheet that Handy was last seen matched up with my calendar as being the same night I was out in a honky-tonk on 75th Street with a big moose named *Tom . . . ,*" Flowers smirked and paused, waiting for a reaction from Brock that never came, before proceeding.

". . . Okay, what do you need me to do?"

"A little telephone eavesdropping."

"Don't you know that's against the law?" Flowers retorted with a sly smile. He was reclining in his chair with his hands folded on his stomach.

Brock sensed the sarcasm and skipped it. "So? How much is your fee to forget that?"

"Gimmee the details."

"There is a certain doctor whose schedule I need to learn, you know, his after-hours habits. But I also need to know, on short notice, when he will be leaving to go somewhere, where he might be alone, or at least alone when he is traveling there. An out-of-town trip to Wichita or Topeka, for instance, would be perfect. I figure if you can get onto his line at home, you can find out for me exactly what I need to know. How much?"

"Okay. Regular rates for now, but if the heat gets on, there may be an increase. I have a friend who bought one of the old phone company vans. The lettering is removed but it still has the right colors. I can borrow it, but it would be nice if I could give him a fifty buck tip, especially if I am going to need it for several nights. So let's say regular rates plus one green & black picture of U.S. Grant for my buddy. Fair enough?"

"Fair enough."

"Fine. Give me a $500 retainer to go for that and the first nine hours. I'll let you know when it is spent. This may take some time or we might get lucky, but you know I won't run up your tab unnecessarily."

"I know. No problem with that," Brock said, laying open the trust checkbook on the edge of the desk and reaching for a pen.

"Hold it, Pal," Frank interrupted. "No checks. My rates were computed with the foreknowledge that you pay in cash."

"Sorry. Forgot. I'll need to drop it by later today. I don't have that much on me."

"That'll be fine. Now give me the name, address, and phone number of this doctor you are interested in. My lady friend at the phone company will have to do a computer run to get me the correct hookups at the central box, but that usually doesn't take long if she's not busy."

Flowers would also employ another old and very reliable investigative trick that can deliver all sorts of clues to personal tastes, alcohol and drug consumption, sex habits, income and business information, listed and especially unlisted phone numbers, and travel. If a garbage bag is curbed, searching through it is legal, and the commandeering of a stuffed Hefty on the right night of the week can be vital and often produce more technical information than a railroad car full of informants, night-vision lenses, infinity bugs, and all the other exotica that feed the mystique of the private investigator. It would be a matter of walking to the Goldman's house, picking up the sack, making a newspaper-stuffed substitution, and taking Goldfinger's garbage back to the office with him for close perusal.

Shortly after dark that evening Frank Flowers had parked a pale green and dull white Chevrolet van next to the cross central telephone box on Mission Road near the Indian Hills Country Club and in his tan attire appeared to any ordinary passer-by every bit as a telephone repair man earning some overtime.

* * * * *

Brock answered his phone at the real estate office two mornings later and heard what was now becoming a familiar greeting from a familiar voice.

"How soon can you be in your branch office?" Bowie asked.

"Give me ten minutes. I need to finish up another call on the other line, and then I'll leave."

Twelve minutes later the phone was ringing as Brock descended the stairs at his "office" at Tijuana Annie's Restaurant. He grabbed it on the second ring.

"Good news," announced Bowie proudly. "Our problems are solved in the Southwest."

Brock immediately grasped that to mean Bowie had completed the Santa Fe mission. He didn't ask for any details. "Did Bill close the sale in Atlanta yet?"

"I don't know. I haven't heard from him since he went south, but I think he made the sale in Birmingham, according to a blurb I heard on the news the other night. But if he hasn't finished with Atlanta yet, I'll pick up another five hundred from him to cover some of my overhead."

"You are having a good time, aren't you?" said Brock.

"Yup. And guess what else. I'm taking a load to Denver in a week or so. How much would you sell me Denver and Cheyenne for?"

Brock laughed. "Well, let's see. You know I was really looking forward to meeting with those two, so you're asking a lot. How about fifty thousand dollars?"

"How about a bottle of Heineken's for each."

"Sold. You drive a hard bargain, but they are all yours. But you've got to come back through here on your way back to Tennessee and give me the blow-by-blow description. You bring the beer, and I will personally grill you the best steak ever, which says a lot. This *is* Kansas City, you know."

"Great. If everything goes smoothly, I'll see you, let's see . . . probably two weeks from this Saturday. I'll let you know."

But things would not go so smoothly in a different locale, and Bowie would see Brock sooner than he expected.

*   *   *   *   *

Even in the early morning Atlanta traffic it took only twenty minutes for the two-car caravan to reach the IRS Service Center at I-85 and Shallowford Road, unbeknownst to Leonard Burr that he was being followed. Banneker pulled in behind them and parked in a handicapped zone front of the building where he could watch Burr and his friend emerge from the Voyager van. As they circled the building to enter, Banneker got out to follow them inside, timing his steps to be a few yards behind them. He was far enough back not to be greeted or acknowledged but close enough to see which office or elevator they entered. The stranger circled into the large open offices at the left. Burr pushed the "Up" button and waited for the elevator. Banneker got on with him, and when Burr pushed "2," Bill nodded a good morning hello and pushed "3." Burr grunted and stared straight ahead. As he noticed Burr's shoes, Bill fought the urge to "run him through" right there, but he knew the door was about to open and had no way of knowing what was waiting on the other side. If there was ever a tell-tale sign of a federal agent, it was those outdated "grandpa" shoes so many wore. Leonard Burr, 45, had another distinguishing and disgusting characteristic. He had long, greasy hair that always appeared as though he had not shampooed in at least a fortnight.

A few seconds later the automatic doors did open, and Bill watched Leonard Burr step to the right. Holding the "open" button for a moment, he watched his prey turn down a short hallway to the left. Bill stepped off the elevator, let the doors close behind him and held still. He heard a muffled buzzer in the distance followed by an amplified male voice coming over an outside speaker.

"Yeah," the voice said.

"Burr," was the solitary word of reply, and a different, louder, more bass-sounding buzzer clacked. Bill heard it stop as he visualized Burr pushing open the secured office door. When the hallway fell silent, he walked around the same corner and saw the words *Criminal Investigation Division* in fading black paint on the upper half of the solid metal door. He decided to leave and find the diner he had noticed at the previous intersection on the ride over. He wanted to have breakfast and think. When the elevator arrived back at the second floor, another man, this one a tall, blond-haired Nordic who wore the same tell-tale footwear strode off without speaking and headed for the familiar hallway. Bill held the door and listened to hear the same exchange as before.

"Yeah!"

"Sharkey" . . . and the buzzer rang and the door was pushed open. Bill heard it slam shut, and the hallway was silent again.

At the Waffle & Burger Shack, Bill ordered coffee and a Western Omelet with all the trimmings. *All this undercover work this early in the morning gives a man an appetite,* he realized when his stomach had growled at him. *What simple security that is to crack. I could probably push the button and say 'Smith' or 'Jones' and one of those clowns would push the inside button like a chimpanzee to let me in.* But what kind of cover story could he use to get Burr up front to blow him away? And if he did, there surely would be a secretary or some other agent there to observe what happened and possibly finger him later. But no, he had never been there before and if he could pull off a big hit, he would never be in Atlanta again either, at least not for a long, long time. He formulated a plan. It was risky beyond the limits within which the three of them had agreed to proceed, but the rewards, if he was successful would be worth it. And if he failed, he would probably be dead.

His breakfast arrived, and while he ate he made his decision. He would proceed full speed ahead but only after taking the necessary precautions to protect his friends. He finished, left a fifty percent tip knowing it might be his last, and drove to a shopping center away from the IRS Service Center and a few miles up Buford Highway. He found a drugstore with a public telephone out front and began thumbing the yellow pages. There had to be one of the easy-rental places in the area. There was, back on frontage road at the interstate. He got directions from a stranger emerging from the drugstore.

The manager of the large rental business was just pushing the sliding gate open to his heavy equipment lot when Bill arrived. He explained to the man that he was from out of town and needed a typewriter and FAX machine for some business transmittals for only a few hours and would return them before noon. Two of each were available. He offered a cash deposit of $500 in lieu of a credit card in order to avoid the record. It was accepted. He returned to his motel room, ten miles up Interstate-85.

He found some faded motel stationery in the desk drawer

and began to type on the back. When he finished the half-page, single-spaced message, he dropped it into the FAX machine and used his own AT&T credit card to keep it off the motel records. He sent a copy to a number in the 615 area and another to 816. Then he burned the sheet in the bathroom and flushed the ashes down the toilet. He drove south again on the interstate, returned the equipment, and collected his deposit.

The black van crept into the parking lot at the Service Center, circled the building, and crept out. This was not the place to park, he already knew, but wanted to case the entranceways and think some more before moving it back across the interstate to the shopping center parking lot where he had just informed his friends it would be.

He pulled on his jacket and stuffed a hand grenade into each pocket. He placed the Uzi with the thirty-shot clip in a sling stirrup under his left shoulder concealed by the coat and left his wallet and keys under the floormat. Before slamming the door, he grabbed an extra 30-shot clip and placed a black stocking cap on his head. He walked across the highway to the IRS offices.

He entered the building for the second time that morning and pressed the button on the elevator. By now there were many people milling around and seated in the lobby, each having taken a number and been asked to wait their turn for their audits. The tax charade was marching on, he thought, as the elevator doors opened. *Will the poor sheep never learn?*

At the CID door on the second floor, Bill pushed the ringer button and waited for the response that he knew was forthcoming.

"Yeah!" said the same male voice he had heard earlier.

"Smith," Bill replied, and the door-opening buzzer rattled.

He pushed the heavy door open and marched in with one hand in his left jacket pocket on the hand grenade. He was surprised to see that no receptionist was at the counter in front of him. No one was in sight anywhere. Whatever personnel were present were lurking behind their cubicles engrossed in whatever these weasels do. He waited for thirty seconds and nobody appeared. He was astounded at the lack of security. Bill now reckoned he, indeed, could have said "Kozlowski" or "Jackie Robinson" and the faceless robot back there would have pushed the buzzer to release the door.

The room was a large one with vacant desks holding typewriters in the center of each, and the walls were lined with a half dozen small cubicles down each side. There was another large one right in front of him which he decided must belong to the "big deal," whoever he was—maybe Burr. He waited for another ten seconds and heard voices but saw no one. He decided this was going to be even easier than he had thought. *Everybody in here is CID. No lackey clerks to worry about. Everyone here is the declared enemy. What the hell, let 'em have it.*

He pulled the pin on the first grenade and hurled it to the back of the room into the farthest cubicle. Three men came scrambling out of the corner office and Bill opened up on them with his automatic weapon. The exploding grenade drew two other men from their desks to the doorways of their cubicles, and as they paused baffledly, two more heads were immediately filled with a burst of lead. Bill pulled the second grenade from his right hand pocket, pulled the pin, and flipped it into the large office in front of him, off of the entrance vestibule. Just before it exploded, Bill thought he heard a door slam in the distance. He exited the big steel door he had entered moments before, as this next eruption set the near end of the room aflame.

He was rounding the corner in the hallway and running for the stairs next to the elevator shaft when an automatic burst of fire whisked by his head and slammed into the wall. It was Leonard Burr who had grabbed his weapon and run out of his side exit into the hallway when the live grenade had hit the floor of his office.

Banneker skipped three steps at a time as he headed down for the lobby. A dozen or more of the people who had been waiting their turns in the lobby had escaped to the front sidewalk when they heard the ruckus. Those already inside the clerical office were cowering behind desks and on the floor. Bill pulled the stocking cap down beyond his ears and covered his face with his arm as he sprinted out front and around the corner into the parking area. Automatic weapon fire broke out from the second story window at the end of the building and Bill Banneker fell on the asphalt with seven slugs in his neck and head. His face was destroyed almost beyond recognition. Leonard Burr had guessed correctly as to which way Banneker would circle the building and had beaten him there on the second floor. By the time the first agent reached Banneker to check the pulse, he was already dead.

Bill Banneker had died fighting for freedom, but none of his friends would ever know the truth of what happened at the Service Center that day. The front page of the Atlanta newspapers the following morning said nothing and page six showed only a small picture of Banneker's dead body against the curb with the small blurb that "an unidentified lone nut set off a detonation device in the IRS Service Center yesterday. The black man, ap-

proximately forty years old, was shot by alert CID agent Leonard
Burr as he tried to escape the scene on foot. No government
personnel were hurt." Talking TV heads quoted government
propaganda about how important the work of the tax collectors
is to the operation of the nation.

Although he had missed his number one target, Bill Banneker
had killed three CID agents and seriously wounded four more,
but the government managed to keep the truth out of the papers
once again. Those in charge felt that too much adverse publicity
would give too many other people the same idea. As much as
they would like to know who this man was, even if they never
found out, the story would be released the next day with a name
and a long history of his psychological problems as well as the
names of several doctors under whose "psychiatric care" he had
been treated for the last decade or more.

When Brock arrived home after six that same evening, the
typed FAX message from Bill was resting in the reception bin on
the back of his machine.

> If no FAX follows this one before noon today, I am dead or
> captured. I am stepping beyond our bounds of risk but our
> potential booty deems the risk worthy. If this is the last corre-
> spondence you receive, you must pick up my van before it is
> impounded. You will find it in the parking lot at the northeast
> corner of I-85 and Shallowford Road in northeast Atlanta. It is
> unlocked, and the keys are under the floormat. I am carrying
> no I.D. and have never been fingerprinted. They cannot iden-
> tify me, and if I survive but am caught, do not worry, I will not
> talk. If I die, you will find my instructions in my papers in my
> desk at home. The trust names Marcel Gautier as 50% benefi-
> ciary and Bowie Crockett with the other half. Brock, I love you,
> Bro, but the last thing you need is more assets, so I named you
> as Trustee. I know you will take care of the others honestly.
> Any further correspondence from me later today negates all
> this maudlin crap.

He had signed it "William Banneker—of sound mind and
body so far this day."

TWENTY-ONE

Brock immediately dialed Bowie's number in Bluff City, knowing he could never be sure when he might find him at home. But the fact that no second FAX had come across to negate Bill's message from late that morning had him concerned—no, more than concerned, by now he was downright worried. Bill had promised to send another unless he was dead or captured. What had he been planning that was going to place him in such jeopardy? Brock hoped that Bowie would know.

Stella answered in that now-familiar east Tennessee twang and told Brock that Bowie had made a short run to Birmingham the day before. "He had a load to dump in Knoxville thiseevnin' and should be home any time now," she twanged in that mountain accent which at any other time Brock would have found amusing.

Having become telephone friends over the last year with Stella taking so many of Brock's messages for her husband, the two chatted a little small talk. Yes, there had been a message from Bill Banneker laying in the bin of their FAX machine, but she hadn't read it. Stella said she never read the stuff and always folded up Bowie's FAX letters and put them on his desk, just to clear the machine for anything new that might be coming through. She knew little of her husband's private business and spoke of it even less. Before hanging up Brock asked for at least the third time that she please have Bowie call him as soon as he got in, and she assured him that she would not forget. It was nearly ten o'clock before Bowie finally returned the call.

"Sorry about being so late, buddy, but I stopped for dinner after I got unloaded in Knoxville. "What's up?"

"Have you read the message from Frank Hamer?"

"Yeah, I'm holding it as we speak."

"That's what's up. I never got another one, did you?

"No. There's nothing else here."

"Then I think the rest of this business should be conducted from our respective branch offices. Can you call me back in ten minutes or should I call you?"

Bowie emitted a long sigh and thought a moment. "Brock, let's wait half an hour. The news is coming on in just a minute, and we may just catch something of interest. You've got cable, don't you?"

"Sure."

"Okay, good, 'cause I don't. So you watch CNN, and I'll flip back and forth on the locals here and call you at your branch at exactly 11:30, 10:30 for you. The Sports and Weather will be on a good ten minutes before then."

CNN had a short, foreboding blurb about a shootout in Atlanta in an IRS parking lot at noon that day. An unidentified but deranged black man was killed by federal agents. No other details were available. Brock had a sick, sinking feeling in his stomach as he pulled the Mercedes into the convenient parking place right across the street from the restaurant and was standing by the phone when it rang.

"Bowie, Did you catch anything on your local news?"

"No. There was nothing. Did you?"

"Are you sitting down?"

"Uh-oh. Yeah. What is it?"

"I'm afraid they got him," Brock replied and told him what he had just learned. "That `unidentified black man' has got to be Bill. We've got to go get his van before they impound it and put two and two together. I hope he sent those FAXes from a secure spot."

Bowie agreed. It sure sounded bad. Bill was too dependable to have left them hanging this long after sending that first FAX. But the second had never come, and that had to spell trouble. They would have to get to Atlanta and quick. At first they talked about Brock flying down there first thing in the morning, but realizing the lateness of the hour already as well as another hour to be lost to the time change, Brock decided to leave right away. He would sleep for an hour or two in the plane once he got on the ground at Knoxville. Bowie agreed to meet him at the airport at sun-up, and the two would fly on south for another hour.

At seven the next morning the *Citation* touched down at Peachtree-Dekalb Airport on the north side of Atlanta with Bowie and Brock aboard. They told the airport attendant to only refuel and chock it as they planned to be back before noon. "I had to fly my friend in to pick up a car," Brock used as a cover story, "and I'm going to shop for a new suit." Then they phoned for a cab to take them to the Shallowford Road exit on I-85 which, most fortuitously, was only a mile away.

As they approached I-85 traveling south on Shallowford, Bowie spotted the black van sitting alone in the parking lot on the left. On the other side of the street was the Waffle & Burger Shack where Bill had eaten breakfast twenty-four hours earlier.

"Pull in there at that breakfast joint," Bowie ordered the driver. "I'm hungry."

Brock had seen the van too, and was cognizant of what his friend was doing. There need not be any cab records of them being dropped off at the van. He paid the $2.90 fare with a fiver and told the driver to keep the change. The two men sat in a booth and ordered breakfast. Before it arrived, Bowie said, "We're wasting time. I'll be right back." Brock said nothing and watched him walk out of the building and across the street toward the van. Five minutes later he had pulled into a parking space at the diner and was seated in the booth again before their orders arrived.

Everything had been just as Bill said it would be with the keys under the mat, and the reality of the fact now that Bill surely must be dead was settling in. Brock saw the tears welling up in the big man's eyes but said nothing as the waitress was setting their plates in front of them. He was saddened too, but Bowie and Bill had gone back a lot further together.

"I'm gonna miss the sumbitch," Bowie muttered between bites. "It hit me when I sat behind the wheel of his van. I wonder what could have happened."

"I don't think we will ever know," Brock replied sober-faced. "Whatever story they report to the media you know we can't believe, and we can't exactly go ask them for details either."

They decided that Bowie should drive the van back to his home in Tennessee and keep it until they could sort out the trust. If Marcel Gautier wanted it, Bowie didn't care one way or the other. The important thing was that the trust lived on in spite of the untimely death of Bill Banneker, and because no probate was forthcoming, no one else need even know that he was dead. The likely prospects of their friend being buried in Atlanta in an unmarked grave bothered both of the men, but it was something that would have to be dealt with later as well as explaining what they could of it to Marcel.

"We've got to tell Marcel," said Bowie, in a low whisper.

Brock thought for a second and replied, "Yeah, but not for awhile yet." Although neither knew him very well, they believed he could be trusted enough and they need not worry about his knowing how Bill had died. He would be proud of his friend for fighting government corruption.

Before flying out of Peachtree-Dekalb, Brock called his voice-mail system in Overland Park and picked up a message from a voice he recognized to be that of Frank Flowers, although the caller did not identify himself by name but with only a few code words.

". . . and your favorite doctor flies to Pensacola, Florida on the early morning flight every Monday and returns late Tuesday night. Call me."

*   *   *   *   *

There had been an incident in Brock's life that had brought Becky Burwell out of the depths of his subconscious and had placed her in his thoughts everyday. For three months he grappled with the mental gymnastics of the absurdity of the situation with logic and realism prevailing only until the folly of fantasy would take over again. He and Becky had never had anything going— he had never even kissed her. She had been merely on a pedestal in his young life, so long ago, and she had never even known it. The unreachable star, his Helen of Troy, Joan of Arc, and a young Elizabeth Taylor all wrapped up into one nebulous dream had long ago evaporated into time. To be thinking about her again was ridiculous folly, he kept telling himself. *She's probably old and gray and wrinkled with a dozen grown children and thirty grandkids by now, and I am but a smashed bug on her windscreen of life,* but the next day he found himself wondering about her again. It had been the brief episode in that hotel bar that night back in May that had messed up his mind again.

While Brock believed strongly in the "Power of Positive Think-ing" as espoused by Peale, Hill, Nightingale, et al., and had taught the same to his sales force as well as his children, he had facetiously belittled on occasion the adage so ardently preached by all of those mentors, "You become what you think about most of the time."

Brock used to jest, "I knew that couldn't be true because if it were, by the time I was sixteen, I would have turned into Becky Burwell."

With all this suddenly rising to the top again after being buried for so long, he wasn't nearly as surprised as he should have been when a comforting note of sympathy arrived at his house:

Dear Brock,

I have been wanting to write to you for some time now. It was only while I was visiting my mother in Independence last month that I learned of the tragic loss of your wife last year and some of the horrifying details.

I experienced a similar loss, though not as shocking, when I found my husband of twenty-two years on the floor of our bedroom closet one morning. He had experienced some heart trouble and had had a triple by-pass the year before, but all this notwithstanding, I was not prepared for it either. I guess one never is. Please accept my heartfelt sympathy, belated as it is.

Sincerely,
Rebecca (Burwell) Ambler

Brock stared at the letter and read it again. This was incredible. Becky had appeared out of nowhere. So she was widowed, but had she remarried? He had to know. She didn't say how long ago this had happened. Twenty-two years since he had seen her would make it 1985, but it had to have been since then because she wasn't married in 1963, and he had no idea when she had become Mrs. Ambler. Should he write her back? The return address on the envelope gave an address on St. Charles Street in New Orleans, Louisiana. No, he would call her. No, that would be too blatant. He would wait awhile. For how long, he didn't know. He read the letter every day until he didn't have to read it anymore. He had every word memorized. Finally, one evening in his office when everyone else had gone home, he changed his mind again and sat down at his typewriter.

"Dear Becky," he began. *No, she signed her name "Rebecca."* *Maybe she prefers to be called by her full name,* he thought, and spun the paper out of the typewriter carriage, trashed it, and inserted another. Before he realized it, an hour had passed, his wastebasket was half-full, and he still had not completed a satisfactory paragraph. *Settle down, Freeman. You're acting like a teenager. You are not writing the great American novel, Dodo. It's just a letter to an old friend. Give her a couple of cordial paragraphs, sign it, and mail the danged thing before you chicken out again.* He chuckled at his self-analysis and this schoolboy foolishness and began to type one more time:

Dear Rebecca,

Thank you for your kind letter. It kindled so many fond memories.

Please let me know the next time you will be visiting your mother. I would like to take you to dinner at whatever is your favorite K.C. eatery.

> Kindest personal regards,
> Brock

He didn't know that Rebecca had been somewhat stressed herself for the past two weeks after mailing the initial letter to Brock, wondering if he would even reply and knowing how foolish she would feel if he did not. Not foolish for writing to him, for her note had been sincere, but for hoping that he would respond. When the colorful envelope from "Freeman International Investments" did finally arrive, she resisted the urge to tear it open while still out on the curb next to the mailbox and waited until she got inside. Then, acting like a schoolgirl herself, she took it upstairs and stretched out on her bed to open it and read it. It was brief, she thought, but, indeed, it had said everything she had hoped it would.

The ball was in her court now, but she decided that if she didn't hit it back, he just might come after it. One evening a month later, she answered the phone in her kitchen while warming up some frozen pizza.

"Rebecca Burwell Ambler?" the male voice said to her.

"Yes, this is she."

"Hi. This is Brock Freeman. How are you?"

"Brock! How wonderful to hear from you. I'm fine. How are you getting along?"

They talked for an hour, catching each other up on the past quarter century. Rebecca had never known Sarah personally but immediately expressed her sympathy once more. Brock thanked her again and told her about Brent and Maria who were both now about to finish college. He learned that she and her husband, an architect on world-wide projects with an international company, had traveled extensively, and they had never had any children. When they had settled in New Orleans in the early eighties, she had set up a small art studio in the front of their home, which enabled her to "scratch an itch" she had acquired while she was a "bored housewife" living in Nice, France. Her pastoral scenes had been a recent hit with the French Quarter shops and elsewhere around the South, and these days she was spending the sunny days with her water colors in Audubon Park. Her husband had died the year before Sarah was killed.

Gradually, the restraints of formality and etiquette broke down, and the two of them were laughing and getting to know each other again, this time as never before.

"I would like to wander into Audubon Park one day and surprise you at work," he said.

"But how would you recognize me?"

"Easy. The most beautiful girl at Independence High cannot have changed that much."

"But I've gained three hundred pounds and have developed these strange green warts on my face," she teased.

"CLICK!" he said.

"What do you mean, click?"

"That was the sound of my phone hanging up," he said, and they had another laugh together.

"Okay," she confessed, "since I brought it up, I will tell you that I have gained some weight since college, but not that much."

"Not *how* much?"

"Not three hundred pounds."

"Okay, since you brought it up, how much?"

"Emmm . . . somewhere between three and three hundred. I must keep up the mystique."

"Yes, in the spirit of wily womanhood, I guess you must."

"Okay, now it's your turn," she returned the fire. "Are you still athletically trim?"

"Of course not. I'm fat, bald, and what few teeth I have left are stained with tobacco juice."

"Oh, Brock," she laughed, "You know I don't believe that!"

"But you can't be sure. So now you've got to hurry back to Kansas City just to find out, don't you?!"

"You're right. I would like to do that."

"It would be great to see you again, Rebecca. I never told you back in the olden days that I thought you were the greatest thing since bread and mayonnaise."

"No, you didn't. But I'll tell you this. I have never been prouder of anyone in my life than I was of you the last time I saw you—that day in The Stables in Lawrence when you vanquished Butch Evans. I want you to know that I've told that story at cocktail parties on five continents, but there is still one thing I have to ask you about that incident."

"What's that?"

"Did you ever collect your other seventy-five cents?"

"No, I never did. I never saw him again. I guess I'm going to finally have to write that off as a bad debt. I'm getting too old to collect it now, so I suppose I really hope deep down that I never run into him again. I imagine somebody has probably killed the bully by now anyway."

They laughed and reminisced and talked more, and when they finally rang off each of them felt refreshed and sensed the *je ne sais quoi*—that little something; that quality that eludes description. Both knew without telling the other that they were on the fringes of a wonderful relationship.

A week later, Rebecca called to say that she was making plans to come see her mother again in a few weeks and that she would let Brock know as soon as she had finalized her travel itinerary.

"Good," he said. "That's real good. I have been racking my brain for some excuse to come to New Orleans. Now maybe I won't have to buy the Superdome after all."

"Oh, I think you should. It's a very impressive piece of real estate. I was down there for three straight nights during the Republican Convention last summer."

"Really? Were you a delegate?"

"No, just part of the local caucus. Steven was a very active Reagan supporter, and his old friends included me this time. It was fun listening to all the campaign rhetoric and the behind-the-scenes chicanery, and being a part of history too, but I really don't get too wrapped up in all that. It seems like nothing changes anyway, whoever gets into office."

"You got that right!" Brock agreed, wondering to himself if he would ever be able to explain to her the piece of history of which he was currently a part. Probably not, but his anticipatory juices were flowing at the thought of finally seeing her again soon after so many years.

*   *   *   *   *

The 1973 supreme court decision legalizing abortions had drawn the battle lines between the "Right to Choice" and "Right to Life" groups. Bombings of abortion clinics had become common. A few perpetrators had been caught and sent to prison for long stretches. New laws were passed to give additional protection to the doctors performing the abortions, but even this had not dissuaded those who believed they were on the side of God. The era may be recorded in history as that of the modern crusades. Some referred to the extermination as the "New Holocaust."

A doctor in Pensacola, Florida was shot to death on the sidewalk in front of his clinic, and the killer immediately surrendered to face the music. He drew a life sentence. The doctor's replacement came two days a week from Jacksonville. A year later he and his assistant were killed and the assistant's wife was seriously wounded in a shotgun attack of much the same fashion as the first. Again, the shotgun-wielding killer, an ordained minister, had made no attempt to hide and at his trial made no apologies. He had not been insane, he had been preventing the future murder of innocent children, he told the court.

Bowie Crockett happened to be in Pensacola a few weeks after the second shooting and the truckstop conversation drifted to that subject over lunch that day. His friend at the table was railing on about the futility of such actions.

"My wife and I sympathize with the pro-lifers," he said. "That is a live human body those doctors are tearing out of that womb, a live human that should be constitutionally protected by 'the right to life.' But those dumb Christians obviously don't know anything about guerilla warfare, and they are damn stupid to just barge in there and throw away their own lives in order to take out one doctor. That's as stupid as shooting one Red Chinese and then getting killed yourself just because you hate communism. They'll just keep on replacing the dead doctors with new ones. They've already got a replacement in this abortuary here in Pensacola with some doc out of Kansas City."

"You're right," said Bowie, more interested up to that point in the large plate of red beans and rice than the conversation. "There are better ways to accomplish that mission and scare hell out of 'em at the same time than with a kamikaze flight. Did you say Kansas City? Who is the new doctor out of Kansas City?"

"Yeah. Dr. Goldman is his name. It was in yesterday's paper, and I made a mental note to remember it because I don't figger he's got long to live either."

Bowie thought, *If it's who I think it is, you don't know the half of it, Buddy!* While trying not to appear overly interested, he said, "What's Goldman's first name?"

"Don't know, can't remember that. But if you really want to know, I'll go get it. It's out in my truck."

"Please. I'd like to know." He had almost added, *"for my own private reasons,"* but stopped in time, realizing it was unnecessary to define *why* he was expressing more than just a casual interest.

"Sure."

In a few minutes Bowie's suspicions were confirmed. Dr. Martin Goldman, a Kansas City OB-GYN, the paper said, would be keeping the clinic open. Dr. Goldman was familiar with the clinic's operations because he had been assisting there two days a week for the past year. He would continue to be in charge of the facility on a part time basis for an indefinite period. Bowie handed the newspaper back to his friend, thanked him, and continued with his meal without commenting.

Bowie did his best thinking on the interstate, and as he rolled out of Mobile up I-65 toward his destination in Montgomery, he pondered whether or not to tell Brock about what he had learned. Brock had wanted first dibs on Goldman, but if Bowie could take care of it for him, what did it matter? Before leaving Pensacola, he had circled by the Woman's Clinic for a little reconnaissance work. There was a perfect spot up on the hill and across the street for a sniper shot of less than three hundred yards. He decided he would do it and leave Brock out of everything. He could read all about it in the papers later. Besides, Brock was busy falling in love again. He had told Bowie as much the last time they talked, something about an old flame who had come back into his life. Brock didn't need to be messing with Marty Goldman right now. Bowie would do it and let Brock owe him one more.

*   *   *   *   *

Brock sat on the sofa in the upstairs lobby of the Crown Center outside of The Peppercorn Duck Club, one of the more exclusive restaurants in Kansas City. Appropriately, the soft strains of "September Song" permeated the warm September evening from the speakers above. Rebecca had preferred to meet him here for the first time rather than at her mother's house in Independence. He understood. Their relationship was still in the embryonic stage, and there was no point in giving the old biddies of the town any more gossip fodder than they already had. But right now he wondered if he would even recognize her, and she him. A few minutes earlier, he had made himself known to the *maitre d'* and slipped him a twenty in exchange for a private table in a secluded corner. He kept getting up and walking past the mirror to be sure that every hair was still in place. God, how long would she keep him waiting. She had said, "Sevenish," and it was five after. Then it was eight after, and she still wasn't there. He sat back down and pretended to relax, as he squirmed and kept looking at his watch.

At seven fifteen, timed to perfection from a woman's perspective, Brock saw the lady in black from the rear as she rode up the escalator, and he knew who it was. Her hair was shoulder length and still dark with slight streaks of gray which he could barely distinguish. Whether it was the artwork of Mother Nature or her hairdresser's magic touch he didn't know for sure and didn't care at this splendid moment. He was as excited and filled with apprehension as he'd been on his first date. At the top step she made the U-turn toward him and he recognized her at once, just as beautiful in maturity as she had been in her youth. He stood as she strode toward him, reflecting a smile of recognition.

She stopped and blew him a quick kiss, just as she had done the very last time she had seen him, and flashed her still-radiant smile. And he noticed at once that those magnificent blue eyes still sparkled.

"Brock, I would have known you anywhere. You haven't changed a bit," she said with her arms extended.

"You're still beautiful, Rebecca, and right now you are a beautiful liar! But thank you. And if you have changed, it's for the better."

They embraced, and when he planted a brotherly kiss on her cheek, she modestly returned it. He held her hand as they entered the restaurant and coyly gave the *maitre d'* his name as if it were the first time he had seen him.

They ordered a bottle of Merlot, Brock having decided he was going to have a steak later, and Rebecca did not object. They postponed the ordering of the main course and settled for appetizers while they talked.

"I've been calling you 'Rebecca' because you signed your letter that way. Do you not go by 'Becky' anymore?" he asked.

"Oh, yes and no. Mom still calls me 'Becky,' and some of my old friends still do, but Steven preferred the more formal name and always introduced me as 'Rebecca,' so that's what everybody else has known me as in recent years. I guess that's why I use it naturally now. Force of habit."

"Which do you prefer?"

"Oh, Brock, it's no big deal. I sign all my work as 'Rebecca Ambler' because 'Becky' is too, you know, blah. But you call me what you like."

"Okay, I'm not going to call you 'Becky' because it's, you know, too blah, and I'm not going to call you 'Rebecca' because it's too formal and, besides, it will tend to remind you of Steven. So I'm going to call you 'Becca' because it's short, almost what I've always remembered you as, and maybe I will be the only one to do so."

"Becca," she said, with a quizzical gaze at the chandelier for a moment. "I like that. You're right. No one has ever called me that."

They had another glass of wine and ordered dinner. Seemingly obsessed with the provenance of its fare, the restaurant—in the strain to appeal to its most discerning customers—listed on its polyglot menu Long Island duckling, Maine lobster, Virginia ham, and enough other place names to fill a gazetteer. Brock ordered their largest K.C. Strip, and Rebecca the small prime rib. She was liking what she was seeing in Brock Freeman. He was handsome—she knew he would still be—but more than that, he was thoughtful, courteous, and scholarly. Strong but gentle. A man of steel and velvet, and a great conversationalist. She felt he would be just as comfortable strolling with her at an art show as he would be drinking beer and screaming with the boys at the Chief's game. She laughed at his quips, not patronizingly but heartily with sincere amusement, enjoying the evening even more than she had hoped she would.

What a lady! Brock was thinking. She was a Royals fan and even played chess, he had just found out. Brock always loved chess, but in his household only Brent had taken an interest. Now the boy had been too busy with college and girls in recent years to even think about challenging his dad to a game.

It was two hours later that they had finished the first bottle of wine with dinner and ordered another glass before dessert. He was in no hurry and wanted to talk more with her, and this would give them more reason to sit there.

"Why did you call me, Brock? Now, I know it is time to admit that I think I remember hoping that you would, but why did you?"

Brock looked at her, glanced away, looked back and pondered for a half minute.

"I've got to tell you something," he finally said, looking her straight in the eye again. "Well, it's more than a something, it's a long story, but it's important to me that I have your undivided attention."

"Okay," she smilingly replied.

"No, I mean it, Becca. This is very serious, very important to me, at least at this moment right now. I have got to tell you something that has been on my heart ever since it happened, and it was the determining factor that brought us here tonight. When I finish you will have the answer to your question."

"All right. I mean, please tell me. If it is important to you, it is important to me. I didn't mean to belittle . . ."

"I know," he interrupted. "I just wanted you to know that the mood here has now gone from trivial to serious, and this is a very personal thing I want to share with you."

"Okay, please tell me, and I promise to listen."

"Thank you. Uhh . . . What I want you to know is that back in May of this year, just six months after Sarah died, I met a young girl. She was very young—only nineteen, I found out. She was clerking in a men's store at Indian Springs Mall. And was she beautiful! She sold me a shirt, and we talked for a minute. She said she was getting off work in a few minutes, and I asked her to meet me at the Baskin-Robbins sidewalk cafe for a malt. I don't know why I was picking on someone so young, she just took me back, and I said to myself, 'What-the-heck, I am free', and well, the truth is that I was mesmerized. She made me young again. In about ten minutes, I was bewitched. Oh, I knew it was the "middle-aged crazies," but I didn't care. She was fun, warm, vibrant, and, well . . . exciting. So I just decided to forget that I was old enough to be her father and pretended I was back in college again. She was fun. Oh, I said that.

"The next day I called her and invited her for a drink over at The Marriott. She met me, and while I sipped beer, she had several whiskey sours. We danced a couple of fast dances and all the slow ones, and I must admit my intentions were anything but honorable as I remembered the old college line, 'Wine is fine, but liquor is quicker.' "

"Brock Freeman, you lecherous old rogue, you!" she could not help interjecting.

"Hold on now, let me finish. It's not what you think. Indeed, I was guilty of the sin of lust in my heart," he smiled smugly, "but that's nothing new since Sarah died. But you have never heard this kind of ending to this kind of story in your life, I guarantee it."

"Brock, as trite as it sounds, I really am on the edge of my seat. Please tell me now."

He was not drunk. But the wine had elevated him to the perfect mood and warm, fuzzy spirit for this conversation—still far short of the level of foolish and clumsy but with inhibitions removed. He was eager to proceed.

"You are not going to believe this," he went on, "but I am going to tell you. Now you've got to understand that this nubile young thing was a movie starlet straight out of the Playboy centerfolds, and I was the envy of every young stud in the place. They were all watching me, or at least her, more than their own dates. In the darkened corner of the dance floor, I kissed her and suggested we get a room upstairs. She readily agreed, and we launched onto another long, movie-type kiss and embrace, the kind Cary Grant would have been proud of, and suddenly the, uh . . . reality of it all hit me like a bus. I mumbled something to her about having to call my answering service and told her I would be back in a minute.

"I went to the men's room and wiped the lipstick off my face and stared at myself in the mirror for a long while. Then I went to the phone in the lobby and did call for my messages. There were a few but not one that needed tending to before the next business day. But I returned to the table, lied and told her there was an emergency that required my attention, and that I would have to call her later. I never have. And I have never told anyone about this until now. I can hear Pottsie and Mozzarella and the other guys at the poker table hooting right now if I ever told them. But you were the only one I could ever tell who might understand. Does this whole thing sound crazy to you?"

"Right now *you* sound a little crazy to me. Now let me be sure I have a grip on this. Here you are with the Playmate of the Year, you've gotten her tipsy enough to agree to go to bed with you, and you suddenly back out of the deal. Am I correct so far?"

"Yep."

"It seems to me that you blew the chance of a lifetime, Freeman!"

"That's what my country club buddies would have said, and that's precisely why I never told them."

"Okay," she said, "and just what was it that 'hit you like a bus?' What changed your mind, and why would I be the only one to understand?"

"That's the crazy part. It's bizarre. The subconscious mind is a strange computer. The second time I kissed her and looked into her eyes in the shadows of that room, I realized all of a sudden what had had me so smitten in the first place. It was the wildest case of *deja vu* anyone could ever experience. Suddenly it was 1959 or so, and—are you ready for this—I was staring right into the eyes of Becky Burwell! Sweetie, she was your twin sister a generation later or could have been your daughter today. And that really scared hell out of me, that it could have been your daughter! Anyway, that's why I ran. I thought about calling her a few times but decided not to. But the more I thought about the scene, the more I began to wonder about you, and I even seriously considered trying to find out where you were and what had ever happened to you. I probably would have eventually. When your letter came, I was convinced that you had been picking up my vibes."

"Maybe I was. I began to think about you a lot after Mother told me what had happened to Sarah. I became seriously concerned with how you were getting along. Now I am debating whether I should be flattered, or if I should club you over the head with this wine bottle and stalk out of here in a jealous rage."

Brock guffawed. "Please, Becca, be flattered. It was you, not her, that I was flipping out over that night, even though I didn't know it at first. Besides, she was an airhead who didn't know a dozen words. And don't forget, I didn't go back."

"But why didn't you, you fool!"

"If I tell you, you'll laugh harder than the guys at the golf club would have."

"No I won't, I promise."

"You promise?"

"I promise. Tell me."

"Because I didn't want to desecrate my fantasy with a cheap imitation. The real thing in my mind was ten times better and had already lasted a thousand times longer than any one-night stand who happened to be a look-alike possibly could. And besides, I had heard all eleven words in her vocabulary."

Rebecca covered her mouth with a grappled napkin and was straining to suppress hysterical laughter.

"Becca, you promised."

Still giggling, she stood up and said, "Brock Freeman, if you don't come over here and kiss me ten times better than you kissed her, I *am* going to hit you over the head with this bottle."

During the next sixty seconds stars and meteors fell to the earth, Roman candles exploded, trumpets sounded, and strobe lights filled the room. But nobody but Brock and Becca saw or heard.

They were married in a quiet ceremony in Mrs. Burwell's living room in Independence the following April, seventeen months after Sarah's death. It was the same house where he had thrown newspapers at the porch a lifetime ago; where he had vainly hoped so many times as he pedaled by that Becky would appear to say hello.

TWENTY-TWO

It was a warm sunny morning as the sun rose over the bay in the eastern sky, beginning a typical day in the Florida panhandle. Vehicles of all sizes rushed like mice through the Pensacola traffic to their respective day-long parking places. Bowie Crockett's towering and bulky body atop the greasy dirt bike appeared almost comical, making the motorcycle look more like a child's training wheels, as he maneuvered from lane to lane through the cars and trucks headed west on Langley Avenue. He had left his "Baby" in the shopping center parking lot in front of Gayfer's with the trailer gate open and the ramp down.

When he spotted the side street he was seeking, he peeled off and headed through a residential section and turned onto the street he had checked out the night before; the one where the vacant house overlooked the Woman's Clinic one block below and slightly down the street. While there he had jimmied the lock. He pulled the motorcycle into the carport and headed it out before killing the engine and parking it. After putting on his gloves, he took the poncho-wrapped rifle from its encasement on the right side and entered the kitchen door. When he opened the kitchen window he had a clear view of the parking lot at the clinic a little more than a furlong away. Perfect. His rifle was honed-in at 250 yards. With the right timing, it would take but one well-placed shot.

Late in the afternoon the previous day, Bowie had brazenly walked into the clinic with the request that he speak to Dr. Goldman. The nurse had said that the doctor was busy, but luckily for Bowie, Goldman had overheard and said, "I just got caught up. Have him come in my office."

Bowie had been brief because he only wanted to be sure what Goldman looked like. He had made up a silly bullshit story about his daughter being pregnant and how he had wanted to hear it from the doctor that an abortion really would not be harmful. In five minutes he had left with the promise to bring her in "in a day or two." He had never given any name to the nurse. From there he had ridden out into the country to fire some target shots in order to precisely sight-in the scope on his rifle.

Now he sat on the kitchen counter sipping the hot cup of coffee he had picked up with the sausage and biscuit at Krystal's drive-up window. It was eight-thirty, and he figured he would have a wait of between twenty and forty minutes. He thought about the last ones, three weeks before in Colorado and Wyoming.

When he had called Brock about the Denver and Cheyenne detail, it was because he had learned of a Freedom Conference that was coming up in Cheyenne, and after locating the right house, the Cheyenne hit had been a piece of cake. He had gone to the man's residence on Saturday afternoon, found he was alone, blown him away in the living room with a single pistol shot to the heart, and was back in the seminar at the hotel before the current speaker had finished. But the previous day's job had required more planning, precise timing, and a lot of luck. Miraculously, all three had fallen into place.

He had registered at the seminar at noon on Friday, paid his fifty bucks, checked into the hotel, and rushed to the Greyhound station to catch the 12:45 Express for Denver. By 3:15 he had called and reached Tom Gage, the Denver member of the government's hit squad. He smiled to himself this day in the house in Pensacola as he recalled it:

"Mr. Gage, I've got to talk to you privately. It concerns "OLLIE," Bowie had said, and Gage had offered no opposition. A few minutes later Gage arrived alone to pick up Bowie at the corner of 19th and Broadway, and the two had driven around the downtown area for a few minutes. Bowie had sidetracked Gage by identifying himself as another operative and engaging him in conversation about the disappearance of Spike Thorsten. Did Gage know? No, he hadn't heard a word, but he had thought it strange that he had not heard from the boss in so long. Bowie then directed Gage to pull into a deserted office parking lot where he choked and beat him into submission before garroting him to death with a guitar string. He had then walked the mile back to the bus station, was back on the next bus for Cheyenne, and made it on time to attend the evening function at 7:30.

Now the time had come to take care of Dr. Goldman, and Brock could handle that Atlanta bastard who had killed Bill Banneker. Leonard Burr would be the last one remaining on the list. If Cochise and the group in the Northwest had done their jobs, everything would be finished, the government's secret assassination team would be totally eliminated.

Bowie sipped the remaining few drops of coffee from his cup as he peered out the open window. A few protestors were milling around with signboards on the street and sidewalk in front of the clinic, but they would not block his view of Goldman's parking space when the baby-killer arrived. Bowie was certain Goldman would soon drive up in the white Pontiac rental car he had observed in the "Reserved for Doctor" space the previous day. *No wonder Goldman could carry out the cold-blooded shooting of Sarah with no apparent remorse, he thought. He ripped little babies apart all day long on Mondays and Tuesdays of every week of the year. The son of a bitch ain't got no conscience.* Indeed, Sarah Freeman had been "just another fetus" in the distorted mind of Marty Goldman, once the Feds had put the hammerlock on him. He had long been inured and hardened away from any contrition or regret regarding such activity. But on the other hand, so had Bowie.

Just a minute or two before 9:00 A.M., the white Pontiac pulled into the correct parking space amid the jeers of the demonstrators. Bowie watched through the telescopic sight as the driver emerged with a briefcase in hand and paused briefly with a baleful eye on the small mob. He had little to fear. The demonstrators by law had to keep off of the private property of the clinic. But the long second his target stood and paused was all Bowie needed. He pulled the trigger on the Chinese-made SKS carbine and delivered an inch-long, 7.62 caliber slug precisely and significantly through the mustache and front teeth of Marty Goldman. The doctor was already writhing in the throes of death on the concrete driveway when the crowd reacted to the delayed reverberation of the shot. They all dropped as one to the grass. No one could be sure exactly whence the weapon had been fired, but most believed it was from somewhere behind them.

Bowie calmly re-holstered the rifle in its case, quietly shut the kitchen door to the carport, strapped the gun back in its place under the poncho, and kick-started the dirtbike. He saw nobody in any of the yards as he roared away. Ten minutes later he was rolling up the rear ramp of his trailer, securing the motorcycle, and locking the door. It was still too early for any shopping traffic at the mall. By the time he finished lunch in Mobile, his rig would be fully loaded and he would be headed for Montgomery in the midst of another normal business day.

Their mission was nearly over, now that only Leonard Burr in Atlanta remained. He would send a FAX to Brock that night to report the news and remind him of what was left to do. Then they would cease for the rest of their lives, leaving the FBI and IRS to wonder forever.

*   *   *   *   *

It was springtime, 1998, and just as they had done once or twice every year, the couple in their late fifties was headed from Kansas City to the northeast to shop and see the sights. This one would be their ninth anniversary celebration trip and, although neither knew it, their last together. He was just over six feet tall and still athletically slender, and despite her telltale lines of age, she was proud of the fact that she could still squeeze into the faded red and blue cheerleading outfit she had kept from her days at Kansas University, where the yearbook had featured her as a "Class Favorite" three years in a row.

Usually they would fly into New York or Boston, but whenever time permitted, they preferred to travel by car—even taking the back roads off of the interstates—in order to meet and talk to new people and see the points of interest. As a lover of American history, he always planned to take at least one extra day visiting several sites on the endless list of battlefield shrines from the Revolutionary and Civil War eras. "It wasn't the 'Civil War'," he had said many times. "There was nothing 'civil' about it. It was the 'War Against Federal Aggression'."

Dusk of this day found them standing in a Virginia pasture watching a beautiful sunset on McLean's Farm on the 137th anniversary of the first Battle of Bull Run. Dreams of a short, bloodless conflict ended here that July 21st, only fifteen miles west of the city of Washington. It was here that an ex-professor from VMI named Thomas Jonathan Jackson had stood "like a stone wall" and rallied weakening rebel troops to the point that the confused clash of inexperienced armies resulted in Confederate victory and Union alarm. General Jackson had been one of the man's life-long heroes who had undoubtedly influenced his own posture in his own private war against federal aggression in the 1980s.

After checking into a hotel in the city and enjoying a late dinner, they decided to park the car, take a walk on this warm night, enjoy the lighted attractions of the memorials, and breathe in the nostalgia along with the sweet-smelling aroma of honeysuckle in the air. It was after ten o'clock before they left the Lincoln Memorial and walked across the knoll to say hello to another old friend and hero, Tom Jefferson, standing majestically under the lighted dome several hundred yards away.

His wife took a quick observation spin through the rotunda before going back out front to sit on the steps at the entrance, have a cigarette, and wait for him. She was used to his habits by now, after so many trips as this, and he to hers.

He spent twenty minutes in the hallowed dome fantasizing himself back into the eighteenth century and imagining what it must have been like to read and write by candlelight, as he strained to read from the dimly lit granite walls the God-inspired wisdom of America's most prolific founder. No one else was there at this late hour, and he felt as if he had been granted a private audience with this giant of history, the presence of whom was accented in the form of an enormous statue standing in the center of the atrium. As the old student circled the open-air room, silently strolling and reading, he lost total contact with the present for several minutes.

Suddenly, his reverie was penetrated by the sound of strange voices approaching, and he turned to see an obviously indigent, coverall-clad, middle-aged little man with a mustache, reverently removing his straw hat as he shuffled into the arena; his wife and seven little stair-stepped children walking behind. Their voices were immediately stifled as they entered and felt the sanctity envelope them.

"How do you do, sir?" he stage-whispered with a nodding, almost bowing demeanor connoting respect if not deference for the taller, better-dressed American; and especially for the hallowed surroundings. His bronze skin and Latino accent telegraphed that his origin was Mexican, probably a migrant worker. The American smiled and nodded, trying to remember if he should respond with *"buenas tardes"* or *"buenas nochas"* at this hour, but the chance passed before he could utter either.

He quietly observed as the polite little man again hushed his children, took the two oldest by the hand, and led them slowly around the panorama. The others fell in behind and were tended by their mother, who, tired and haggard, managed a sober-faced head-nod and a moving of her lips as she strode by, which the American man took as a greeting from one who spoke no *Inglés*. He could readily see that, despite her lack of beauty care, she was still a naturally pretty woman. She was wearing a wrinkled, faded-cotton, print dress, and somehow he knew it to be her only one.

He stared at the wall pretending to continue to read again what he had already been over as he inched along beside the family, eavesdropping on this poor, proud man's instruction to his children on the laws of freedom. The little man's grasp of English was more than adequate—far better than the others, the observer surmised—but sometimes, when he would come to a word he didn't understand or which was giving him trouble pronouncing correctly, he would substitute the Spanish translation or an English synonym to help further clarify his meaning to his young students.

" 'We hold these Truths to be self-evident that all men are created equal, . . .' " he read, then turned to his children and said, "No one in the world has more rights than you. These rights are God-given and protected by the United States Constitution. We know these are true things—that all men are born free and equal, that no man can steal away what God gave you because, see, here . . . 'they are endowed by their Creator with certain . . . un-take-away-able Rights.' " He wandered to the next panel, his family in tow, "And here, . . . that among these are life, liberty, and the . . . uh . . . getting of happiness. *Comprendes?*" And after they all nodded . . . *"Bueno!"*

The American was standing close to them now, and the father stopped and looked at him pleadingly as if to say, *Please confirm this for me, rich American man who has spent his whole life in this paradise. I am telling my children the truth, aren't I?*

The American quickly realized that, by third world standards, he, Brock Freeman, who even if he had been but the owner of a struggling hardware store in western Missouri, indeed, was the rich man, the land owner, the governor who could give these remarks that desired cachet. His heart and soul screamed everything he had ever heard on the subject when he was growing up. *Yes, you can be anything you want to be in America. The American free enterprise system which allows you to keep the fruits of your labors is alive and well. Do your own thing. Stake your claim. Work harder and longer than your competitor and you will become financially free.* His heart and soul yelled it, but his brain refused to let him perjure himself. Rationalizing away his reticence with the thought that he shouldn't usurp the little man's authority— shouldn't destroy his hope—he just smiled and nodded in assumed agreement. But even with that slight gesture, Brock felt a little guilty, just a tad censurable, knowing that he had helped confirm the lie. The great American Dream of his youth no longer existed, and he knew it. He knew exactly how it had been stolen, too. And he knew that this poor man was doomed to indentured servitude, regardless of what the politicians said.

He followed the family outside and watched them descend the marble steps. As they slowly walked across the lighted lawn, the poor Mexican turned and waved with his straw hat to the rich American before placing it back on his head. Brock stood at the top step, waved back to them, and continued to watch as they all climbed into a post-war, paint-faded pickup truck—the wife and the smallest child in the cab with the proud patriarch, the other children in the crudely covered back bed—and chugged down the street.

"Let's go, honey," he said, reaching for her hand to help her up.

Becca paused for a final drag of smoke and snuffed out her third cigarette in a large, standing ashtray. She stood and smoothed her skirt with a brushing sweep from her other hand as she leaned over to pick up her purse. Then she noticed the tears streaming down her husband's cheeks. "Brock, why are you . . . ," she said before pausing to measure her words. As he put his arm around her, they started down the steps toward their shiny new Mercedes. Having already discerned the answer to her question before she finished asking it, she hugged him around the waist with one hand, passed him a kleenex with the other, and said no more.

TWENTY-THREE

The snow had finally stopped falling after depositing a healthy eighteen inches on the world outside. The air was cold, but from inside the day appeared almost spring-like. The mid-morning sky was clear blue, and the bright sunlight bouncing from the niveous powder was illuminating an exquisite winter wonderland. The city maintenance crews had been on the job since before daylight—the two men had heard the sounds of the motorized equipment when they finally went to bed—and by early afternoon, the ultra-modern implements of the era would have the traffic on the main thoroughfares of the city moving almost as if there had been no storm at all.

The young writer had labelled the 90-minute tapes "One" through "Six" and was seated at the dining room table installing a new tape in his recorder when the old man came ambling down the stairs in his silk robe.

"Good morning, Mr. Freeman!"

"Good morning. Did you fix us some coffee yet?"

"No sir, I didn't. I haven't been up long myself, and I really didn't know where to look for it."

The older man went into the kitchen, filled the coffee maker with the two necessary ingredients, and returned to the table. They talked about little more than the weather, and in a few minutes they could hear the coffee pot's groaning of its final overtures from the other room. The old man arose again.

"How do you like your coffee?" he said.

"Let me do it," the young man said, getting up to follow, "because I like a little of this and a little of that."

They tended to it together and returned to the table.

"I'll fix us up a little breakfast after I get my motor running a little better," the old man told him.

"How do you feel about everything you revealed to me last night? I mean is there anything that I should edit?" asked the writer.

He pondered briefly. "No, while I am not necessarily proud of what we did, I am not ashamed of it either. It wasn't something that I went around bragging about, you know. I never even told Becca about it, although I thought about doing so many times over the years. But she was so sick and pathetic those last few months, I wouldn't have considered adding to her misery then." He paused and digressed. "I'm glad to see that you don't smoke. That lung cancer is a dehumanizing way to die. Any slow death is, I guess." But he wouldn't dwell on that, and proceeded.

"The Lord has promised to forgive our trespasses, but I never thought of my actions against His enemies as being that which would require forgiveness. I always felt we were His soldiers. That we had His blessings.

"During the French Revolution the tyrant Marat was deceived and murdered by Charlotte Corday, a patriot for the cause of freedom from government oppression. On her way to the guillotine she announced to the cheering throng, 'It is I who killed Marat. I alone am responsible. I killed one man to save a hundred thousand; a villain, to save the innocent; a savage, a wild beast, to save my country.' You could say that we acted accordingly in a similar situation.

"What we call society today is a vast network of mutual agreements. We cheerfully trust our lives to total strangers in the persons of airline pilots, steamship captains, taxi drivers, traffic cops, and unhesitatingly consign all our worldly goods to bankers, lawyers, and insurance companies. Ninety-nine percent of the people we deal with everyday are personally trustworthy. But what happens when a whole society is deceived? It rots that society with its cancerous lies, that's what. Without an honest system of just weights and measures, nobody knows what Truth is anymore. And our society is flooded with a multitude of publications written by a bunch of charlatans who view themselves as Messengers of Truth from Valhalla.

In fact, they are either totally deceived themselves or are of the few who are paid handsomely to perpetuate the deception over the rest of us.

"Bowie, Bill, and I performed an operation on a tiny portion of a cancer on society, that's all; and the operation was a success, I might add. The enemy has pulled some dastardly acts in recent years—such as that Oklahoma City hoax—but as far as I know, they haven't tried to come up with any more OLLIE-type assassination teams. We terrified them out of that idea for a decade or two. They must have thought there were thousands of us retaliating against them. But I later realized I had actually overestimated the enemy. Their bombings of the New York Trade Center and the Murrah Building in Oklahoma City demonstrated their sick fear of us—to the point that they would kill even baby children of federal employees to make us look bad and to justify our legal lynching.

"Would you do it again?"

"Not before tomorrow. I'm kind of tired today."

The young writer grinned and said, "I would take that to mean that you would not think twice about it."

"And you would be right on. Matter of fact, I believe I would have fewer qualms about it today. Elbert Hubbard said that the greatest mistake you can make is to be continually fearing that you will make one. Brent and Maria are grown with their own families, Becca's gone now, and I have sold my businesses and am completely out of usury. And even though it appears to be in remission, I've still got this damned Hodgkins. So what kind of mistake would I have to fear about doing God's work? I know that He would surround me with His cloak of angels again just as before, but it won't be a willful decision on my part to do anything anymore. Besides that, the American people are so brainwashed they don't give a damn. As long as the majority continues to believe the hoax about a deficit and balancing the budget and that the IRS collects money from them in order to run the country, they will always be slaves praising their wonderful freedom. Fiat money is slavery. Only the gangsters who create it change from election to election or generation to generation."

Brock paused and sipped his coffee, collecting his thoughts.

"The American people are up against such a vicious enemy they cannot even fathom it. The silent opposition has acquired such unimaginable power that the fact that the FBI paid more than a million bucks to have the World Trade Center blown up was reported in *The New York Times, The Los Angeles Times, Reuters,* and others, and yet almost nobody is even aware of it. That's total mind control. If that Trade Center bomb had been properly placed, it would have toppled one tower into the other and killed a hundred thousand people or more. Do you think the FBI gave a damn?

"That was when they learned that Americans wouldn't get upset enough anyway with any kind of catastrophe that might happen in New York, so they took it to the Christian heartland and blew up the Murrah Building in Oklahoma City and tried to blame it on anybody and everybody but themselves.

"But no, it is no longer time for fighting, it is time for waiting and watching this thing collapse. You know something?

My dad hated Franklin Roosevelt. Now if he and his contemporaries had done in the Roosevelt era what Banneker, Crockett,
and I did in the eighties, we wouldn't be having these problems
now, but we came along too late. We made a contribution, but it
was too little, too late.

"I guess there are only two things that could ever set me off
on an offensive course again. If they try to fool around with me
again or if this illness recurs. Either one would be a death sentence. I know there are a few of them left who would love to get
me into Springfield and give me a dose of AIDS or something,
and there are a few of them left out there that we missed—like
Joe Day, who took care of himself—and others that have popped
up since. But I am not one to hold malice in my heart for the
low-living sons of bitches. I guess I am saying that, the situation
being right, I could be recruited for duty again. Meanwhile, I'm
in a defensive mode and just want to be left alone to live out my
days in peace."

The young writer was somewhat dubious of this mystical
stuff, having always been taught in the government schools to
dismiss it as religious hocus-pocus. He asked, "But if God's angels were protecting the mission, why didn't Bill Banneker make
it through?"

"That was between him and God. I hope someday one of
them will tell me."

The young man had awakened that morning with his next
question and was waiting to grasp an opening. "Last night I
mentioned Larry McDonald, and you put me off. Can you tell
me about him now?"

"Sure. It was one of the classic cover-ups of the times. Larry
was a medical doctor who, like everybody else, thought he could
change things from the inside. In the mid-seventies, he cam-
paigned from door-to-door in his north Georgia district and got
himself elected to Congress, in spite of dreadfully hostile media
opposition. He was a brilliant man, but he didn't understand the
power of the beast and the lengths to which the enemy could
stretch, until maybe at the very last moments when it was too
late. Oh, he understood the intricacies of the sophisticated dis-
mantling of our culture and liberties better than anyone, and he
knew that when the authors of the Declaration and the Constitution spoke of law, they meant the Law of God revealed in the
Bible. But I don't believe he imagined how *totally* the world's
media, politics, education, police, and nations are controlled. All
earthly authority is in the hands of those who rule the world's
monetary system.

"Dr. Lawrence P. McDonald was a fifth-term congressman and very popular in his conservative district when he boarded that now-infamous Korean Air Lines flight 007 from New York to Korea on August 31, 1983, as you know. But you probably don't know that he originally had reservations on a Pan-Am flight that was cancelled at the last minute. Because he had to make a speaking engagement in Seoul, he felt at the time he was very lucky to get on that 007 flight. They stopped for refueling in Anchorage, and some very high-profile people were taken off the flight, not Congressman McDonald, however.

"The initial news reports we heard told us that KAL-007 had mistakenly entered Soviet territory, had ignored warnings, and had been shot down by two Russian fighter planes, but landed safely on Sakhalin Island. Everybody in Atlanta went to bed relieved. But then the next morning they awoke to the news that the plane had indeed gone down and all 269 people were killed.

"It was all government balderdash. Actually, the plane had a hole blown in its side from which four people were sucked out by the decompression. Then it was forced down and landed safely on Sakhalin Island. 265 survived and were all taken prisoner. Big Red learned the truth in a matter of days from his CIA buddies.

"Now any thinking person should have been suspicious of the details when the initial reports coming from the FAA saying that their Japanese radar had confirmed the safe landing were refuted by the world media the next day. Bowie confirmed it all later through one of his former CIA contacts who had seen McDonald and some of the others two years later in a prison camp. The contact told us that when the divers went down to retrieve the 'black box' from the cockpit of the plane, they were amazed that there were no dead bodies on board and no luggage in the hold. The truth was that the plane had been towed into the bay and sunk after it was unloaded. The FAA also had radio transmission tapes from the pilot confirming the safe landing on Sakhalin. The tapes were turned over to the U.S. State Department and systematically destroyed."

"But did you or did you not personally talk to Dr. McDonald later?"

"Yes, we did. Bowie and I found McDonald in 1992 after the Soviet Union had opened up, but he was not in prison and had not been for seven or eight years. He was in good health and even doing well financially, comparatively speaking, as a government doctor. They had almost starved and tortured him to death during the first two years in an attempt to make him denounce the United States and repudiate his former anti-communist stand, but they could not succeed. Finally when they realized they would not be able to break him, they made him a deal. He could practice medicine in the Soviet Union, remarry, and live well the rest of his life, as long as he was a 'good boy'; and that's exactly what he has done. He really had no choice.

"How long were you with him?"

"Just one afternoon. We visited with him for a few hours in his home and met his young wife. She is a lovely Russian woman who spoke English pretty well, thanks to Dr. McDonald. They even had a couple of young children at the time. We offered to take him out of there, but we could already see that he would refuse before we offered. He was under a death sentence for any escape attempt and, besides, what would he do if we got him back safely? The American government would have seen to it that he disappeared within 24 hours if he attempted to open his mouth about the truth. He was a dead man if he did anything other than what he was doing, and we all three knew it."

"What was the fate of the others?"

"The children were separated from their parents and safely hidden in various orphan houses of one of the Soviet Middle Asian republics. Their parents were taken with the others to a KGB-guarded camp on the mainland—Soviet Gavan—while McDonald was sent incognito and strictly guarded to Moscow, along with the plane's pilots.

"Incidentally, in November of that year after the supposed shootdown of McDonald's plane, they had a special election to fill his unexpired term because he had, of course, been declared dead. Here was one of the most blatant examples in history of how it is possible to have eighty percent of the electorate conservative in a small district and still have liberal politicians. McDonald's replacement was a left-wing government lackey—a lawyer and former prosecutor who knew how to play the game—and he was the only one given any decent media exposure. Even McDonald's wife was attempting to fill his unexpired term, but the people were hardly aware that anyone else other than the 'Chosen One' was even running. They named the damned highway from Atlanta to Marietta after him, but almost no one of the younger generation even knows who Larry McDonald was anymore."

"What ever happened to Bowie Crockett?"

"He and Stella are alive and well, but they don't live in east Tennessee anymore. He retired from the road after he collected his inheritance. They sold their farm and bought a big motorhome and just lost themselves in the world. They stopped to see me about a year ago, and they send me postcards on occasion, but he's unreachable. He has adopted a whole new I.D., and he wouldn't talk to you anyway, even if you could find him. He's got too much to lose."

"What about Joe Day? Was he ever tried by the People's Court?"

"Not in Nevada, but in his own mind, yes. He was the archetype of the message found in James 1:8: 'A double-minded man is unstable in all his ways.' He tried to operate on both sides of the fence, and it blew up in his face. He was left with no friends on either side. After the IRS used him up, they threw him into the federal nuthouse in Springfield without a trial and kept him there for more than a year. Some trumped-up contempt of court charge. When he finally got out he was a broken man—physically, mentally, and financially—and stayed drunk about half the time. He went back to practicing dentistry, but they tell me he was a paranoid wreck—ostracized both socially and professionally and barely able to make a living. Bowie added to his fears and misery by mailing him news clippings every few months about the various disappearances of the IRS agents around the country. There would always be a note attached about Joe being next. Around five years later, one night in his office after drinking a half-bottle of rum, he finally stuck a shotgun down his own throat and pulled the trigger."

"And Cochise?"

"Haven't heard from him or about him in years. He'd be about seventy now, and if he's still alive, I can guarantee he is still fighting them in one way or another. The man was more dedicated to freedom than anyone I have ever known. I cannot begin to imagine what he would have done to Washington, D.C., if it had been his wife they murdered instead of mine. Probably would have leveled it. The man had a whole different moral code from that of any of us. I am sure it was his heritage, but 'an eye for an eye' would never have made sense to him. It just wouldn't balance or compute. For him it was more like 'You take my eye and I kill you, burn your wife and kids along with your house and crops, and, for as long as I live, kill everybody I ever find later who bears your name.'"

"What was the story with the 747?"

"There really wasn't much to that. It got blown out of proportion later when the guy flew his plane into the White House and scared the crap out of Bill and Hillary. That was when the Secret Service came to see me the last time, but they never got farther than the front porch. They had a file on me from the letter I had sent to the Secretary of the Treasury several years before and wanted to know if I had known this dead pilot."

"What had you said in your letter to the Secretary?"

"I told them that I knew that agents of the United States government had murdered my wife and still wanted to murder me, and that if they tried again, they had better succeed, because I knew I could not hold off their awesome power forever. Besides that, I was diagnosed with Hodgkins, so I would have nothing to lose. I told them that I still had my old TWA uniforms in storage and that I could be sitting in the cockpit of a 747 at any airport in the country within fifteen minutes. In short, if they didn't leave me alone, I would have no choice but to pay them a visit at 550 miles an hour."

"Didn't they perceive that as a threat?"

"Of course they did, but they obviously decided it would be more prudent on their part to just leave me alone rather than try to prosecute me and have the truth about their assassination team exposed in court."

"How could you have done that without jeopardizing yourself?"

"Good question. I thought about that myself for quite a while and realized I had two options. It would have been a simple matter to have extracted a hand-written affidavit from Don Handy telling all and naming names, before he was hunted and shot. That wimp would have done anything we asked. But I had a stronger ace-in-the-hole too, if my Hodgkins had flared up again at the time. In that case, I would have been willing to tell the court everything under oath then that I am telling you now because I would have been under a death sentence anyway. They would have done anything to keep the truth about OLLIE from coming out. After I talked with them, they grilled me about Spike's disappearance, but it so happened that I had had a real estate closing in Kansas City on the same morning that Bill Banneker sent them Thorsten's head from Louisville, and there was my notarized signature on the papers to prove it. Investigation concluded!"

"So they left you alone."

"Pretty much. Oh, they still keep an eye on me, but they have too much to lose to try anything drastic. I told them I had Spike Thorsten's sworn statement filed with several people ready to expose it, if anything out of the ordinary happened to me. It was a bluff, but it was more than they could afford to risk. So, yeah, they left me alone. Time has always been on their side. The enemy has always been very patient.

"The New World Order is in full swing now. Americans are placidly wallowing in the same misery and squalor that their parents ridiculed in the Soviet Union only a generation ago. These parents were the same people who uttered to dissenters time and time again, 'If you don't like it here in America, why don't you move to Russia.' Today we, their children, have found that exact world without packing up and moving anywhere. The rise of atheism in the last quarter of the twentieth century has thus provided unlimited license for tyranny in the twenty-first. Once the State found no morally binding standard, it became god and we subjects mere beasts of bureaucratic burden."

Brock Freeman was launching into a litany of rhetoric that led the writer to believe was one of his undelivered speeches that had been saved for this moment. He quickly turned on the recorder again to capture one last gem, for whatever it might be worth.

"The government that rejects God's law becomes a terror. But who is God? While He may differ in spirit by what Muslims, Buddhists, Hindus, and Christians believe, all of those religions have an orderly and moral code of laws. To say that we need new laws to fit our new technological age and the Bible is not adequate is to denigrate and deny the Word of God in its all sufficient regulating power. The civil government has not the power to add to or take away from the Law as it is already written. When that government uses its sword from any other standard than the standard of the Word of God, it will fall upon the head of the righteous, and therefore no righteous, law-abiding citizen will be safe in the United States. Whenever the civil government claims to be God and claims ownership and sovereignty and we do not stand and oppose that claim but simply go along with it, it is because we wear the Mark of the Beast.

"America is one big prison camp. Those of us not actually behind the walls might as well be. Taxes are at confiscatory levels and beyond. The hyper-inflation of the money may soon require us to pay for a restaurant meal in advance, before the price increases while we eat it. Total collapse of the monetary system is just around the corner. Those who work for the bureaucracy survive. Those who do not will starve. People who were formerly model citizens will be caught and executed for stealing a loaf of bread or a can of soup. While otherwise honorable people will do strange things when their children are hungry, it is more amazing to see to what depths the 'Roman soldiers' will stoop in order to mete out punishment in the name of the State. Civilian informers for the government are everywhere. No one can be trusted not to inform on his neighbor. And yet nobody knows exactly how all this happened or why. They only know it wasn't the America of their youth.

"Most Americans are unaware of the religious and political persecution that went on in their country during the Reagan and Bush administrations of the 1980s. Nor do most of the older citizens know how the federal government managed to amass such enormous power during their lifetimes under the guise of 'providing more freedom.' The younger ones have no reason to know or care. They were educated in the public school system to believe that the State is omnipotent, and their parents were too busy making ends meet in a two-job household to find the time to teach them any differently.

"That the daddy had to seek permission to enclose a garage, in order to add a room onto his house, would have scandalized the founding fathers. But the new and neutered generation of Americans submits like a lamb to any and all demands the government puts on it. Most of the wimpy piss ants would go downtown and apply for a Walking License, if the wicked bureaucrats required it today. The federal government has finally won the fight for the land, but it was not without struggle. Nor was it without bloodshed, but they managed to keep most of those details of their own bloodshed out of the controlled press during that struggle."

Brock fixed a gargantuan breakfast of bacon, sausage, eggs, toast, and pancakes, and the two men talked discursively about many things. A generation apart they shared a common respect: the younger man for the erudition of the older; the older man for the courage of the younger.

When they had finished and he was loading up his things in preparation for the enormous task ahead of him, the young writer realized that this day was the very last one of the century— New Year's Eve, 1999. The next sunrise would bring with it a new millennium and whatever that held in store for the people.

"Thanks again, Mr. Freeman," he said, standing in the same doorway where Sarah had been killed more than eleven years before. "I'll be in touch."

"Call me anytime," Brock replied. "I'm not going anywhere . . . for awhile, I hope."

"Good! When I get a first draft completed, I'll be back to spend some time with you so we can check the facts."

As the young writer started his car and pulled onto Ward Parkway and into the twenty-first century, the words John Maynard Keynes penned in 1920 kept ringing in his ears, and he peered at his notes to read the passage one more time:

By a continuing process of inflation, governments can
confiscate, secretly and unobserved, an important part of
the wealth of their citizens. There is no subtler, no surer
means of overturning the existing basis of society than to
debauch the currency. The process engages all the hidden forces of economic law on the side of destruction,
and does it in a manner which *not one man in a million is
able to diagnose.*

Had I not spent that long night talking with a very wise man, he
said to himself, *I would never have understood it either. He is, indeed,
that "One in a Million."*